PRENTICE HALL

Small Business

MODEL LETTER BOOK

WILBUR CROSS

PRENTICE HALL
Englewood Cliffs, New Jersey 07632

Prentice-Hall International (UK) Limited, *London*
Prentice-Hall of Australia Pty. Limited, *Sydney*
Prentice-Hall Canada, Inc., *Toronto*
Prentice-Hall Hispanoamericana, S.A., *Mexico*
Prentice-Hall of India Private Limited, *New Delhi*
Prentice-Hall of Japan, Inc., *Tokyo*
Simon & Schuster Asia Pte. Ltd., *Singapore*
Editora Prentice-Hall do Brasil, Ltda., *Rio de Janeiro*

© 1992 *by*

PRENTICE-HALL, Inc.

Englewood Cliffs, NJ

This publication is designed to provide accurate and
authoritative information in regard to the subject matter covered. It is sold with the understanding that the
publisher is not engaged in rendering legal, accounting, or other professional service. If legal advice or
other expert assistance is required, the services of a
competent professional person should be sought.

From a Declaration of Principles jointly adopted by a
Committee of the American Bar Association and a
Committee of Publishers

10 9 8 7 6 5 4 3 2 1

Library of Congress Cataloging-in-Publication Data

Cross, Wilbur.
    Prentice Hall small business model letter book / Wilbur Cross.
       p.   cm.
    Includes index.
    ISBN 0-13-718602-9 :
    1. Commercial correspondence—Handbooks, manuals, etc. 2. Small
business—Handbooks, manuals, etc. I. Title. II. Title: Small
business model letter book.
HF5726.C87 1992   92–22702
651.7′5—dc20   CIP

ISBN 0-13-718602-9

PRENTICE HALL
Professional Publishing
Englewood Cliffs, NJ 07632
Simon & Schuster, A Paramount Communications Company

PRINTED IN THE UNITED STATES OF AMERICA

DEDICATION

Dedicated to the memory of my late grandfather,
Wilbur Cross, Sr.,
Formerly Dean of the Yale Graduate School,
Governor of the State of Connecticut,
author of numerous books,
and a dedicated and prolific writer of letters.

$\mathcal{W}$HAT THIS BOOK WILL DO FOR YOU

Here is a book of model letters that has been researched, compiled, and written especially for people who are involved with small businesses. It not only tells you how to write good letters, but provides over 500 easy-to-use models for you to follow. It is intended for owners, managers, staff executives, or others who must—frequently or occasionally—communicate by letter in order to keep their businesses thriving and growing. By using the *Prentice Hall Small-Business Model Letter Book* to its fullest extent, you can accomplish just about any letter-writing objective you have in mind, including such matters as increasing sales; announcing business events and programs; activating delinquent accounts; hiring, firing, and other personnel issues; handling legal problems; providing data about products and services; improving your marketing contacts; and answering complaints.

Special Features Tailored to Your Needs

The chapters in this book have been arranged to make it easy for you to find the subjects and contents of the kinds of letters you want to write. Simple, direct instructions assure that you will have both the information and the confidence you need to write better, more effective letters by using a constructive and positive approach. Do the following comments sound familar to you?

- I put off writing letters I know I should send because I'm not a very good writer.
- *Starting* a letter is difficult for me because I don't know how to get into the subject quickly enough.
- How dull! I think when I reread a letter I've written. Maybe it's better not to send it at all.
- I can write an informative letter pretty well. But I just can't face the truth if I have to broach a touchy subject—like rebuking a supplier for messing up an order.

- Sales letters are supposed to *sell*! But when I write one it sounds as though I couldn't care less.

- I began, stopped, began again, and tore up four notes before I could get one off that expressed my grief over the death of a client's son.

- Sometimes I think I'd rather lose the money than write a customer implying that we think he's a deadbeat.

- I'm really envious of some of my business friends who can write legal letters that sound professional; mine never seem to have the right tone.

- I'd like to send memos and notes to any of my employees who should be praised for good work or going out of their way to help someone, but my words seem so *mushy*.

- When I try to write an informative company memo describing new technical equipment we're acquiring, I get so tangled up in terms and phrases that even I can't understand what I've written.

The *Prentice Hall Small-Business Model Letter Book* has been designed to meet such writing problems head on. In the following pages, you will be shown, among many other things, just how you can write an opening sentence that will grab the reader's attention, focus on exactly the right amount of text for your primary message, and combine tact and persuasion when trying to turn an adversary into an ally.

Chapter-by-Chapter Guidance

As you anticipate your needs for writing letters on certain subjects, you will naturally turn to the chapters that are the most pertinent. Thus, you'll want to peruse the chapter on *employment* if you are actively recruiting or are forced to take people off the payroll. You'll look to the chapter on *finance* if you need to correspond frequently about money management. And you'll find the chapter on *billing problems* filled with formulas for making light work of some of the most unwelcome writing chores.

In each of these, and other chapters, the introductions have been carefully organized and presented to guide you as you select model letters whose contents cover the subjects and thoughts you most want to express. You will be aided by specific guidelines such as these:

1. How to do it
2. Opening leads
3. Closing statements
4. Appropriate lengths
5. Using attachments and enclosures

Picturing Your Reader

Do you have any mental image of the person(s) to whom you are writing? What do you do if you know very little about the intended recipient of your letter(s)?

First, bear in mind that people who are regular and enthusiastic writers of personal letters derive much of the enjoyment from the fact that they can picture the individual at the other end of the line who opens the envelope and begins to read. Thus they tailor the letter to the situation, always anticipating the reaction. Humor and lighthearted comments are aimed at those who may be shut in or down in the dumps about life, a tone of nostalgia for old schoolmates long out of touch, terms of endearment for someone loved and very close, or admonition and scolding for correspondents who have failed to honor a commitment or communicate properly.

Much of the enjoyment of letter writing is akin to that of conversation over a long-awaited luncheon or a casual get-together for a drink. But when it comes to writing *business* letters or those that have deadlines or purposeful intent, even the most prolific writers of personal letters seem to shrink from the task at hand. And those who are poor or skittish correspondents go to pieces or try to delegate the assignment to someone else. When they do take pen, typewriter, or dictating instruments in hand, they seldom try to visualize the persons to whom they are addressing their messages.

You do not need personal profiles or detailed résumés of persons you are writing to, but it helps to have at least a smattering of information, particularly when your letters are other than routine and when the nature and scope of the replies are important to your business or professional interests.

Write the Unpleasant Letters First, and Don't Delay

If you are a successful owner or manager, you accept it as all part of the business mix. There are good days and bad days, productive discussions and meaningless hassles, rewards and busts, bright ideas and stupid notions, hits and flops, ups and downs. Letter-writing is no different. Correspondence one day can be a joy and the next day drudgery. The *Prentice Hall Small-Business Model Letter Book* will help take the drudgery out of your letter-writing.

A study of recipients of business letters turned up more complaints than compliments. Here are typical examples. In the chapter on complaints and adjustments and in the index under headings for those, and related, subjects, you'll find references to model letters written in response to such gripes that will help you avoid receiving such complaints in the future.

- "I wrote for technical information that was not in the literature packaged with electronic products, saying clearly I was an electrician and could make better installations with this knowledge. What did I get? A form letter suggesting I read the owner's manual! My response was to send the shipment back and order a competing brand."

- "I applied for a job with a small company having trouble recruiting qualified employees. My résumé was well organized and precise. Apparently nobody bothered to study it because the position they offered was way out of line with my experience. Who wants this kind of employer?"

- "Because of serious injury and hospitalization in my family, I got behind in my bills. I knew I'd catch up and, in fact, wrote short notes to several creditors apologizing for the delay. When I got back on my feet, do you know which ones I paid off first? Naturally, those who were sympathetic and understood my plight rather than the ones who harassed me and threatened to ruin my credit rating."

- "My father was a fine booster of our community and, as a local retailer himself, active in organizations like the Chamber of Commerce and Better Business Bureau. When he died, we must have received 100 letters from business friends. But not more than 10 showed any real awareness of his nature, his philosophy of life, or even his contributions to society. What do you have to do to make your mark in life?"

- "When we wrote to the chairman of a hospital fund drive to voice distaste over high-pressure tactics being used by members of his drive, we didn't even receive an apology. Instead, he sent us what was little more than a form letter pressuring us still more to make a pledge to 'a worthy cause.' Worthy or not, I'm sending my donations elsewhere."

- "Having made a name for myself in politics, I am constantly being asked by local entrepreneurs to recommend them for positions that would enhance their stature. From the nature of the requests and the manner in which they address me, I'd say about two-thirds of the letter writers haven't taken the time to determine where I stand on current issues, or even which party I represent. The only thing I'd recommend them for is an adult education class on how to do your homework!"

Did these stories bring to mind some familiar examples of letters you too have received in the mail? Did they make you wonder how the writer could have been so far off target, if not downright stupid?

As an author, I can cite dozens of occasions in which I have been frustrated and irritated after writing for information, each time with a basic objective specified. In the cases I have in mind, I have not only been explicit in defining what I was seeking, but have tried to make it easier for the recipient by providing a thumbnail biography and my qualifications in the subject field at hand. The answering letters all but ignored what I was saying but managed to provide total non sequiturs. Many thanked me kindly for "applying for a position" and expressed regret that my "résumé" did not fit any of the job openings available.

All of which is but a smidgeon of the weighty mass of proof that people are prone to ignore their audiences when writing letters and talking about whatever happens to be on their minds—regardless.

How to Select the Right Letter to the Right Person about the Right Topic

The *Prentice Hall Small-Business Model Letter Book* will help you avoid these unpardonable errors that can create financial setbacks, cause you to lose customers, and at the very least create embarrassment. A primary criterion for writing an effective letter is to know as much as possible about the recipient, and then select the approach and wording that are appropriate and geared to your objective. The book recognizes the realistic truth that you cannot always write individual letters to everyone you want to reach when you are, say, drafting a sales letter or expressing a business policy. The more recipients there are for any particular communication, however, the more diluted the effect of the message will be. But, after selecting the model letter that best suits the situation, you can usually add some kind of personal touch, especially now that computerized editing and personalizing are readily available.

About the Appendix

In the back of the book, you will find specific data and references that can be of great help to you in using model letters, as well as in improving your letter-writing skills. These sections include

- *Structure and Format*: what you should know about the elements that comprise a good letter
- *Proper Forms of Address*: how to use correct titles, terms, and designations in addresses and salutations
- *Glossary of Terms Relating to Correspondence*: words and phrases that will help your understanding and usage when you are studying model letters or writing on your own
- *Suggested Reading*: a selected list of books you might want to refer to

when composing correspondence or writing other forms of business communication

- *Index*: key words that will help you find exactly the model letters or information you want in the book. Many letters are cross-indexed so you can locate them by subject, category, geographic locations, proper names, and reference to related topics.

As the title suggests, the *Prentice Hall Small-Business Model Letter Book* has been designed to be of particular interest to entrepreneurs, people with small businesses or business interests, managers, owners, and professionals who must write letters and memoranda in order to succeed. But the book, with over 500 model letters to select from, can help to improve the personal communications of just about anyone who needs to make written contacts with others in order to achieve goals.

$\mathcal{C}$ONTENTS

CHAPTER 8 FINANCIAL CORRESPONDENCE 166

CHAPTER 9 LEGAL CORRESPONDENCE 188

TRANSMITTAL LETTERS 190

AGREEMENTS AND CONTRACTS 193

LEGAL ACTIONS 199

TAXES 214

TRANSPORTATION 216

REGULATORY ISSUES 221

RECOMMENDATIONS 223

INQUIRIES AND REQUESTS FOR INFORMATION 227

CHAPTER 12   COMMUNITY INVOLVEMENT   264

CHAPTER 13 PERSONAL BUSINESS CORRESPONDENCE 289

$\mathcal{P}$ROVIDING AND REQUESTING INFORMATION

In their efforts to make sure that they have provided enough information, most correspondents go overboard. They say too much, are repetitious, and often confuse the issue rather than clarify it. Not infrequently, they bombard the recipient with so much data that they fail to supply the exact information requested in the first place. As one editorial consultant explained the situation, "It's like opening a fire hydrant to water a geranium but leaving the plant on the upper landing!"

In order of sequence and importance, consider the following steps:

1. Make sure you know what information is being requested. Financial data? A product description? Geographical locations? Names and titles of people? A brochure? Tear sheets describing a situation? Addresses of suppliers? Description of available services?

2. If you do not already know the persons who are requesting information, try to picture what they are like and what their needs may be. Bear in mind that *they* may be at fault for not making their wants clear to you. Yet if you have some idea of their age, sex, circumstances, and fields of interest, as well as location, you may be able to provide just what they are looking for, regardless of their fuzzy language.

3. Draft an initial reply; then review what you have said, and ask yourself whether it would really be clear to a person unfamiliar with the kinds of facts you might have readily at your fingertips.

4. Shorten your response. Make it as brief as possible without omitting essential information. You do not have to explain why you are qualified to provide facts or suggest all kinds of alternate evidence or proof of accuracy.

5. Provide an enclosure only if requested or if it will clarify the subject more quickly—such as a product photograph, map, or chart.

6. Avoid stuffing the envelope with all kinds of related materials, no matter how eager you are to show the extent of your knowledge about a subject.

7. Suggest an alternative source if you find that you cannot fulfill the request. Be as specific as possible in the matter of phone numbers, addresses, and contacts.

8. Select the mailing category or delivery service according to the urgency (or lack of it) implied by the request received.

Putting the shoe on the other foot, *requesting* data or information can be frustrating and time consuming if you do not pay attention to the basics. Again, in order of sequence and importance, consider the following:

1. If you are not already familiar with the organization that can best supply the information you want, do enough homework to determine that fact.

2. When possible, address your correspondence to a specific individual, if not by name at least by position or title.

3. Make it very clear exactly what you want. Product information and prices? Names and addresses? A map? Printed matter? Technological specifications?

4. If the reason for your request might heighten the interest of the recipient and hasten the response, include it. If not, avoid comments.

5. Draft an initial letter, and then shorten it. At the same time, make sure your tone is courteous, not curt. Avoid asking for several pieces of information at the same time unless they are very closely related.

6. Enclose a stamped, self-addressed return envelope when appropriate, particularly if you are putting an individual to personal effort and/or cost.

7. If your request is urgent, make this clear, but do not send a fourth-class inquiry and expect the recipient to reply by express mail! If you want a reply by phone, have the courtesy to suggest that the charges be reversed, even if you are contacting a well-heeled corporation.

8. Ask for suggested sources of information when appropriate, but only if you feel that the recipient of your request might not be able to fulfill it.

Always write a thank you note for information received, with special appreciation if the sender seems to have gone to extra trouble or expense to supply what you asked for. You never know when you may have further requests or would like cooperation from the individuals or organizations contacted.

What do you do if you have been very specific in stating your request for information and you receive something totally off base, useless, or overwhelming?

Double-check to make sure that you have (1) addressed the right organization and individual, (2) stated your needs precisely, (3) made a reasonable request, and (4) kept your communication brief enough so it received a complete and proper reading rather than a casual glance.

If everything seems in order at your end, hide your annoyance and ask again. You might even swallow your pride and apologize that you did not specify clearly enough what you really wanted and are sorry, but perhaps, and so on.

Keep in mind whenever you write a letter, whether for information or any other purpose, that the opening and closing sentences are likely to be the most important in establishing a good rapport with your correspondents.

HOW TO DO IT

1. Select the proper person with whom to communicate.

2. Be precise when requesting or providing data.

3. Keep your message brief and to the point.

4. Limit your request, if asking for information.

5. Consider using an insert or data sheet when providing information.

COVER LETTERS

The purpose of a cover letter is to introduce a chart, publication, or other material enclosed with it. A cover letter should be brief, but it can also contain a summary explanation about the enclosure.

Brochure

Dear Zeke:

We are patting ourselves on the back. We are touting our accomplishments. We are being anything but modest. However, please skip all that (after all, we are in public relations!) and look on page 22. There you'll see a complete list of the people who really deserve the credit—you among them. It was truly a well-coordinated effort. And the real reason why we have published this brochure has been to call the community's attention to the continuing need for water conservation and what can be accomplished when a lot of determined and dedicated individuals get behind the wheel and give it a big push.

Thanks again for your help.

Cordially,

Newsletter

Dear Jim:

You might be interested in the item at the bottom of page 2, marked with a yellow highlighter. In about 50 words, it says more than I could in a half hour about the insect-repellent qualities of the new liquid pine balm we have just started to market. I'd be happy to send you a sample. And, as the copy in the newsletter states, if you can find a mosquito approaching within 30 feet of a pine-balmed body, we'll give you a $10 gift certificate.

Note also the other items I marked, on pages 3 and 4. Interesting?

Regards,

Product Information

Dear Mr. Robbins:

Per your request, I enclose a booklet describing our CPT-8500 series. All workstations may be used to enter text and then communicate that text to a variety of typesetters for output. In most instances, standard software is used in such a way that coding may be entered in the text and transmitted to the typesetter, although this generally requires development of appropriate software at the typesetter to translate the codes.

I have also included data about our newer products that support desktop publishing and provide laser output. The CPT-9000 series was introduced last year, providing a full-page, high-resolution, black-on-white display similar to the one you are already familiar with in your work.

If, after reading the enclosed leaflets and fact sheets, you have any questions, you can obtain almost immediate answers by calling the toll-free "800" number on this letterhead at any time between 8:00 A.M. and 6:00 P.M., Eastern Time.

Sincerely,

POSTCARDS

By their very nature, postcards must be brief. As in the following examples, they are generally used to impart a single item of information.

Change of Address

This is to inform you that we have changed our address and phone number, effective March 1. Please make a note on your records to avoid any delays in reaching us by phone or mail. Our new address is

10 Orchard Place
Suite 106A
Pineville, NY 14873
Telephone: (914) 789-2345
Fax: (914) 789-5678

Acknowledging Order

Your order of 4/7/92 has been received and is being processed.

Please note that there will be a shipping delay of approximately one week, since the color you requested is temporarily out of stock and has been ordered from the manufacturer.

Thank you for shopping by mail with Blank's, Inc.

Announcing New Staff Member

We are pleased to announce that Johnson Henning has joined our firm as the new Director of Information. He will be pleased to provide whatever data or materials you may need for use in news features and articles about the latest air purification equipment and water filtration supplies available through our firm.

For further information, please call him any time at our local number: 789-2300, ext. 47.

Thank you,

Clarifying Business Name

Dear Customer:

Please note that Johnson Marine is not affiliated with Johnson Motors, Inc., the national corporation. While we do carry Johnson products, along with those of other major outboard producers, we are an independent, local business that was founded 10 years ago to serve the Lakeside community and surrounding areas. Inquiries about Johnson warranties should be addressed directly to the manufacturer.

Yours truly,

PRODUCT INFORMATION

A product information letter is most effective when it can be limited to a single subject—whether requesting data or supplying information in response to a request. In answering requests for information that requires a lengthy or complex explanation, it is sometimes better to write a brief cover letter and enclose printed or visual material.

Office Equipment and Services

Dear Ms. Bondi:

The name of your shop was given to me by one of my former law associates at

McLearn & McKay as one that could offer the kinds of equipment and furnishings I need when establishing my new office in the Eastridge Building. I plan to start my practice there on or about October first and thus would like to get established within the next few weeks.

You were recommended because, as I understand it, you offer consulting services in interior design and decor at no extra charge for customers whose purchases exceed a certain minimum. Quite frankly, I need assistance when it comes to selecting materials, harmonizing colors, and deciding which furniture blends good looks with easy care. The space I am furnishing consists of two offices 10 feet × 12 feet, a secretary/reception area 9 feet × 11 feet, a lavatory, a short hall, and a storage room 6 feet × 7 feet.

If you feel that you could assist me, both with the equipment and furnishings and with professional counsel as part of the "package," I would like to hear from you within the next two or three days.

Sincerely,

Requesting Computer Software

Dear Ms. Cowley:

You may recall that you have in the past sent me information about IBM AT-compatible hardware for use in the writing, editing, and graphics I have been preparing for my clients. I am interested in knowing more about your Ventura Publishing software that allows text and graphics to be incorporated into a single document, one that can be produced in "close-to-typeset" formats.

Please keep in mind that my goal in most circumstances is to prepare material quickly that will provide an accurate simulation of the finished publication, yet without delays or extra expense. In many cases, the clients I serve are not accustomed to looking at conventional advertising layouts and rough drafts and visualizing the final results.

Sincerely,

Product Specifications

Dear Mr. Shortliffe:

When I spoke to your production manager on the phone, I provided all the details he needs to process our order for the 75 12-foot sailboat hulls we discussed. However, I would like to emphasize two points here on paper that are of critical importance:

1. The adhesives, sealants, and paints applied in your shop must contain *no* metals of any kind. My customer is an environmentalist and has decreed this in *no* uncertain terms.

2. The delivery *must* be made no later than July 20. It will take me three days to mount sails, fittings, rigging, and other accoutrements, and my customer has already arranged to accept the shipment July 24.

Failure to meet these specifications to the "T" would abort the entire order—his and ours both.

Sincerely,

Engineering Specifications

Dear Mr. Creame:

Al Donick, our plant manager, asked me to provide data for you about our operations building that apparently was skipped on the information sheet we supplied you for the plant revisions.

The production line is located in a building that has no basement. All of our heavy equipment is fixed with steel bolts to the slab floor, which is reinforced concrete and is no less than 3 feet thick in any section. The slab rests on 10 feet of pebble and cinder fill that cannot be affected by frost or ice in the winter. Since the building is situated high on a gentle slope and is well drained, there are no problems with water or moisture accumulations.

I trust this provides the data needed for your planning.

Sincerely,

New Product Information to Employees

TO: All Employees
FROM: Al Stocker, Public Relations
RE: New Products

Management has asked me to keep you informed about new products or improvements in existing ones, and this is the first in a series of memos to do just that. You are in a better position to promote the company, the brands, and the individual merchandise if you know what you are talking about.

Right after Memorial Day, the Skin Enhancement Division will start marketing SunTurn, which as the name implies contains oils that turn away the harmful rays of the sun, while at the same time permit a smooth tan. The product will be packaged as a cream in tubes and as a lotion in bottles. Both will use our familiar blue-and-white design and logo.

Samples can be obtained by employees after May 15 at the reception desk, where a three-dimensional product display stand will also be presented.

Change in Product for Customer

Dear Bernie:

Without a great stretch of the imagination, I can see questions being raised by you and others on your landscape purchasing staff as you read the headlines about pesticide control legislation in Georgia.

If the bill goes through—and we are all convinced it will—our entire 4HDA line will have to be modified before the next calendar year to eliminate the toners that have come under the fire of the ecologists. Our chief agronomist has recommended that we replace them with "R"-type neutrals rather than with active agents. The bad news is that dry mixes, packed in bags and cartons, will be prone to lumpiness if exposed to any moisture. But the good news is that the price will definitely not increase and may even be a shade lower.

If you have any questions after the bill's curtailments are spelled out, we'll be happy to answer them.

With best regards,

Mechanical Engineering Data

Dear Mr. Probish:

By now you will have received the four steel tie rods that represent the type my firm is about to produce for the Hart Engineering Company bridge project. Would you please perform both heat and stress tests on these, in much the same manner that you did for our circular rods last month.

It is important that we have the results in writing, certified, and stamped so we can affix the document to our contract with Hart.

If possible, we'd appreciate these data by no later than March 15.

Sincerely,

Additional Information—Warranty

Dear Mrs. Turnbull:

When your firm recently installed a new heat pump for our offices, you gave us a copy of the ten-year warranty, which explains in considerable detail what is covered in the event of product or duct failures. However, we are not clear about the extent of the warranty in the event that we should add to the system in the future to increase the capacity. We plan on doing just that when we add a wing to the north side of our building, two years hence. Would the warranty then be extended for two years, covering both the present system and the addition? Or would we end up with eight years to go on the old equipment and ten on the new installation?

Any information you can provide would be appreciated.

Sincerely,

False Product Claims

Dear Customers:

You are advised to be alert to the operations of a con artist who has been reaping in the bucks by selling a liquid formulation that he claims will "banish baldness forever." He is very convincing and has even made sales to professional pharmacists, as well as multitudes of barber shops, by showing "before" and "after" photographs. These not only appear to document the stimulation and growth of hair but are signed and notarized by supposedly prominent people, including the "chief researcher" of a nonexistent drug company. The salesman also presents convincing-looking bank references and offers full refunds to any purchasers not totally satisfied.

We have analyzed this "magic formulation" and have found it to be about as effective for growing hair on a bald head as if the user were to apply salad oil.

Sincerely,

PRICES

When writing a letter to request price information, make sure you specify clearly what you want regarding such matters as retail price, discounts, quantities, and related costs. When responding to requests for information, bear in mind that accuracy is all important. If you misquote a price unfavorable to you, it is possible that you can be held to that figure, despite a later correction.

Catering Service

Dear Mrs. Farley:

The accompanying printout lists the hors d'oeuvres, soups, entrees, desserts, salads, breads, accoutrements, and side dishes that we prepare in our gourmet kitchens. Most of our items are sold by servings, for which we suggest average sizes and weights, depending upon the occasion. It is our policy to offer *non* resort prices because we want our customers to feel that they've received exceptional values—enough to stimulate their interest in placing orders for small dinner parties or simple family affairs, as well as those that normally call for a catering service.

We further pledge our money-back commitment to your complete satisfaction.

In so doing, we promise only the finest and freshest ingredients and the promptest service.

Yours in good health,

Packaging Materials

Dear Mr. Preising:

I am the owner of a small local business supplying boxes, crates, cartons, and other containers to merchants in western Tennessee. Our business thrives on the fact that we can keep large and varied inventories of these items in our warehouse and then supply needed items quickly and in small lots to our many customers, thus making it easier for them to allocate more of their store space to display and sales and less to storage. During the last couple of years we have seen two basic problems developing: steady price boosts and a decline in the quality and strength of the materials used by our suppliers.

We are getting in touch with you and other potential suppliers because of the article I read with interest in the June issue of *American Packager* about new fiber sheetings that are stronger and cheaper than other materials and are also biodegradable. If you can supply these new types of cartons, we'd like information, prices, and samples.

Sincerely,

Increasing Order—Requote Prices

Dear Powell:

Because of a new contract in our production schedules, we would like to increase our order for the Heavyweight #36 shipping cartons from 2,080 to 3,600. Since we anticipate even further increases within the next six months in all our production departments, we are now reviewing our sources of supply and price lists.

Sam and I would appreciate it if you could revise your price quotes at this time and let me know what discounts would apply to increased orders for all of the sizes and types of cartons you have been supplying regularly.

As I recall from past conversations, we might also be eligible for discounts if we allow you to select delivery times and keep them flexible. What kinds of savings would be effected, for example, if from time to time you piggybacked our order on that of someone else to whom you were making deliveries in this area?

Sincerely,

Requesting a Discount

Dear Ms. Henderson:

We greatly appreciated the time your representative, Sam Scott, gave to us in estimating the cost of repainting, carpeting, and improving the lighting in our offices. As we explained to him at the time, we were also obtaining price quotations from two other prospective contractors.

Now that we have had a chance to review the estimates and specifications provided by all three firms, we find that your costs fall in the middle—higher than one and lower than the other. Quite frankly, we would prefer to give the contract for the work to you, since Mr. Scott seemed to grasp our needs better than your competitors did and since his specifications were more exacting.

We are torn between this decision and the temptation to effect the improvements at a lower cost. Is it possible that you could give us a 15% discount and thus solve our dilemma?

Sincerely,

PROFESSIONAL QUALIFICATIONS

One of the challenges facing letter writers providing information about their personal qualifications is to emphasize positive capabilities and achievements, without seeming to be too self-promoting or self-serving. For this reason, the best letter is the one that is factual and businesslike and that lists qualifications in order of their significance. Give priority to the essentials that are pertinent to the recipient of the letter, not necessarily the ones of which you are most proud.

Attorney

Dear Judge Sembarton:

I am delighted that you are going to chair the quarterly *Fidelis* meeting and will thus be introducing me as the keynote speaker. The following data should be sufficient to provide the career "highlights" you want, without putting the audience to sleep before I even get started:

- Earned her law degree at St. John's Law School
- Earned her doctorate at Wharton
- Worked for two years in her hometown, Portland, Maine, as clerk of the county court
- Moved to Philadelphia to work for five years with Caine & Caine

- Married one of the partners and took a three-year leave to start raising a family (now two daughters)
- Established her own law office in Philadelphia with two fellow graduates from Wharton.

I am looking forward to the occasion with enthusiasm.

With kind regards,

School Founder

Dear Mrs. Bamleigh:

I was interested to read the item in *School Newsline* about the opening of the Crowell Academy for the Disadvantaged. You might want to complement it sometime soon with a brief profile of Dr. Amadeus Crowell. Here are some highlights in his educational career:

- Graduated with a B.A. from Wesleyan in 1965
- Earned his doctorate at Columbia in 1970
- Served four years as assistant provost at Rugby, in England, 1971-1975
- Held an instructors's position, later an associate professorship at Duke University from 1975 until 1982
- Directed a program for the disadvantaged in the Houston public school system from 1982 until 1986
- Completed a three-year advanced study program in psychology and teaching at Columbia from 1986 until 1989.

At the end of 1989, having developed long-range plans for more than five years, Dr. Crowell opened the Crowell Academy. In this, he was supported financially by the Smithers Foundation, as well as with a special grant from Columbia.

If you need further details on any aspect of Dr. Crowell's distinguished career, please let me know.

Sincerely,

Consultant

Dear Dr. Sorensen:

As your associate, David Pratt, has probably mentioned to you, I have submitted a proposal to your agency to undertake a survey of the market potential for compact disk players among men and women in the 30- to 45-year-old age bracket. He requested that I inform you of my qualifications.

Before starting my own consulting firm two years ago, I was with a polling organization for five years as a field supervisor. During that period, I was responsible for hiring part-time interviewers and supervising their assignments as they conducted surveys and reported results. My work included studies involving a number of types of products, such as electronic equipment, cameras, small appliances, and sporting goods. Now, as an independent consultant, I not only act as a supervisor in this sense, but take responsibility for preparing all interview questions, researching the areas to be covered, and selection proper cross sections of people to be interviewed.

I am a graduate of the American Statistical School and have authored six published papers on the science of selection and statistics. I am also a member of the National Statistical Society (NSS) and for the past three years have been its recording secretary.

If you would like further biographical details, I'd be more than happy to furnish them at any time.

Sincerely,

Accountant

Dear Messrs. Richardson and Coker:

We have 16 accountants on our payroll, and normally when one of our clients indicates a preference, pro or con, we reassign personnel accordingly. In your case, however, I strongly suggest that you stick with my choice, Gertrude Trice. I make this recommendation for a number of reasons, despite the fact that you are concerned about her youth and question her experience in the chemical industry, which is the mainstay of your business.

In the first place, Ms. Trice has been a practicing Certified Public Accountant (CPA) for nine years, which may surprise you. She not only looks younger than she is, but was bright enough to be about two years ahead of most students her age when she was at Penn State and later in graduate studies at Baxter. She spent four years in the comptroller's office at Allied Chemical where she was a financial analyst and for two other years was in Houston with the Internal Revenue Service. Since joining our firm three years ago, she has worked with clients in at least a dozen different industries, always with a strong grasp of their specific, and sometimes singular, problems.

My suggestion is that you let Ms. Trice work with your accounting department through the initial evaluation period, which will give you a realistic overview of her qualifications, attitude, and procedures. Then, if you have the slightest hesitation about continuing with her, I will step in and take over the assignment myself.

As you can judge, I am convinced that such a step will not be necessary or advisable.

Cordially,

Technician

Dear Mr. Dooley:

This letter will, I hope, serve to set your mind at ease regarding the professional qualifications of Roberta Shackley, whom we assigned to your account to service your electronic tracking gear. Ms. Shackley is completely familiar with the equipment and even went so far as to inform me that she would have to be on your site for three and a half days in order to (1) study the problem, (2) adjust the circuits, and (3) test the recurrent cycles thereafter.

You may be more confident about her when I add that she is a graduate of M.I.T., completed an advance training seminar at AT&T last year, and for three years was the technical field maintenance supervisor for the U.S. Meteorological Service, in a division with tracking instruments not unlike yours.

Sincerely,

INTEROFFICE COMMUNICATIONS

When writing an interoffice memo or notice, the four most important requirements are (1) keep the message brief, (2) make it clear, (3) stick to one subject, and (4) don't try to be chatty or humorous.

Change in Company Plans and Goals

TO: Depot Managers
FROM: Tom Streeter
SUBJECT: Change in Truck and Trailer Rental Goals

During the past four years, we have been moderately successful in persuading the public to rent our small, single-hitch trailers. They have been popular with consumers because they are considerably less expensive to rent than trucks, and because they can often be backed into a narrow driveway space where nonprofessional drivers are afraid to navigate with wide-bodied trucks.

After serious consideration, however, we are going to phase out the trailer business. We'll start by eliminating all mentions in newspaper ads and the Yellow Pages, and we'll gradually sell off our trailers or take them out of service. The reason? There have been too many accidents with trailers, some caused by faulty hitching and some by top-heaviness as a result of improper loading. As a consequence, we are facing rapidly rising costs for insurance policies. While we could pass these along to our customers, our rates would soon be out of sight and would play havoc with our claim that we are the most economical rental agency in our region.

So please bear this change in mind and start converting your own sales and promotional efforts to trucks, instead of trailers. To aid in this effort, we hope soon to make available a fleet of smaller, lighter-weight vehicles we'll refer to as "minitrucks."

Proposing Employee Orientation Program

TO: Roger Barstow
FROM: Stan Rayfield
SUBJECT: Orientation

During the last year, we have seen a marked increase in the number of production runs that have had to be scrapped and reworked because of poor quality or outright errors. I've been keeping records to try to determine why this downtrend should have occurred and have pinpointed the problem as follows: The quality of the professionalism in our ranks has declined for two basic reasons: (1) As experienced journeymen have retired, their replacements have largely been apprentices who have not had anywhere near the same level of training or experience, and (2) the pay scales are such that we cannot attract people who are as qualified as the applicants we used to draw.

We have discussed remuneration before and have pretty much agreed that we cannot stretch the budget any further without raising prices out of sight. So my solution is this: Let's allocate a modest investment of time and money in an internal orientation program focused specifically on production and the manufacturing processes, procedures, and quality controls we employ. By complementing our know-how with that of an outside consulting engineer who would be better able to look objectively at the problems, we should be able to get back on track. I'm positive the investment would pay off in terms of better quality, fewer rejected production runs, and even improved morale.

With your approval, I'd like to outline the subjects that should be covered, in order, and then discuss a detailed plan of action.

Announcing Employee Orientation Program

TO: Production Department Employees
FROM: Production Manager
SUBJECT: Orientation

During the last year, we have seen a marked increase in the number of production runs that have had to be scrapped and reworked because of poor quality or outright errors. Our information records indicate that the problem has been caused, at least to a substantial degree, by a lack of familiarity with some of the new equipment and materials we now have in our plant. To solve this problem, we have hired an outside production consultant who will conduct an in-house orientation program. This will focus on production and the manufacturing processes, procedures, and quality controls we employ.

Within the next ten days, you will receive a schedule outlining the subjects to be covered and listing the hours during which classes will be held. Since the entire program will be held during regular working hours, everyone in the production department is expected to attend.

Requesting Preferential Treatment

Dear Mrs. Kellogg:

By the time you receive this letter, you will also have received our supervisor's applications from computer operators listing their preferences for weekday morning schedules for using mainframe time. One of the entries that will undoubtedly strike your eye is my "priority" request for the most popular 9:00 and 10:00 A.M. openings on Mondays, Wednesdays, and Fridays.

Please take into consideration that my request is not based on either personal convenience or office preference but on the fact that my time has been so completely assigned to the controller's office on those three days that I have no other hours at my disposal. The only alternative would be for you to talk to my department manager and have her coordinate the schedules to suit your needs.

Sincerely,

Explaining Expense Report

Dear Harlan:

After reviewing my expense report as you requested, I see no reason for reducing it in any way. We have complete documentation for all the entries. The vouchers and figures on the report match, dollar for dollar and cent for cent. And the supporting data are accurate and pertinent.

You are concerned because (1) there is one entry for a major expenditure of a type that has not occurred on past expense reports and (2) that expenditure bears that red-flag tag, "entertainment." You can set your mind at rest regarding the former: it was for the big, two-day pitch we made for the National Baker's account, which is really paying off. As for the latter, change the nomenclature to "financial research."

With best regards,

Warning to Employees About Scams and Ripoffs

Dear Grace:

If we are not alert and informed, we run the risk of getting bilked by a new breed of con artist now making the rounds. Please warn any and all of your buyers, or prospects, of a scam that could cost them—and all of us—a potful of money. We have just learned that a con man known variously as "Professor Ruggles," "Dr. Halbert," and "Judge Bergmann" has been peddling bogus contracts for Indonesian fabrics at huge discounts. He uses the ploy that a shipload of the goods arrived on the West Coast destined for a buyer who had gone bankrupt. As the tale goes, the consignor was desperate to unload the goods before having to face long-term dockage and warehouse fees.

The "Professor," "Doctor," "Judge," or whatever else he may be calling himself is very persuasive, assuring prospective buyers that he is "merely trying to help a friend in need." To assure delivery of the fabrics at his astonishingly low price, he requires only a 10% cash advance. And he has an attache case filled with official-looking documents, bank references, fabric specifications, and—you name it—to prove the transaction is bona fide.

Of course, he is playing on the inherent greed of suckers to believe they can get something for nothing. I hope that does not include any of us.

Cordially,

Monthly Meeting Schedule

Dear Lorraine:

As we agreed at the last meeting, our joint discussions are vital if we are to have the kind of coordination we need in the agency. After running the data through the computer, we have come up with the following combination. The *first* order of business on the *first* Monday of each month will be designated our *"First Order"* parlay and will take place in the *first floor* conference room. It will take place promptly at the *first* hour of normal business, 9:00 A.M., and will run until 11:00 A.M. Each of us will present or describe just one project, the *first* on our priority list.

Could anything be clearer than that?

I hope this will eliminate past confusion, and since Monday mornings are usually shunned by clients, we should have few, if any, schedule conflicts.

Sincerely,

DELAYS AND ERRORS

If you have been guilty of delays or errors in the delivery of goods or the promptness of service, your letter should contain the following elements:

1. Apology for the problem, no matter who is at fault
2. Explanation of the reason for the problem, but *only* if it will serve a positive purpose for future business
3. Your solution to correcting the problem or offering acceptable alternatives.
4. A conclusion that ends on an upbeat note

Merchandise Order—Instructions

Dear Dr. Dembarton:

Following the mixup last month in the order for sterile products we sent to your laboratories, our shipping supervisor apologized to me for having misread the invoice. However, when I reviewed the situation to make sure that it does not recur, something struck my eye that should be called to the attention of your chief technician. She had specified the totals in *pounds* rather than *kilograms*, as printed on the order blanks. Hence, the totals were different from what you expected.

This resulted in an inconvenience rather than a crisis. However, such a mixup could be serious, even threatening, if the order called for blending or amalgamating liquids and powders before delivery. Over and beyond that, we want you always to be pleased with our products and our service.

Sincerely,

Explaining Late Shipment

Dear Jake:

Just a note to alert you to the fact that the next scheduled delivery of propane gas to your plant will be delayed by what we now estimate to be four days. We received a notice from AmGas that the refinery fire in Tulsa resulted in greater damage than expected and has severely slowed production.

I phoned the marketing manager immediately and asked for top priority, both as a longtime purchaser and the supplier of critical materials. I told him, in effect, that one shipment (yours) was earmarked for a critical defense industry and thus rated special consideration. I intend to phone him again at the end of this month and expedite the delivery. So rest assured that we have your interests in mind and will do everything we can to avoid delays.

Cordially,

Incorrect Shipment

Dear Warren:

I haven't goofed so badly since I sent my grandfather a green plaid shirt to wear with checkered orange slacks and a purple striped cap. Well, I guess it was just one of those days. I had carefully selected and arranged the wallpaper samples for your office, along with those I knew would be in keeping with the decor for Allan and Desmond. So what did I do? I wrapped them lovingly and meticulously, identified as to price and specifications—and sent them off by messenger to the Mayor's office!

What you and your partners received were intended for the hearing room at the village court, the sheriff's office, and for all I know in my present failing state of mind, the fire department ready room! I apologize ten times over.

Shamefacedly,

Explaining a Delay in Construction Schedule

Dear Stewart:

When we negotiated the contract for the construction of your minishops at the Arcade Mall, I promised to alert you to any problems that would delay their completion well before the Christmas shopping season. So I am doing just that.

Late last evening, I received a phone call from my plumbing subcontractor to the effect that the city had placed a moratorium on the laying of waste disposal lines throughout all uncompleted sections of the Mall. This gave me a very bad night, I'll tell you. So, first thing in the morning, I contacted Selectman Skinner, who chairs the Approval Board, and asked him what kind of rug the bureaucrats are pulling out from under us this time. Skinner was more apologetic than informative, but after a lot of nagging, I got him to admit that "somebody" in the building codes section had goofed and permitted the installation of sewer lines that were too small. I think I scared him by prophesying that the city would be in deep trouble should the Mall tenants suffer serious financial losses as a result of mistakes made by City Hall.

The bottom line is that he all but promised that the condition would be corrected "within five days" and that we could then continue our work in time to avoid a monetary disaster. If this is correct, we have no problem. Should the situation worsen, I'll let you know. Pronto!

Sincerely,

Apologizing for a Missed Deadline

Dear Roger:

I was one day late. Then two days late. Then three days late. I don't want to take the time to make excuses and thus be four days late.

You will have the manuscript three and a half days late. But it will need practically no editing, thus saving you that same amount of time.

Apologetically,

Providing Missing Information

Dear Charlie:

I goofed. I told you we would be moving our meetings henceforth from the former Landmark Society Building to the new conference room at the Lion's Club. But I forgot to tell you *when* this would go into effect. The answer is simple. The next time you attend, go to the Lion's. See you there.

Cordially,

Correcting Erroneous Information

Dear Dr. Carrier:

Your correspondence of January 17 was misdirected and we are sorry for the delay in responding to your request for our Acme Medical Supply catalog.

We are located, as this letterhead indicates, at *10981* Seaside Boulevard. The mistake is understandable. Your letter went to 348 Seaside, which is the location of Acme Photo Supply, and did not reach us until today.

In order to serve you better, we are sending the enclosed catalog by priority mail rather than second class. When we hear from you, we'll make sure your order is processed promptly. But please note our correct address on your records.

Sincerely,

Enclosure

ADVICE AND INFORMATION

When asking for information, and particularly advice, limit your request to the subject that takes top priority. Don't try to overload a single letter with multiple appeals. When responding to a plea for advice, provide only what is asked for and do not digress into other subjects, dear though they may be to your heart. If you do not have the proper data, or feel that you are not qualified to provide the kind of counsel desired, be frank in saying so.

Potential of a Franchise

Dear Fran:

Some 20 years ago, I opened what I thought was the finest, most promising bookstore on the West Coast. One good year followed after another, but then the inroads of cut-rate bookstores, television, and videotapes took their toll. Last year, I didn't realize even enough profit to repaint the fading walls and scoured shelves. So where to go?

Recently, I read that children's bookstores might be the coming thing, based on the burgeoning interest in juvenile books. One of my associates advised me to look into a franchise for a children's bookstore. A study had revealed that children's bookstores were leading the rest of the publishing industry in dollar sales by 20%.

My two questions: (1) Based on your experience as a children's book editor, does this figure sound realistic? And (2) if you were in my shoes, would you consider investing in a children's bookstore franchise?

Sincerely,

Educational Objectives

Dear Mr. Paddington:

My name is Hiram Short. You do not know me, but two months from now, I would hope that you would see the name and say, "Oh, Hiram Short. Of course! He's the fellow who...."

I am about to start a unique new venture. It is a service that is much needed, has news value, lends itself well to photographs, and should attract a considerable amount of public interest. If I had the capital, I would hire Paddington & Co. to represent me as a client and launch a stimulating public relations campaign that would immediately put my little company, Short Circuit, on the map. For the moment, however, I have to be content with a do-it-yourself operation, until that magic moment when I can become a paying client.

Which brings me—at last—to the point of this letter. As I drew up plans for my new enterprise, I also outlined time for a public relations program to get my name, company, and objectives known to prospective purchasers of my service. This plan included a week or so during which I would educate myself about publicity, promotion, press relations, and related functions. There is only one hitch. Despite exhaustive research and a great deal of homework, I could not find a single professional seminar or practical course in the subject anywhere within reasonable commuting distance.

Did I overlook something? Are such courses hidden under ambiguous names? Does one have to take membership in the Public Relations Society of America to enroll?

What would you do if you were in my shoes?

Sincerely,

Drinking and Alcoholism Programs

Dear Mr. Wilds:

When our firm was small, we were more or less a family operation in which we all knew each other and filled our employee needs through personal recommendations. In relatively short time, we doubled in size and then quadrupled when we acquired another trucking firm that was facing bankruptcy. As a consequence, it became increasingly difficult for me, or my four state managers, to keep track of drivers and load handlers and know which ones were reliable and which were not. Substance abuse began to loom as one of the major problems, and we early on had to establish strict rules about such matters as drug use and drinking prior to going on the road.

Although our program has been moderately effective, we feel that it needs a total overhaul and most probably a better orientation and education program to complement it. We would, therefore, appreciate it if you could send us whatever printed material you may have on hand about company programs. I am also wondering whether it would be possible for you to put me in touch with two or three other managers in the trucking and transportation field who have initiated programs that have proved to be effective and rewarding.

Sincerely,

Data Processing

Dear Ms. Downright:

As the owner and manager of a horticultural service in a region that covers about 100 square miles here in central Virginia, I maintain a large file of data about such pertinent matters as species of plants, growing seasons, pest control, nutriments, pruning, and soil conditions. I also keep detailed records about my customers, their plantings and lawns, and preferences during the various seasons. The extent of this valuable information has reached such proportions that I am certain we could well use a computerized data processing system to maintain better control and provide more reliable service to our customers.

With these considerations in mind, I would greatly appreciate it if you would recommend a reliable source I could turn to for information about specific makes and models of electronic equipment. I am so inexperienced in this field that I could easily be talked into purchasing the wrong equipment or paying an exorbitant price for a system that was greatly overqualified.

Perhaps my first step should be to enroll in an adult education course in computers.

Your suggestions would be most welcome.

Sincerely,

Advertising

Dear Professor Ruddick:

You may recall that I was one of some 15 students in your "Over-50" advertising seminar at the State U. summer program five years ago. Since then, my wife and I have taken over a defunct hostelry in the northwestern mountain region of North Carolina (described in the enclosed brochure). We knew from the start it was a mad venture, but we have always wanted to be innkeepers—and here we are. Thus far, we have been quite successful and have built up a small, but loyal clientele.

I am writing you because I particularly recall that you dearly loved a challenge, especially if it were one in which advertising might effect an about-face and transform failure into success. Our immediate hurdle is this: How do we attract more off-season visitors, short of lowering rates to the "loss" column of the books?

Believing that you might accept such a challenge, I offer you and your wife a weekend in our Blue Ridge Suite in return for just one good idea.

Whether you can make it or not, I do want you to know that I enjoyed your seminar and have already applied some of your advertising principles to good effect.

Cordially,

Public Relations

Dear Messrs. Simpson & Burdick:

By way of introduction, I am the owner of what was a defunct hostelry in the northwestern mountain region of North Carolina (described in the enclosed brochure). My wife and partner in the venture knew from the start it was a mad venture, but we have always wanted to be innkeepers—and here we are. Thus far, we have been quite successful and have built up a small, but loyal clientele.

We need help, however, and wonder if you are interested in a challenge, especially if it were one in which you might effect an about-face and transform failure into success. Our immediate hurdle is this: How do we attract more off-season guests, short of lowering rates to the "loss" column of the books?

Believing that you might accept such a challenge, I offer you both (with your wives) a weekend at our inn to discuss ways in which you might help, and at what cost. If you come up with ideas, you'll get our business. If not, at least we guarantee you'll all enjoy a memorable weekend.

Cordially,

Marketing Information

Dear Mr. Hammrick:

To introduce myself, I am the business manager of a small firm that my husband recently established to provide consultation, equipment, and products for the treatment of water that is too hard, contaminated with organic materials, or overladen with mineral contents. He is an engineer and will handle the technical side; I will supervise marketing and sales.

As a member of the Southeast Marketing Association, I attended the one-week seminar last fall in Greensboro on Marketing and Merchandising Principles and Procedures. During the sessions, numerous chalkboard charts and checklists were used to emphasize the subjects under discussion. This kind of material and data would be extremely useful to me now, and I am wondering whether SMA has published any brochure(s) on the subject that you could send me. If not, would any of this material be available in loose-leaf form, which would be permissible for me to copy. If so, I'd be happy to pay someone to make copies. Or, if that is not feasible, I could visit your office and make the copies myself.

Any suggestions you have about other marketing materials that would be pertinent to our new business would be welcome.

Sincerely,

Environmental Data

Dear Dr. Thorsen:

I was interested to read in the *Daily Ledger* that your research laboratory has recently completed a study on stack emissions and pollution in the Savannah River Basin. Since our company is about to install a new heat-treating furnace, we want to make certain that the one we select will meet the most stringent environmental requirements.

Is it possible to obtain a copy of your complete report? If so, we need to know not only the cost but whether we would have approval to cite the study in our request and application to the municipal antipollution board.

Sincerely,

Demographics

Dear Mrs. Sagarro:

A mutual friend of ours, Elayne Demetrius, gave me your name as the best person to write to for information about West Columbus. I am a professional interior decorator, graduate of the New School in New York, and owner of a home furnishings shop that has been successfully in operation for almost ten years. Because my husband is being transferred to your area, I am moving my business and trying to determine which of four community locations would be the most feasible for professional reasons and the most pleasant for personal reasons.

I'd greatly appreciate it, therefore, if you could send me demographic data about West Columbus and any other information you think would influence my decision. I should add, too, that I am very active in civic affairs and volunteer programs and so would be interested in knowing where such opportunities lie.

Cordially yours,

New Product Line

Dear Ray:

As I may have mentioned to you, I am thinking of writing policies for a number of small businesses in town whose owners have expressed interest in the right combination of personal service and reliability—something they seem to find lacking in large agencies. My first impression was that this would be an effective way to expand my business and build a coterie of customers who might also turn to me for other kinds of coverage.

After further thought, I began wrestling with some doubts. Small businesses have a high rate of bankruptcies. They are frequently the targets of break-ins and vandalism. Their premises are not always adequately protected against fires, floods, and other natural disasters. So I might end up with a choice between two evils: (1) citing rates that are statistically realistic but financially too rich for my prospects' pocketbooks or (2) keeping rates low but hiking the risks I'd have to assume to protect my policyholders.

You have been in business a long time and can look at both sides of the fence objectively. What would you advise?

Cordially

Community Profile and Demographics—Prospective Business

Dear Aaron Grohman:

Thanks for writing the Rotary Club about your proposed move. Your inquiry has been passed along to me since I operate a regional travel bureau and am the Rotary's volunteer public relations manager. I have lived here for more than 25 years and have run my travel agency most of that time, and so I am familiar with situations and circumstances that relate to your field of business. You have come to the right place if you are looking for a neighborly midwestern town in which to open a country inn and restaurant. Because we attract large numbers of tourists to our lakes, rivers, and recreation areas, we are constantly in need of better, more attractive accommodations for visitors, of the type you have described. Also, since we have a fairly large permanent population of retired people, it is always a welcome sight for them to see new restaurant facilities and home cooking being made available.

We suggest that you come and visit us soon and see firsthand what our town has to offer. My wife's first cousin operates a comfortable bed-and-breakfast lodge, and we can assure you that you'll feel right at home there. It also has an excellent view of the surrounding mountains and forests.

Sincerely,

Thank You Note, Providing Directions and Map

Dear Mr. Gatlinger:

My associates and I are delighted that you will be paying us a visit Monday to inspect our clinical facilities and discuss plans for implementing your employee medical and health program.

For your information, I have enclosed a map showing the most convenient and direct route from Rochester to Austin. The distance is 49 miles and thus should require no more than an hour's drive. The road construction taking place near Dexter is negligible. The only place where you might get mixed up is at the approach to town. Bear to the right when you see the Austin City Limits sign. Barker Drive will be the first right turn after that, and you will find our office and clinic on the circle at the far end of the street.

We'll expect you around 10:00, but do not be at all concerned should you encounter any delay. We are here to serve you, at your convenience.

Sincerely,

RESPONDING TO REQUESTS FOR INFORMATION

The first example is a note of transmittal by a person who has been asked to complete a questionnaire from the Chamber of Commerce. Not wishing to comply fully, yet still wanting to be cooperative, the letter writer is gracious and restrained. The second letter is more blunt, making it clear that the writer feels imposed upon and is not in accord with the purpose of the request. The third letter not only provides the information requested, but adds a note—altogether proper here—of appreciation. The final letter is a simple request for relief from continual solicitation.

Side-Stepping a Request for Confidential Information

Dear Pete:

As requested, we have provided most of the information specified in the questionnaire. However, we have skipped questions 14 through 19 because we feel that the answers would release certain data supplied to us by our clients as private and confidential information. I trust that this will not greatly diminish the value of the survey, which we feel is well planned and will be useful to all of us who are members of the local Chamber.

Sincerely,

Submitting Business and Professional Forms—Under Protest

Dear Chairman Daniels:

My partner and I have spent the better part of the morning filling out the six forms that we received last week from the Town Planning Commission. We do so, however, with a note of protest, first, that we are obligated to participate in this project as "responsible members of the business community" (the term used in your covering letter) and, second, that the data requested seem so remote from what we were led to believe are the objectives of your Commission.

If the forms are examples of the Commission's "planning" organization and skills, then I'm afraid the town has a cloudy and unpredictable future. We suggest that, as a first step, you eliminate at least half the forms, streamline the rest, clarify the nature of the information you want, and restrict the recipients to organizations who are much more qualified than we are to make judgments and recommendations about architectural, structural, technological, environmental, and legal issues.

Sincerely,

To Police—Burglary

Dear Inspector Kearney:

The engineering manager explained to me that you need a complete list of the items stolen during the break-in at our offices last night. Since the equipment was all from the electronics department that I supervise, I was judged to be the one who could provide the most accurate details. As I understand it, you would like serial numbers and any other identifying features so that your detectives could check out dealers known to have purchased stolen goods in the past.

Attached is a list of missing items, including serial numbers, model numbers, and years of manufacture. For several of the most expensive pieces of equipment, we have also added pictures, photocopied from our maintenance manuals.

To the best of my knowledge, this list is complete. But if we discover that anything else has been stolen, I'll let you know immediately.

We appreciate your prompt response to our manager's phone call this morning and the thoroughness with which your officers investigated the break-in. They impressed us with their professional composure and polite, but no-nonsense manner.

Sincerely,

Requesting a Favor

Dear Abe:

One favor. A personal favor.

As the owner of my own enterprise, I seem to get on the list of everyone in town (or out of it for that matter) who is looking for large corporate donations to support worthy causes. Since our business is small and since I have already selected those few causes to which we contribute, these solicitors are barking up the wrong tree.

I understand there are ways of having one's name removed from these lists, and I'd appreciate it if you'd let me know how we go about discouraging the flood of mail we receive.

Thanks,

*M*AKING AND ANSWERING COMPLAINTS AND EFFECTING ADJUSTMENTS

It would be a fantasy land if small businesses could function without complaints—both on issuing and receiving them. Most business owners and managers cringe at the thought of complaints, whether they take them on the chin or have to dish them out. Yet, in a broad sense, these supposedly negative aspects of business are among the most important in the whole structure of commercial growth and development. The letter writers who bear this truth in mind are likely to have far less trouble composing and/or answering letters of complaint. And once they address these matters, they are more able to effect the kinds of adjustments and modifications that can renew customers' faith in the firm and its products or services.

Letters, more than phone calls or personal service visits, are the most effective dialog in the long run, when they are well written and tailored to the recipients. They can be written and dispatched in quantity. And they can serve as messages of goodwill as well as solutions to common problems.

HOW TO DO IT

Making Complaints

1. Describe the situation completely and accurately.
2. Restrain your emotions.
3. Tone down any impulse to be aggressive.
4. Avoid ultimatums and baseless threats.
5. Stick to the point.

6. Specify clearly what you expect to be done to resolve the problem.

7. Express a positive belief that there is a solution.

Complaint letters are basically negative; that is, they are not likely to be either complimentary or favorable. Yet they can be positive in the way they express your opinions. In some instances, they can even anticipate that a meaningful response will help to develop a better business or professional relationship than existed before. Ending a complaint letter on an upbeat note is often the most productive way of generating the kind of response and action you are hoping for.

Answering Complaints

1. Consider that the complainer may be justified.

2. Weigh the pros and cons of the issue.

3. Suggest a mutually advantageous solution.

4. Answer promptly to prevent resentments from arising.

5. If there will be a delay in reaching a conclusion or resolving a problem, say as much and estimate when and what you will do.

6. Be firm, but courteous if you are convinced you are in the right and the complaint is unjustified.

7. Request further information if you need it to reach a decision or resolve the issue.

8. Call in a third party when an issue is controversial or you need another opinion.

9. Be restrained in your language and tone, even if you can prove that the complaint is meaningless.

10. Make it clear, in closing, what you intend to do—or not do.

Answering an honest complaint in a positive and productive manner can sometimes prove to be excellent public relations and help to polish your and your firm's, image. A successful merchant once told me that he purposely made little errors to certain customers so he could correct them and make a good impression. While this is not recommended, it does show that you can turn a negative into a positive with a bit of ingenuity and imagination.

When answering complaints, use positive statements whenever possible— the kind you yourself would like to receive after making a complaint. If you cannot satisfy the complainer in the way expected, make an alternate suggestion. If you have to turn the matter over to someone else, state why this is to the complainer's benefit and not simply passing the buck.

Making Adjustments

1. Be congenial and gracious when making adjustments, whether they involve the repair of a product, replacement of goods, providing additional service to compensate for an inefficiency, or offering financial compensation.

2. Explain why the adjustment was needed in the first place, if there is good reason, but don't make weak excuses.

3. Offer a reasonable alternative in the event the adjustment proposed is not acceptable.

4. Follow through later with a note of thanks for being considerate and/or patient in the matter.

In any small venture that entails dealing with clients, customers, suppliers, contractors, consultants, patrons, employees, the public, or any other individuals or groups, complaints are just part of the business. The owners and managers, and professionals who fare best are those who recognize this and treat it the way they might any other kind of business challenge. And when dialog and action are needed, letters are often the best instrument you can have at your disposal. The model letters that follow cover some of the more commonplace subjects in this genre. Most are easily adaptable to your needs.

MAKING COMPLAINTS

The following model letters are examples of effective ways of making a variety of complaints. You can readily adapt them to complaints you might have, whether on these subjects or others. Note that the letters each focus on a specific complaint, are restrained and businesslike in tone, and make clear what the writer expects the recipient to do to alleviate the situation.

Failure to Honor a Commitment

Dear Mr. Gammond:

We were both surprised and dismayed to learn that you were not going to provide bus service for our employees for the annual fall tour and picnic, as you had in the past. We had counted on this transportation, and when we found out at the last minute that we would have to make an alternate plan, we had to pay a premium price to get what amounted to limousine service. Also, since the capacity of the vehicles was limited, a number of employees were forced to use their own cars, thus diminishing the purpose of the event: to get as many employees as possible together in a group.

We trust that, in the future, you will coordinate your planning a little better—that is, if you expect to stav in business and provide reliable service.

Sincerely,

Transportation Problems

Dear Mr. Dominick:

Two years ago, when we purchased our building from you and mutually signed the covenants relating to Northwood Park, it was with the understanding that certain benefits would come with this investment. One was that there would be regular, and reliable, transportation to and from the center of the city and outlying residential areas. That was one of the important advantages cited by you as a reason for us to move from our former urban location to this less congested locale.

Where are the regularly scheduled municipal buses that were to provide transportation for employees during the morning and evening commuter hours? They are overcrowded, unreliable, and poorly dispatched.

Where is the private van service that was to pick up patients and customers in town and bring them to our offices with convenient round-trip schedules? You keep giving us endless excuses for the delay in inaugurating the service.

Where are the Northwood shuttle omnibuses that were to circulate from one end of the park to the other and to shops along the fringe? There is only one such vehicle, and it seems to spend most of its life in the repair shop.

Thus far, you have failed to live up to your claims, which were clearly specified in your proposal. Transportation here is miserable! Even trying to obtain taxi service in emergencies is frustrating. As a consequence, our tenants are losing patients and customers they once had and are failing to attract prospective ones they had hoped for.

Unless you can effect a major turnaround in this situation and provide the transportation promised, within the next six months, we intend to join with other landowners and leaseholders in the Park in a lawsuit against you.

Very truly yours,

Noisy Construction Crew

Dear Mr. Contana:

The other day, I dictated a memo to my secretary on an audiocassette. After she had transcribed it, she suggested we get new tapes or a new player because the playback was of such poor quality she could hardly hear my words above the discord of background noises and interference. When I listened to the tape, I realized what the problem was: the screeching blare of radios from the lot next door coming right through my open window. One of the worst offenders had been barely 20 feet away on the back of a pickup truck with Contana Construction painted on the side. Out of curiosity, I toured five or six Contana construction sites in town and found the same situation: radio noise levels that can only be classified as "air pollution."

In talking to people, I've heard the same story repeated. "Oh, we've asked Contana crews to turn down the volume. They do, but the next day they're at it again!" If I were in your shoes, I certainly wouldn't want my name associated with this kind of invasive disturbance any longer.

Sincerely,

Inexperienced Service People

Dear Ms. Danforth:

How many times do I have to call your attention to the sloppy performances of your workers who are supposed to be keeping our offices tidy and clean? Each time we complained, we have received assurances from you that the situation would be improved. These promises are the kind that can only be referred to as "empty."

In case you have forgotten what kind of service you are supposed to be giving your customers, I enclose a copy of the neat little pamphlet you mailed us when you were promoting your firm. The assurances therein are hardly in keeping with the conditions on the job. We are herewith taking the stand that your pledges about reliability and satisfaction are deceptive and may even be cause for legal action, since we can lose business here when prospective clients arrive and find a messy office. If you cannot live up to your commitments, please say so and we'll sign up with another cleaning service.

Sincerely,

Computer Hardware Problem

Dear Jerry:

As I explained on the phone, the problems we have been having with the operation of the CPT-8510 are threefold:

1. The text on the screen jiggles and sometimes fades when the operator is typing at the same time the Rotary VIII Printer is in operation. This variation suggests a loose internal connection that may be subject to vibration when the printer is running off copies.

2. If we want to erase an entire disk, we have to do it one page at a time. The

"0,5" code does not function for more than one page. This is very time consuming. Is it possible that there is a different erase code in our system?

3. The Alphanumeric Sort has trouble alphabetizing lists that are more than 100 lines in length.

If your technician has any questions, I expect to be here from about 11 A.M. until 6 P.M. the rest of the week.

Thanks,

Repeated Breakdowns of Equipment

Dear Mr. Abbatello:

I understand from a reliable source that you are responsible for writing the copy in the ads for the X-5638B Duplex photocopying machine, one of which was installed seven months ago in the office of the secretarial pool I manage. One of your ads is on the desk before me, and I take the liberty of suggesting a few changes in the wording. These changes are based not on semantics or creative phraseology but on the performance of the very machine you have so unstintingly been glorifying.

In the headline, instead of "state-of-the-art technology," it would be more accurate to say "seat-of-the-pants guesswork."

In line 1, I suggest that you replace "reliable" with a more accurate word, "undependable."

In line 3, try "touch-and-go" instead of "steady."

At the end of the first paragraph delete "maintenance-free" and substitute "spotty performance."

Where you show the machine about to be put in use, place a placard on the tray saying "Out of Order."

Finally, where you quote a secretary saying, "What I really love most about the job is our X-5638B Duplex," you would be better advised to have her say, "I've come to love our X-5638B serviceman—he's here to keep us company so often."

If you'd like further suggestions, why don't you drop by our office some day and hear what the members of the secretarial pool have to say. Of course, you might have to censor their remarks.

Sincerely,

Defective Workmanship

Dear Mr. Guillot:

We've been ordering plumbing supplies and fixtures from Union Plumbing for the past 16 years and have for the most part been completely satisfied with both the products and your service. Therefore, it was with considerable surprise that I was informed by my installation technician that we had a very serious problem. At least half the valves you supplied us with last fall for the heating and air conditioning system have been faulty. When I inspected three of the ones he had dismantled for examination, I was dismayed to find that the grommets on them were made of acrylic, which is far less resistant to temperature-change stress than fiberglass (used in previous valves). Also, it was obvious to me that the workmanship was inferior. The adjustment nodes were not seated properly and, in two cases, were the wrong size.

We know from past experience with Union that you always make good on parts and materials that fail to live up to what is expected of them. To be on the safe side, we would like to replace all 86 valves in the system and would appreciate it if you would see to it that the new lot is carefully inspected for both material quality and workmanship before delivery.

Sincerely,

Unsafe Construction—Slippery Floors

Dear Ms. Armand-Fugeot:

When you designed the interior of Chase Towers, you did so, I'm sure, with beauty and distinctiveness in mind. There is no doubt that the lobby sparkles with good looks and has elicited some rave reviews from passers-by. However, I'm afraid this is a case of Beauty and the Beast, the "beast" being the monster the floor turns into when it becomes wet. The other day, when we had an all-day rainfall and many soaked feet trod the marble slabs, the surface became as treacherous as ice. We were fortunate indeed that, despite numerous falls, no serious injuries were sustained.

Won't you please see what can be done to coat the surface with a nonskid substance. Surely there must be some way to preserve the beauty yet eliminate the threats to life and limb. Our insurance company insists on this action.

Sincerely,

Dangerous Sidewalk Conditions

Dear Mr. Pierson:

One of our employees slipped and fell on the sidewalk leading from our east entranceway to the parking lot. She, fortunately, suffered no more than bruises on her left arm. But our inspection showed that the walk had not been properly cleared, nor had it been treated with any deicing chemicals. We must remind you that our lease calls for proper measures to counteract icing and other problems arising from weather conditions, as well as general cleaning and maintenance. Under the terms, you are fully responsible for any accidents that take place in the exterior of our building.

Over and beyond the monetary penalty, we are more concerned with the safety and well-being of our employees. In the future, I hope you will be likewise.

Sincerely,

Inferior Installation

Dear Mr. Blount:

Two months ago, we purchased on sale 970 square feet of vinyl carpeting, which your people installed in several of our offices and hallways as part of your special cash payment service. One month later, my office manager phoned the salesperson who had filled the order to complain that the carpeting in two of the offices was badly wrinkled. The two installers who had laid the carpet were dispatched the next day, when they worked for several hours smoothing the material and reattaching it along the walls. Within a matter of days, it was just as wrinkled as ever.

This time, I phoned the salesperson myself to suggest that the padding might be at fault. But she replied that there was nothing more that could be done. There must be a problem with the floor being uneven, she suggested. That is not true, since the building was completed only four years ago, and it can be seen that the floors are perfectly straight. But what really got me was when she informed me that, since we had bought the carpeting "on sale," it could not be replaced nor could we get a refund.

The problem was not with the material we bought, it was with the way your people—supposedly professionals—installed it. This is to inform you that, unless the job can be completed correctly, we expect full compensation.

Sincerely,

Delivery of Wrong Materials

Dear Mr. Forrest:

As a former salesman myself, I dislike to go over the head of the person who is supposedly servicing our account, particularly since your products themselves have been reliable and effective. But now the situation has reached a point where we can no longer abide it. We either resolve it immediately or look for another supplier.

The problem is a dual one. First, on the last ten orders, we received merchandise that we did not request or that had already been shipped to us. Second, the inventory lists and financial statements have been totally different from the actual shipments, making it necessary for our stockroom to double-check every incoming container.

Since phone calls and correspondence to your regional office here have failed to correct the problem, I would like to find out how we can resolve this to our mutual satisfaction and get on with our business.

Sincerely,

Deceptive Advertising

Dear Colonel Travers:

Consider this letter a request to cease and desist the statements you are now making in your radio and television commercials concerning the burial allowance you offer to the families of deceased veterans of U.S. military forces not on active duty. You imply in your advertising that your company, Briarcrest Cemeteries, Inc., will deduct up to $300 from burial costs for families of former military personnel, as your own expression of goodwill for their duty to their country.

Please be advised that it is clearly stated by the Department of Veterans Affairs that deceased veterans of wartime or peacetime service are eligible for a plot or interment allowance of that amount, up to $300 to be specific, to be reimbursed by the government itself.

Furthermore, it is deceptive for you to imply that you yourself were an active colonel in the U.S. military service when your title is purely an honorary one awarded for duty as a deputy police training officer.

If you continue to employ deceptive advertising to make consumers believe that you are offering a payment out of pocket, we will have no recourse but to seek an injunction against your continued operation in business.

Sincerely,

Unreliable Mailing Lists

Dear Mr. Fletcher:

Three months ago, you sold us a list of prospective buyers of sporting goods which you had promoted as "a well-tested and reliable list of people in the upper-third income level who regularly purchase goods and equipment as active sports participants."

Well, these people must also be active in selling their homes and moving because no less than 19%—almost one out of every five—of the mailings were returned by the post office with the notation MOVED—NOT FORWARDABLE or similar pronouncement. In view of this, we are herewith requesting that you refund 19% of the payment we made to you at the time of purchase.

Sincerely,

Thank You for Handling a Complaint

Dear Celia:

 I happened to run into our valued customer, Sandra Dalley, at a luncheon yesterday. She had really been miffed when she received the wrong order for the cross-rib taffeta—and two days late at that. But she so appreciated your prompt action and your full acceptance of responsibility. And she was favorably impressed by the little gift you sent her for her daughter's engagement shower.

 So thanks for making amends so quickly—and so well.

Best,

ESTABLISHING COMPANY POLICIES

Communications about company policies should be written only after you have made a list of subjects that are timely and significant and should be called to the attention of employees or outsiders who are likely to be involved. Issuing too many statements of policy, or stressing ones that are of questionable importance, can result in a diminishing response on the part of the recipients. Make sure (1) that you have stated the policy clearly, (2) that you are addressing your words to a suitable audience, and (3) that the timing is right.

To Managers—Rude Salespersons

TO: The Managers of "Mall 36" Shops
FROM: Mall 36 Management
SUBJECT: Complaints About Rude Salespersons

 Although everyone is happy that business throughout the mall has climbed 75% since our opening three years ago, we are dismayed that another statistic—an unwelcome one—has also climbed. I am talking about complaints received in the mall reception office and elsewhere about salespeople who are rude, indifferent, and sometimes downright insulting. We do realize much of the fault lies in the fact that it is tough these days to recruit adequate help, and we all have to "make do" with employees who are untrained, little motivated, and sometimes on edge because of substance abuse problems.

 However, our own past experience has shown that the situation can be greatly improved if owners and managers are willing to devote half an hour or so of their personal time to indoctrinating new personnel about manners in general and their own policies and procedures in particular. Complaints often originate with misunderstandings rather than outright rudeness or indifference. To take a positive approach, we are instituting two steps that should be helpful:

1. We have acquired the services of an outside consultant, Marcia DeLong, who is a specialist in manners and etiquette. Ms. DeLong will make herself available to any manager who desires her services on an hourly basis, either to provide instruction or to evaluate problems. Because we are so concerned about making an improvement, Mall 36 management will pick up the tab for half the cost.

2. Under Ms. DeLong's direction, we are going to take monthly surveys and make "Sales Personality" awards to those who exhibit special traits of courtesy and consideration to customers.

If you have questions or care to make suggestions to counter this problem, our door is always open, as well as our ears.

Thank you.

To Warehouse Employees—Careless Packing and Shipping

TO: Handlers of Company Merchandise
FROM: Warehouse Management
RE: Careless Handling

If we could improve our handling, packing, and shipping procedures and habits by about 75%, we could save enough money in one year to give each and every employee in the building a bonus of $200! As things stand right now, we have an unusually high rate of return from customers because of rough handling or breakage in improperly padded packages. Another cause of loss has been the slashing of contents when handlers have hurriedly or heedlessly used knives improperly when opening cartons.

To offset this problem, we have scheduled a one-hour package orientation workshop on September 20 at 10:00 A.M. in the main warehouse. All employees who have anything to do with packing and shipping are expect to attend.

For the Management,

To Warehouse Manager—Faulty Merchandise

Dear Millie:

Looking through our recent marketing files, as I do from time to time, I was surprised to note a distressing fact about letters we have been receiving that demand adjustments for faulty merchandise. These communications have been increasing at the rate of almost 10% per month for the last six months. A little arithmetic shows that, at this rate, we'll soon be out of business entirely.

By way of correcting the problem, I suggest we set up a series of short orientation programs for all employees who are responsible for checking orders, confirming them, and packing cartons to ship to our mail-order customers. If you have any other suggestions for ways to improve our track record, let's discuss them.

Cordially,

To Professional Organization—Industrywide Standards

Dear Ross:

Your public relations committee has not been very active of late, but now we are faced with a problem I think you and your group might be helpful in solving. An increasing number of members have reported that their employees just don't know how to handle complaints from customers and thus tend to ignore them instead of trying to deal with them. This makes customers even madder and often results in a loss of repeat business.

We cannot ignore complaints, whether justified or imagined. So what should we do? My opinion is that your group could come up with some kind of "formula" for answering the most common gripes, such as delays, high prices, failure to remove spots, or discourtesy. You might also give thought to a printed slip that could be attached to the identity tags, soliciting suggestions from patrons. What do you think?

With best regards,

ANSWERING COMPLAINTS

Answering complaints is a chore that is high on the list of duties that are placed on the "back burner." The best way to cope with the situation is to follow this formula: (1) Respond immediately. (2) Acknowledge responsibility, if your company is at fault. (3) State what you intend to do to correct the problem. The following letters will show how some typical complaints were handled.

Faulty Products

Dear Ms. Farbrow:

We were distressed to learn that the order we delivered to you last month was not satisfactory because the swivel ball rollers on 8 of the office chairs were defective and much too tight. I have personally inspected the 14 similar chairs we still have in our warehouse stock and found that all but 3 of them have the same problem. Our repair technician tried to adjust them and came to the conclusion that the defect lies in the tooling of the part itself, not in the installation or alignment.

I have contacted the manufacturer and described the problem. He is shipping us replacements, which we will deliver to you immediately upon receipt. Unfortunately, this will take a week. I apologize sincerely, both for the faulty products and for the delay, since it is our aim to achieve customer satisfaction with each and every order we ship.

Cordially,

Faulty Clock Radio

Dear Mrs. Semple:

We are sorry to hear that the new clock radio you purchased from us two weeks ago has a faulty alarm timer and mechanism. We have been selling this model for almost a year and have had no previous complaints. There is always a "lemon" sooner or later on any assembly line, and you, unfortunately, have been a victim this time.

Please bring the defective product in next time you are shopping in this area, and we'll replace it. As compensation for your trouble, we'll also give you a handy program selector for your TV.

Sincerely,

Poor Service

Dear Dr. and Mrs. Chivas:

We appreciated your taking time to complete our little questionnaire during your holiday weekend at the Primrose Inn. Your views are most important to us, since they help us to improve our facilities and our service, as well as make any adjustments that are called for.

The problem you mentioned has been discussed with our chief housekeeper, who has asked me to apologize for the untidiness you found in the bathroom. There is no way that she—or we—can excuse sloppy housekeeping in any way. We are so sorry for letting you leave our premises with a sour note. But we promise, promise, promise that it will never happen again.

And we do thank you for calling the matter to our attention.

With best wishes,

Inadequate Accommodations

Dear Dr. Holderness:

The pleasure of my short holiday trip to visit a daughter ended on a sour note when I returned to Beaufort and discovered from my manager that there had been some confusion about your reservations and you and Mrs. Holderness were not able to stay in the West Wing that you have always preferred. Had I known at the time, I would have instructed the Desk to put you in the Fairway Cottage, which, ironically, was vacant. I should not have to apologize for a manager who is a professional and a graduate of the Cornell Hotel Institute. However, he is new to the region and just arrived on the job last week. Otherwise, he would have been more imaginative in righting an obvious wrong. Please forgive us this once. And please accept the enclosed certificate for a complimentary night on the house the next time you come to Beaufort.

Cordially,

Delays in Serving Guests

Dear Mrs. Comley:

You were very patient to put up with the service problems that plagued your outdoor buffet last Saturday, and I apologize again for having let you and your guests down. I should never have left the last-minute arrangements to my assistant who, though very conscientious, has not had enough catering experience.

I can assure you that such a defection will not occur again and hope that you will use our service in the future.

Sincerely,

Mixup in an Order

Dear Sebastian:

If we had wanted to screw up an important assignment for a longtime artist friend and customer, we could not have achieved it any more effectively than we did. Only after you arrived on location, ready to go to work, did I discover that the chisel points you had ordered were for *stone* and the ones we shipped were for *wood*. I hope that our overnight express shipment of the proper tools reached you in time to avoid any serious delay in your work. It does no good for me to make any excuses, but believe me there is one red-faced shipping clerk in our storeroom who has not been very popular around here the last couple of days.

Sincerely,

Shipping and Billing Errors

Dear Mrs. Tomlinson:

We were dismayed to receive your letter and the sample computer printout that documented the confusion that has been occurring in your shop as a result of the billing procedures used by our marketing department. I have looked into this situation personally and am convinced that the problem lies in our company's computer programming setup and not in the marketing operations per se.

Our entire system is being checked and reviewed by an outside consulting firm, and I am confident that we will resolve the problem to your complete satisfaction.

In the meantime, I have a submitted a voucher to our accounting department to reimburse you for the costs incurred when you had to crate and return duplicate merchandise.

Thanks for your patience.

With best regards,

Business Hours and Schedules

Dear Mr. Snively:

We appreciate your calling to our attention the fact that you have had a problem reaching your insurance agent early enough in the morning. Our policy is to be available at all times particularly when there is an emergency. Our regular opening office hour is indeed 9:30, but for a reason. After we opened an office in Denver last year, we discovered that we could serve our policyholders better by keeping the Boston office open until 7:00 P.M., instead of closing at 5:00, to accommodate Mountain Time clientele. So, despite the slightly later hour of opening, our staff members actually work longer hours than they would in most other offices.

Naturally, if there is an emergency, you can reach us at any time of the day or night, seven days a week. Just use the toll-free "800" number on this letterhead.

Sincerely,

Unjustified Complaint—Missed Deadline

Dear Dr. Eckard:

We are certainly sorry that your monthly newsletter, *Medigram,* had to be mailed almost a week late, causing some problems in your association's schedules of events. Rather than blame my pressman for the delay, however, you should be talking to your art director. He delivered the sketches and diagrams for the first and last pages almost three days behind the art deadline we had jointly agreed upon. There was no way we could reschedule the *Medigram* press run without usurping a time period from some other customer, which would have been grossly unfair—and not exactly conducive to getting repeat business. The only solution would have been overtime, and you, yourself, have instructed us never to choose an option that would put any month's publication over your budget.

Let's reexamine our deadlines for next month.

Sincerely,

Poor Preparation—Convention

Dear Malcolm:

One of my convention committee associates relayed to me your comments that the housing plans for our firm's session seem to be "much inferior" to those that were arranged for the participants last year. I must state here and now that you are absolutely right. The plans are second rate. But please don't place the blame on the shoulders of the committee. When we were given our budget for the meetings, our treasurer's housing allowance per participant was *23 percent lower* than last year. Add to that the fact that the room rates at the Lodge are *11 percent higher* than they were 12 months ago.

With a percentage cutback equaling 34 percent, how could you expect more luxurious accommodations? Maybe we should cut the liquor budget. Or the food budget. Or get there by bus instead of by jet. Our company committee is stretching things as best we can.

Cordially,

Response to Stockholder's Letter

Dear Mrs. Agnew:

We appreciated your writing to inform us that your recent securities report arrived in a wrinkled condition, yet without any notification from the post office that it had been damaged in handling. Since we received two other complaints about the same problem, we are referring the matter to the postmaster here and will do our best to eliminate any similar occurrences in the future.

In the meantime, I enclose a replacement for the report, along with our thanks for your courtesy.

Sincerely,

Problems Caused by Road Work

Dear Mr. and Mrs. Strawbridge:

As the owner of Blake Road Contractors, Inc., I hasten to respond to your letter expressing fears about unsightly excavations and traffic tie-ups in your neighborhood. Please understand that the trenches being dug are the narrowest that can possibly be cut for the installation of television conduits, that the end result will be better cable TV transmission in your area, and that there will be absolutely no unsightly scars along the roadway or pavement. Also, my construction foreman assures me the job will be completed in only a few days rather than the "weeks upon weeks" you were alarmed about.

It is our company policy in all construction work we undertake to leave the site more attractive after our work than before we started.

Sincerely,

Commercials on Rented Videotapes

Dear Customers:

Thanks for your note of protest. We'd rather have compliments than complaints, but we do appreciate your letting us know your feelings about our merchandise and service. We have discussed the matter of videotape commercials with two of our suppliers. The bad news is we can't do anything much to change the picture. But the good news is that—as they pointed out to me—the money paid by advertisers for these commercials does reduce the prices they charge and in the end results in a small savings for our customers.

We suggest you start the videos at "fast forward" until you are past the commercials. By way of thanking you for the time you took to write, we'll deduct $2.00 from your next rental. Just bring this letter and show it at the checkout desk.

Thanks,

Inability to Issue Insurance Policy

Dear Travis:

You have every reason to be upset that I cannot write you a homeowner's policy for your Arizona residence similar to the one you had in Cleveland. I certainly wish that I could, but in the insurance business we are restricted geographically and cannot do business outside of prescribed limits. As it happens, your former underwriter, Community Mutual, engages in business in only six midwestern states. So there would be no chance of transferring your original policy, even if I could extend my business boundaries.

However, a former associate of mine, Jack Downs, moved to Prescott three years ago and transferred his office there. I enclose his business card. Please give him a ring, and I'm sure you'll be delighted with his rates and his brand of personal service.

With every good wish,

ADJUSTMENTS

Treat requests for adjustment like any other kind of complaint, but follow through with reasonable action, the sooner the better.

Truck Repairs

Dear Buck:

This is both (1) a complaint about unsatisfactory maintenance and repair and (2) a petition for a substantial adjustment in our monthly bill. As you know, we undertake periodic formal spot checks on all our company trucks and vans, a custom that benefits us with reduced annual insurance premiums. Our inspectors have observed during the past two months that the automotive maintenance program which we have with you under contract has been increasingly inefficient. We have found, for example, several instances in which lubrication has been overlooked and at least two cases of trucks with badly corroded exhaust pipes and mufflers.

I realize you—as well as a good many automotive service shops—have difficulty recruiting and keeping well-qualified and experienced mechanics. However, our insurance agent is not inclined to accept excuses. If we find that our premium rates are increasing, we'll have to ask you to absorb the difference.

With my regards,

Returning Products

Dear Mr. Farthingale:

The four mail sorters we ordered from you last week have been returned under separate cover via United Parcel Service. It would be understandable if one of these were defective, but not all four. The problem is that the automatic sorting levers function erratically. They might work for an hour or two, or longer. But eventually, they kick off and cause a pileup of envelopes being processed. This is not only time consuming for our personnel who have to shut down the equipment and feed the mailings manually, but in several instances the malfunctions have resulted in damaged envelopes and contents.

Unless you can replace these with machines that you can guarantee unconditionally, we'll have to take our business elsewhere.

Sincerely,

Damaged Merchandise

Dear Mrs. Krantz:

This is to acknowledge receipt of your letter of June 10, in which you pointed out that you should be credited for the storage rack that was damaged in transit.

We are sorry for our failure to make this adjustment on our records. Please advise us as to your preference. We can credit your account, replace the merchandise you wanted, or send you a refund check. No matter which you elect, we will still honor the 20% discount coupon for future purchases.

Thank you for your patience and understanding.

Very truly yours,

Sloppy Construction Work

Dear Salvatore:

When our firm hired you as the contractor to replace our parking area, driveways, and ramps, it was with the belief that your "Vacuumatic" method of trimming and removing loose cement and asphalt would eliminate flying grit and dust around the premises. It was with considerable consternation, therefore, that I turned from a business trip to find the job completed but our building encrusted on two sides with asphalt granules and grime.

Steam Kleeners, Inc., has given us an estimate of $730 to clean the affected surfaces. We are offering you two alternatives: (1) to reimburse us for this cost or (2) to undertake the cleaning yourself. In either case, we will be satisfied, but will be left with a less than flattering impression of your touted process.

Very truly yours,

$\mathcal{S}$ALES AND PROMOTION STAFFS AND OUTSIDE VENDORS

Sales and advertising letters are powerful tools, when used wisely and with purpose. They are particularly important to the owners and managers of small businesses who realize that they cannot compete with the marketing and advertising campaigns of large corporations and chains. From the standpoint of correspondence, letters in this category, which also include effective written communication with your vendors, are likely to be the ones used most frequently in your day-to-day business. In the average small business, such letters probably equal in frequency all other types of letters combined. Therefore, it is vital that small-business owners devote continual attention to letters relating to sales, advertising, and vending, whether they are selling products or services, establishing better coordination, or simply bolstering faith in their organization and its operations.

KEY FACTS YOU SHOULD KNOW ABOUT SALES AND ADVERTISING LETTERS

As you select model letters from this book and adapt them to your own use, keep foremost in mind that they must

1. Be coordinated with all other sales, marketing, and advertising activities.
2. Base statements, claims, and reports on your ability to meet forseeable demands realistically.
3. Address themselves to a need on the part of prospective customers and clients.
4. Be scheduled to reach their destinations at favorable times.

5. Be persuasive, but not insistent.

6. Open with a sentence that will immediately spark the reader's interest.

7. Provide the necessary details without being wordy or preachy.

8. Convince the reader that the offer beats the competition.

9. Clearly list addresses, phone numbers, and (if appropriate) a person to contact.

10. Close with an action statement so the reader knows what to do to take advantage of the offer.

ENHANCE YOUR OWN PERSONAL STYLE

You don't have to be a professional author or a grammarian to write an effective letter that will promote your company and what you have to offer. But you do have to develop a *style*—that is, a way of expressing yourself that is forthright and convincing and uses words that are appropriate to the subject at hand and the nature of your company. You try to accomplish as much when you speak or make presentations to get favorable reactions. So why not work this into the letters you write so they are extensions of your personality and outlook?

Ask yourself in each case; How appropriate is my style to the subject of my letter? A letter promoting books to an intellectual audience, for instance, will be poles apart from a letter trying to sell rods and reels to sports fishermen or apparel to young women.

MAKE YOURSELF CLEAR AND CREDIBLE

You should use language that will be easily understood by your intended audience. But, be careful. Never talk down to readers or attempt to make them feel inferior because they do not own a prestigious product you are marketing, or are out of step because they cannot provide instant supplies and service. Use words and phrases that are positive, rather than negative, promoting products and services on the basis of what they can do for prospects, rather than on what people will be missing in their lives if they do not react favorably to your message.

Emotion can be effective in motivating people in certain instances, as in the case of, say, selecting gifts that will demonstrate the giver's love and affection. But the most effective use of emotions is likely to be when your message is low key and certainly when it has a ring of sincerity.

LIMIT YOUR POINTS AND REFERENCES

Before writing a sales letter, an advertising letter, or a message to synchronize your supply plans with vendors, carefully list the primary points you want to make. These might include

- The advantages of a product or line
- Documentation of excellent service
- Attractive pricing
- A special offer
- Improved coordination of supply and delivery
- Testimonials from satisfied users
- The addition of facilities and capabilities

Once you have jotted down a few appropriate topics, pare the list to its bare essentials, bearing in mind what the reader of your letter is likely to be most interested in. Many letters that intend to be promotional in nature lose prospective clients and customers because they attempt to cover too much territory.

HOW LONG SHOULD A LETTER BE?

There is no formula for length. But experience shows that most small-business owners and managers are not skilled enough to write a letter that is more than one page of single-spaced type. If the message, for one reason or another, *has to* be long, you should consider getting professional help in its composition and approach. This is particularly vital if your recipients are people who are specialists or professionals and are likely to relate credibility to your skill with words.

When describing a product or service that is specialized or highly technical and requires a detailed summary, it is usually best to make the primary letter short and to the point and enclose an insert. An attractive, well-designed envelope stuffer, printed by the supplier, is generally more convincing than a typewritten description in the body of a letter.

OPENERS AND CLOSINGS

The model letters that follow contain openers and closers that have been effective and can be easily adapted to your specific needs. Here are some other sample openers:

- Do you want to know how to get $100 worth of groceries for only $38?

- You've probably driven down Main Street dozens of times this year—but here's something extraordinary I'll bet you missed.
- Can you remember what the major headline was in yesterday's paper?
- You'd almost welcome inflation once you know this surprising way of beating it.
- Have your toes ever hurt so much you just wanted to take your shoes off and put your feet in a hot tub?
- Buying just one of our new suits is almost unheard of—our customers always want at least two.
- Our service not only pays for itself, it will pay you just to try it.
- For the first time in memory, you can avoid sales taxes *legally*.
- You never need to be annoyed again at blaring radios and other sound pollution.
- When you shop with us, you don't have to bring cash, check, or credit card.
- Here are some sample closings:
- If you write or phone before July 10, we have a special gift for you.
- We guarantee satisfaction—in writing.
- Come in any evening before 7:00 P.M. and enjoy the first course on us.
- The fun is yours, the work, ours.
- Return the card before the date stamped on it and we'll mail you a free sample.
- Just ask for me, Randy, when you phone and I'll make sure the job is done at *your* convenience.
- This postcard is your certificate for a 15% discount on all products not included in our annual sale.
- Bring this letter with you, and we'll approve an immediate credit account in your name.
- Walk into our shop with this magic number, and you'll walk out with a complimentary bag of plant food.
- Don't postpone your chance to get a free evaluation, since our estimator will be here, and available, this week only.

Remember, the first sentence and the last sentence may be the most important in every sales or advertising letter you write. As for correspondence with your vendors, these openings and closings are significant, too. No matter what a specific letter topic may be, in the long run you are continually trying to "sell" them on your company one way or another in order to obtain supplies more promptly, keep costs down, and coordinate deliveries so you always have enough stocks on hand but are never overloaded with inventories.

HOW TO DO IT

1. Select the right person to whom to address your letter or other message.
2. Put yourself in your recipient's place and use the opening you yourself would find to be most attention getting.
3. Focus on the single strongest point you want to make.
4. Document your statements, if necessary.
5. Make it clear what you expect from the recipient.

PERSONALIZED SALES LETTERS

Selling is one of the most personal aspects of any small business that has products or services to offer the public. Personality plays an important role. Some people are "born" salespersons and are successful on the strength of their own charistmatic appeal. Other people, perhaps more experienced and knowledgeable, have to struggle to make sales because they are less affable and congenial than are some of their colleagues. One area of letter writing in which you can improve your relationships with prospective customers and clients relates to personal letters and notes that you may send in a casual way. Use these to display your interest in the recipient—just as was done by the composers of the following letters.

Enclosing Newspaper Clipping

This letter is aimed at molding the opinion of one interested, but undecided, customer.

Dear Mr. Lockard:

Since you and I have discussed the subject, I knew you'd be interested in the enclosed clipping from yesterday's *Eagle* about the savings that can be effected through the gas company's Off-Peak Energy Plan. We can install a water heater that is approved under this plan and that we guarantee will save you at least 18% a month in water-heating bills.

At that rate, you would end up with a brand-new, large-capacity unit that would literally pay for itself in ten months.

The article tells very clearly why this is so. I'd be happy to answer any questions you have. Just call me whenever convenient.

Sincerely,

Description of Services—Home Repair

The writer of this letter has just read a letter the recipients had sent to the local newspaper.

Dear Mr. and Mrs. Kelbaugh:

Your letter to the editor, published in today's *Globe*, was of great interest to me. I could not agree more that homeowners today are at a distinct disadvantage. They find themselves increasingly at the mercy of "high-tech" appliances and electronic marvels that they can hardly cope with when the devices are functioning properly, let alone when they sputter, blink, and break down. Then comes the shock, with the arrival of the space age technician (formerly known as a repairman) who can charge outlandish fees for time, service, and parts.

It was this very situation that motivated my partners and me to go into business three years ago to supply a reliable service that would get results without bankrupting our clients. Our firm, TechRepair ©, provides an annual service contract that will cover everything in your home that you feel might at one time or another need servicing, repair, or replacement. *You* select the items you want covered, the nature of the services you desire, and the cost restrictions. We do the rest.

I would be happy to visit your home and discuss our qualifications and experience or send you a sample contract that spells out all the details. But, first, I suggest that you contact two of your neighbors, Mr. and Mrs. Swetenberg and Mrs. Richard Ervin. They have been clients of ours for two years and will tell you honestly what they think of our service.

Respectfully yours,

Selling a Service—Marketing

Dear Captain Sandifer:

What costs 56¢ to produce, can be mailed in a 7¢ envelope for 29¢ in postage, and will bring a favorable reply from more than one-third of all the people to whom you mail it?

The answer: One of our HiMarx © door-opener mailers.

We tailor these to the individual market and goals of each firm with which we do business. In your case, we would promote boat sales and marine services according to your objectives. Past experience has shown that an effective HiMarx© mailing piece will end up with substantial purchases from about one out of every eight people who receive it. That's a record worth looking into.

May we show you samples?

Sincerely,

Responding to Request for Information

Dear Mr. and Mrs. Irving:

We share your concern over the rising costs of energy, particularly electricity, in our area. While we cannot pinpoint exactly how strongly these costs will affect you and other customers by the end of the next quarter, we assure you the increase will have very little effect on consumer rates—even six months from now.

Why can we make such an optimistic assurance? Because the Energy Conservation Board is putting into effect a new peak-load plan that will spread the demand for power more evenly across the board during all hours of the day and night. This will more than offset rate increases. If you want to stop by our shop some day, I'd be glad to show you a chart we have that projects both the increases and the savings.

Sincerely,

Turning Down Prospective Business

Dear Keryn:

It may be poor salesmanship for me to advise you to take a step that will lessen my chance of doing business with you again in the near future. But I can only give one answer in response to your inquiry about the Continental's employee profit-sharing program: By all means, allocate as much of your salary as you reasonable can to this planned investment program. If the company is matching your investment dollar for dollar (up to 4%, I believe), the chances are you'll do better in the long run than with an outside program. Besides, it is always beneficial to support the company you work for, especially when your company is supporting you.

Of course, any time I can be of service to you in the future in building your portfolio, by all means get in touch.

Cordially,

Offering Special Services and Discounts

Dear Mrs. Coggeshall:

As we discussed on the phone, Southern Repro is centrally located, has two branch offices, and offers quick, reliable pick-up and delivery service. To our regular customers we offer substantial discounts, based on both the frequency and quantity of orders. This letter will confirm my assurance to you that your agency would be eligible for such discounts, and quite often complimentary overruns of material.

Our capabilities and services include full-color laser copying, blueprinting, photocopying, surveying, fax service, oversize and undersize transitions, and general printing, as well as a full line of drafting supplies and equipment, forms, writing materials, and professional stationery.

We stand ready to serve you.

Sincerely,

Requesting Appointment

Dear Mr. Butterfield:

If you were to look east from the third floor boardroom of your corporation, you might barely notice a white, two-story colonial-style building with twin chimneys that sits on a hill by the Contoocook River. It was built in 1812 and qualifies as one of the area's historical heritage sites. In its earliest days, it was a general store. To some extent, it is still a store today, but the wares we are selling here are somewhat more sophisticated. We are recent MBA graduates, we design and produce innovative software, and we specialize particularly in training programs of the kind your group sales and marketing managers have been developing for better familiarization with new merchandising techniques.

How do I know this? Because my partners and I have talked with a number of your managers, done our homework, and are completely familiar with the kinds of hardware you use in your seminars. If you will give me 12 minutes of your time, I will convince you that our approach can measurably improve the effectiveness of any seminar in which you want to test it out. You have nothing to lose and everything to gain.

I'll phone you for an appointment, with the expectation that curiosity alone might prompt you to risk 12 minutes of your time to see what a group of young people with an 1812 heritage have up their sleeves.

Sincerely,

Setting an Appointment

Dear Kenneth:

As we discussed briefly when I ran into you at the town committee meeting, I'd very much like to get together with you for lunch so we could discuss ways in which our firm could assist you in the county water conservation project. I suggest that we set a date in mid-September, at which time I would bring along Julian Bookhart, our foundation engineer. He will just have returned from the Pace Polytechnic Institute seminar on soils and should have some interesting observations to make on soil and water retention.

I'll plan on phoning you next week to see what date and time would be most feasible.

With best regards,

Confirming an Appointment

Dear Mr. and Mrs. Bonner:

This will confirm my appointment with you on Thursday, November 15, to take you on a tour of the development we are now completing at Powder Point. I will pick you up at your hotel at 11:30 and have also made arrangements to have you as my guests for lunch at 1:00 at the Powder Point Inn.

It so happens that November 15 is a notable anniversary for me. On that day, 20 years ago, I sold the first home in my first development. That home is still owned by the same family, which is quite typical of the more than 3,000 homes we have designed and built over the past two decades.

Sincerely,

Accepting a Dinner Invitation

The writer has been asked by a college classmate to attend a regional dinner being given by alumni. He sees this as a good opportunity to mention his professional services.

Dear Chick:

It has been about two decades since last we had any communication, and I was delighted to hear from you. I'd very much enjoy attending the dinner in honor of Dr. Goudge. He was one of my favorite teachers, and his arrival in town should add new life and spark to the community.

I noticed on your letterhead that you are now in real estate. My partners and

I work very closely with real estate agencies, since our business is renovating older homes to fit new design concepts. I'll tell you more about it when we meet at the dinner.

Cordially,

Accepting a Sports Invitation

Dear Terry:

My business partner and I enjoyed playing tennis with your two clients when they were here for your meetings. At the time, they mentioned the possibility of an informal intercompany tennis tournament when we all go down to Port Royal for the marketing seminars and said they would draft a proposal for recreational activities.

When you next talk with them, please mention that we are interested in participating in a tennis tournament and would probably have six entrants from our firm.

What an enjoyable way to do business!

Sincerely,

Postponing an Important Business Presentation

Dear Vernon:

You were most patient with me when I insisted that you light a fuse under the planning committee and schedule the meeting earlier than everyone wanted. I used the phrase "time was of the essence" and asserted we should address ourselves to the matters at hand as soon as possible.

How can I now come back to you and say—*whimper* might be more descriptive— that I myself (that diabolical foe of procrastination!) am requesting a delay?

Well, the fact of the matter is that our top client, who seldom consults with me about personal agenda, has scheduled me to lead a two-week seminar at a time directly conflicting with our planned meeting date. I have thought of quitting my job. Breaking my leg. Anything. But all I can do now is crawl back and say, "Gee, fellas...."

I leave my future in your hands.

Dejectedly,

Providing Directions

Even a simple form letter can be tailored to stimulate business.

Dear Mrs. and Ms. Jackmer:

We appreciate your inquiry and are looking forward to having you visit our model showrooms. You will find us very easy to reach by car. Simply follow Interstate 89 south to exit 23 at Burbury. Turn *left* onto state highway 67A and drive for exactly 4 miles. On your *right*, you will see a tall green water tower, and just past that you turn *right* onto Wintergreen Road. Drive for half a mile and you will see our entrance sign.

Should you need further information of any kind or road assistance in the event of car trouble (which we certainly hope will not be necessary!), phone us at 789-5200. We want to make sure everyone arrives promptly and safely.

Oh yes, and before browsing, stop by our Hospitality Room at the entrance, for a cup of freshly-brewed coffee or a soft drink—with our compliments.

We look forward with pleasure to your visit.

Sincerely,

Requesting Extension of Deadline

Dear Mrs. Longstreet:

The Lexington highboy reproduction you ordered will not reach you the week after Thanksgiving, as you had hoped. However, I can turn that bad news into good news by telling you the reason for the delay. As you'll recall, we had agreed to substitute marsh mahogany for teak, because of the cost and unavailability of the latter in the golden tone you desired. Through a fortunate coincidence, I heard rumors of a supply of teak in a Sydney yard, which sounded just right in the matter of color, grain, and age. I took the liberty of ordering it and, after several delays, the shipment is on its way.

You will be delighted with the results, I assure you, and will treasure this piece forever.

Cordially,

TARGETED SALES LETTERS

These letters are less casual than those in the previous section, yet they, too, require a degree of personalization. The rule here is to make sure that your "target" is a legitimate event, circumstance, or offer. Don't fabricate invitations or offers as a means of getting attention. Most recipients will see the message for what it is and will respond—or fail to respond—accordingly.

Selling a Development Community

The recipients were carefully screened so that the sales points would be meaningful to them. They were all widows who had lived in the community a long time, and had shown concern about crime at town meetings or elsewhere.

Dear Mrs. Palmer:

Like you, we have been distressed to read in the *Daily Bugle* about the apparent increase in break-ins and vandalism that have disrupted our lovely and once crime-free town. Not a few residents have considered moving and leaving behind friendships and associations built over many years, even generations.

If you are having such reservations yourself, I assure you that there is a better answer. My 22-year-old firm, Acme Real Estate, which you are familiar with as a local business, has just signed a contract to act as agent for Golden Acres, a complex of fine town houses being constructed in the wooded section of nearby Highland Hills. Not only will these gracious homes be attractive and reasonably priced, but they will offer the very best in state-of-the-art security and trouble-free living—and close to the friends and acquaintances who are already dear to you.

May I make an appointment to show you in person and at your convenience what Golden Acres could offer you? There is no obligation, of course.

Sincerely,

Launching a New Business—House Sitting Service

Dear Mr. and Mrs. Potter:

By way of introduction, we are a semiretired couple living in your community who have started a house-sitting service for people who are away and would like the comfort and assurance of knowing that their home and possessions are in competent, friendly hands during their absence. Between us, we have all the basic homemaking skills—firsthand knowledge and experiences with plumbing, electricity, leaks, pest control, communications systems, fire and burglar alarms, heating and air-conditioning systems and equipment, appliances large and small, cleaning materials, the care and control of pets, and just about everything else under the roof or in the yard. We can even effect minor repairs and adjustments, should such services be desired while you are away. More important, we are tidy, caring people with a fondness for our own home and a respect for the homes of others. We enjoy being helpful and, in fact, started our business in an informal way as a kind of neighborly hobby.

We won't try to enumerate here everything we can do for you in our professional capacity as SIT, Inc. But drop us a note or give us a ring when you make your next going-away plans, and we'll give you all the necessary details.

Cordially,

PS: You'll like our friendly rates, too.

Soliciting New Customers—Interior Decorating

Here, and in the following letters, the writer uses names of new home buyers announced in the local newspaper to develop new clients.

Dear Mr. and Mrs. Leahy:

Congratulations on your purchase of your new home.

You will find the people in our community pleasant, congenial, and responsive to your needs—and that certainly includes my colleagues and me at Bramley Interiors. We invite you to visit our office at any time in the future that you would like help with decorating ideas and services. We have a small staff of just three people. But all of us have lived in the village for many years and have enjoyed the kind of professional reputation we hoped to establish when we went into business eight years ago.

The enclosed discount certificate is our way of saying that we would welcome your business at any time. We want you to know that our door is always open and the "Welcome" sign out.

Cordially,

Soliciting New Customers—Lending Library

Dear Mrs. Thorndike:

You are more than likely to receive a warm welcome in Fredericksville. So we hope that you, in turn, will welcome a chance to make every possible use of our lending library. We keep well stocked with current books, as well as with the classics and reference works. We also offer a book exchange service, both for paperbacks and hard-cover books, where for a minimal fee you can bring in volumes you no longer want and go away with ones you do.

Enclosed are discount coupons so you can get off to a good start with some of our better bargains right away. We look forward to serving you.

Sincerely,

Soliciting New Customers—Insurance

The writer has checked automotive records to determine who might be good prospects for a policy.

Dear Ms. Baladon:

Your automobile insurance policy will soon be due for renewal. So perhaps this is a good time to find out how you can get the same coverage for less money and with assurance of the best in service.

Just fill out the enclosed card describing your present coverage, and we'll quote our rates and conditions. At the same time, we'll tell you just what our policyholders think of our response, especially during emergencies. Our agency is small and our service is personal and attentive.

Sincerely,

Invitation to an Open House—From Company President

Dear Dr. and Mrs. Severense:

When I established this company ten years ago I did so because my wife, relatives, and neighbors were constantly complaining that it was impossible to find a supplier of major appliances that could guarantee quick, reliable service. Even those that took a stab at it required preposterous service fees just to arrive on your doorstep, though they might have spent barely 4 minutes locating a faulty fuse. And, of course, the unhappy owners of the appliances were told, when they asked about an appointment, that the repair person would arrive "somewhere between 7:30 A.M. and 5:00 P.M.!" All that changed when I founded this firm, and I appreciate the many customers who have thanked us for emerging from the Dark Ages.

At any rate, this is a long way round to say that I am holding an Open House for a few of our most valued customers—you among them—on Friday, April 15, from 3:00 until 6:00 P.M. Please join us and inspect our brand-new Small Appliance Hall.

Sincerely,

Invitation to an Open House—Local Merchant Groups

Dear Mr. and Mrs. Northinger:

If you selected Martinsville as a retirement community because you felt it would be hospitable, peopled with congenial neighbors, and compatible with your needs and desires, you have certainly come to the right place.

We'd like you to attend the community Open House buffet at the Civic Center on Saturday at 5:30 P.M. as a guest of Hospitality House.

One of the ways in which we welcome newcomers is through our Hospitality House program, which introduces you to local merchants by offering a sampling of our members goods and services—all complimentary. The enclosed coupon book makes it possible for you to enjoy our hospitality whenever and wherever you like. There is no charge, no obligation, and we assure you that no salespeople will call.

I look forward to meeting you.

Welcome!

Letter to Purchasers of Similar Products

Dear Mr. and Mrs. Oliver:

Your names were included in a list of people who have purchased gourmet foods by mail during the past two years.

Quite frankly, as a consumer myself and owner of a small family business, I am deluged with "junk" mail and do not have much faith in mailing lists. But, noting your address and knowing the kind of people who live in your community, I thought you might just be somewhat like me and interested in what we have to offer.

My wife and I sell top-quality homemade products. Last summer, while driving through the lovely Blue Ridge country of the Carolinas, we stopped at a farmhouse stand where a sassy woman in her mid-eighties was selling jars of her special Peppersass Sauce.

Well, we couldn't resist tasting a sample and we were so intrigued that we made a deal with her, on the spot, to purchase all of that Peppersass Sauce she and her three daughters could produce prior to the Christmas season.

Unfortunately, we can't send you a sample that would retain its zestiness and be fair to Sue-Helen Lacey, the creator of this wonderful sauce. But we'll ship you any one of the Peppersass packages (described in the little leaflet we hastily put together and have enclosed) on a guaranteed money-back basis.

If you don't think this sauce is *the very best of its kind* you ever tasted, keep what's left and we'll give you your money back the instant we hear from you.

Sincerely yours,

Wooing Competitor's Customers—Special Offer

The writer has a list of customers who buy largely, and in quantity, from a competitor and is trying to get each of them to switch to his product line.

Dear Dr. and Mrs. Northrop:

You may be perfectly happy with the performance of the cleaning and polishing products you have been purchasing and using in your home for many years. Brand loyalty is important to most of us, and I always have a feeling of guilt when I suggest that someone abandon an old "friend" and switch to a competitor.

But the time has come when I just have to tell people about Sparkle Q© cleaning and polishing aids. When our store manager was approached by the company's representative, he could not believe the claims that the man made. But we tested each and every one of the products in the line and were nothing short of amazed. For the first time in 15 years, I made a major brand switch on our own shelves. We invite you to stop by and see for yourselves how well these products work.

And they all have a "no questions, money-back" warranty.

Very truly yours,

Announcing New Line of Products

Dear Arlen:

Customers like you have certainly helped us to establish our business throughout the Springfield area, and we hope to continue giving you the kind of service that keeps your water purification at a top level. We have had so many favorable comments, in fact, that we recently made the decision to offer *air* filters as well as water filters in our product lines.

After considerable investigation, research, and testing, we elected to represent the High Star Manufacturing Group, whose products have received top ratings in objective consumer tests. We'd like an opportunity to demonstrate the many ways in which the H/S line could improve the quality of the air you breathe in your offices, reduce production problems caused by undesirable particulates, and actually extend the life of plant equipment and machinery.

Please take 5 minutes to glance through the enclosed product leaflet. I'll give your secretary a ring next week to see when it might be convenient for you to see me.

Sincerely,

Offering Local Businesses Employee Discounts—Stationery

Dear Mrs. Carradine:

As a former office manager, I am quite familiar with the fact that companies have to purchase about twice as many office stationery supplies as are really necessary for the conduct of business. Why? Because employees think nothing of one of the most common "perks" supplementing their desks at home with paper, pens, pencils, envelopes, and other such necessities as they can easily slip into their pockets or briefcases when homeward bound. Is there any solution?

One way is to make it attractive for employees to *buy* many of these items. And we can help you do just that by offering your employees the following:

- 20% discounts on all stationery supplies they buy from us
- Free imprinting of their names on such items as pens, pencils, and rulers
- Free imprinting of their letterheads on writing paper and envelopes in quantities of 100 or more
- Gift certificates at a cost of 25% less than the face value
- Free delivery to home or office

With your approval, under separate cover, we will send you attractive posters and coupons that can be used by all employees who want to participate. We think you'll be pleased with the results.

Sincerely,

PS: Don't overlook us for your own office supplies, too. Our discounts are very competitive.

Announcing Change in Policy to Existing Customers

Dear Mrs. McIntosh:

A sales manager asked me at a luncheon meeting last week why *Woman's Home Life* endorses your cosmetic products rather than those that he is merchandising. This came as a complete surprise to me and, since that time, I have been leafing through past issues to determine what he was driving at. And he really does have a legitimate gripe. It appears that, while the editorial style used by your copywriters is perfectly straightforward, the layout and type faces are so close to ours that readers confuse editorial pages with some advertising pages. Hence, it is very easy for a reader to think that an endorsement for, say, your hair rinse, was written by our fashion editor rather than your ad agency.

We could solve the confusion by increasing the boldness and size of the "ADVERTISEMENT" designation at the top of each advertising page. However, I think that a more constructive solution would be for your agency to design pages and spreads that do not emulate WHL layouts.

How do you feel about this?

Sincerely,

MEETING CUSTOMERS' SPECIAL NEEDS

An important part of letter writing is doing your homework. If, for example, you keep your eyes and ears open to the activities of customers and prospects, you will find plenty of opportunities to communicate ideas and facts that eventually may result in more business. The following are characteristic examples of what can be done.

Plant Layout and Description

Dear Mr. Armitage:

People normally do not associate the increasingly common phrase "state of the art" with something as fundamental and seemingly nontechnical as a mailing room. But the fact of the matter is that an effective layout, proper spacing, and automated handling can do wonders when it comes to speeding mail on its way, not only much, much faster, but with astonishing reductions in cost and an almost total lack of misdirectional errors. What you see before you on the 8" × 10" enclosure is a "portrait" of our Post-O-Matic® layout, so functional and streamlined it can process more than 10,000 pieces of mail in as many as ten different sizes and shapes in a single hour.

Seeing is believing. We invite you to visit our mailing center at any time that suits you, between 8:00 A.M. and 7:30 P.M. on weekdays. We'll even run a sample mailing through for you, before your very eyes, with our compliments.

Sincerely,

Hardware Meeting

Since many of this hardware distributor's products are seasonal in nature, he has decided to launch a program to sell more products off season as well as on season.

Dear Jean and Pete MacKay:

You are one of our valued customers and, as such, are eligible, at no charge, for our new "Round-the-Calendar" sales program. This is designed to lesson the problems of seasonal selling and, in fact, increase the sale of products off season. Our program consists of the following:

- A computerized evaluation of the products we supply you to show seasonal ups and downs
- Plans for promoting products off season—after the normal season and before
- A buy-back program, whereby we market products to other areas by mail on your behalf, so you don't have unsold inventories in stock

- Warehousing at cost, to put your unsold products in "mothballs" away from your store and thus free up your shelf space and storage rooms for more productive uses

If you are interested in knowing more about ways we can help you overcome "seasonal-itis," just fill out the enclosed card or call our "800" number and we'll tell you more about this innovative and valuable program.

Sincerely,

Office Furniture

Dear Mr. Lembke:

Yesterday, I accompanied one of my transportation crews to your office building to deliver 32 chairs, 12 tables, and 2 serving counters to your cafeteria. We thank you for the order and were delighted that we were able to make the delivery right on schedule. You will be pleased with the quality and durability of these items, which we guarantee unconditionally for three years.

While the crew was unpacking the crates, I took the liberty of strolling through the cafeteria and chatting with several members of the staff about meal schedules and the flow of traffic. As I understand it, the increase in the number of employees hired this year has caused a serious logjam, most notably between the hours from noon to about 2:30. Your chef mentioned that thought had been given to establishing an auxiliary cafeteria near the warehouse section, which would take care of more people but cause something of a logistics problem.

Before leaving, I obtained a first-floor layout from the building management office and spent some time studying the cafeteria and the access routes to it. I have evolved a plan that I feel would provide a solution to your problem. It would not require any auxiliary facilities, but merely the addition of four serving counters, a few additional tables and chairs, and three food-relay racks. I'd like to show you a simple sketch and explain my plan. It could solve your traffic problem, provide service to more people—even with continuing employee increases—and cut your operational costs.

Could I stop by your office and discuss this, at your convenience?

Sincerely,

FOLLOW-UP LETTERS THAT PROMOTE SALES

A proper follow-up letter is not only tactful and polite, but in many cases an expression of interest on your part that can lead to new, or repeat, business. Begin your letter with a statement that will quickly associate you with the subject at hand—just in case your recipient is forgetful or did not initially catch your name or business. How much you need to say will be determined somewhat by how long it has been since your prior contact with the addressee. Follow this reminder with brief, pertinent facts that should be of interest. Then conclude with an action statement or proposal.

Confirming Travel Arrangements

The travel agent writing this letter not only verifies data about transportation and accommodations, but uses what is nothing but a routine letter to stimulate an initial desire for additional travel.

Dear Mrs. and Ms. Trumbull:

You have been confirmed on Delta Flight #6039, leaving at 8:30 A.M. October 30 from LaGuardia for Honolulu. And you'll be glad to know that we were able to change your reservations at the Kahala Inn so that you have adjoining rooms bordering on the Japanese garden and reflecting pond, instead of near the swimming pool.

We have some very good news for you. Because of the three-week tour of the English Lake District you took last year, the week in the Virgin Islands two years ago, and the forthcoming trip to Hawaii, you will end up this year with 455 bonus points. That means that our agency will give you a credit of almost $1,000 toward whatever travel arrangements we handle for you next year.

I'll have some fascinating suggestions for you, after you return from the Pacific.

With very best regards,

Questionnaire—Travel Preferences

Dear Dr. and Mrs. Cookson:

We have been delighted to serve you in the past and look forward to helping you plan rewarding and exciting trips in the future. With clients like you in mind, we are constantly on the alert for ways to provide more memorable tours, select the kinds of accommodations and transportation that will be most enjoyable, and keep the costs reasonable, even with inflation and unfavorable fluctuations in foreign exchange rates.

Since we rely more and more heavily on computers to supply quick and reliable data, we also regularly update our files to provide you with more accurate data. It would be helpful to us at present, as well as to you in the future, if you would be kind enough to answer the following questions:

1. Would you be interested in knowing about occasional "short-notice" tours, which might give you only four to eight weeks to plan for but which would take considerable advantage of market fluctuations that gave you more for your money with no sacrifice in comfort or quality?

2. In the matter of transportation, are you more interested in getting to places quickly by air or in alternate carriers, such as trains, buses, and boats, that take longer to reach destinations but offer more scenic enjoyment en route?

3. If costs were about the same, would you prefer to travel (a) individually? (b) as a couple? (c) in small groups of not more than six? or (d) in larger groups?

4. What would your preference be in question 3 if the cost declined progressively with the number of people on a tour?

5. What time(s) of the year do you prefer to travel?

Please feel free to make any other comments you might have about tours and travel. The more data about preferences we can feed into our computers, the better we will be able to serve you.

Sincerely,

To a Satisfied Customer—Home Furnishings

Dear Mr. and Mrs. Paley:

You were thoughtful to tell my sales representative that you and your customers are delighted with the colors and designs we have selected for our All-Weather® tables, chairs, and accessories. We can't wait to send you copies of our new spring catalog, which will be off the press in about three weeks. Visually, it is the most appealing catalog we have produced in our 13 years in business.

More important, though, I'd like to point out something that is all but *invisible* in our products, yet of great importance. Last year, our Paint and Plastic Division spent more than 120,000 man hours and some $245,000 researching and perfecting a very tough metallic surfacing we have named WonderWeld™. It will be featured in the catalog, along with our unconditional five-year guarantee against chipping, fading, or discoloration. That should prove to be a very favorable selling point, along with our new look in outdoor living comfort.

So thanks for your good wishes. We'll stand behind you and your customers all the way.

Sincerely,

Thank You Note to New Customer—Homebuilding Products

Dear Mr. Pollack:

Welcome to Pine Falls! And congratulations on your decision to move to our community this spring. As you have probably already discovered, the popularity of our village rests in part on the reputation our local stores and shops have earned for prompt, reliable service to residents and visitors alike. We can assure you that, while our prices are very competitive, our standards are high, and we hope that we can continue to serve you long after you have made your move. To that end, we have opened an account in your name should you desire to purchase additional homebuilding products at any time. Not only is there no charge or monthly interest for this service, but you qualify for the 15% discount we make available to our regular customers.

With our best wishes,

Welcoming a New Charge Account Customer—Shoe Store

Dear Mrs. Perritt:

Your new charge account is more than simply a means of purchasing shoes conveniently—and with a money-back guarantee. It is the key to a whole new world of foot comfort, improved health, and high fashion.

Most of our customers are astonished that they can buy the very best at prices that are affordable—shoes from some of the country's finest manufacturers, with all-leather insoles, soft leather linings, and designs that let the feet breathe, even in hot, sultry weather. One of our secrets to customer satisfaction is that we provide exacting specifications to our suppliers. We demand layers of foam cushion rather than cork fillers. And we reject any shoe that has not been broken in by the manufacturer, so that it is soft, pliant, and flexible the instant a customer tries it on.

Best of all, just compare our prices with those of the finest luxury shoe stores, and you will see that ours are from 30% to 70% lower for exactly the same models.

Thanks for joining us.

Sincerely,

Thank You for Referral—Veterinarian

Dear Ms. Calhoun:

Thank you for the kind words you said to Mr. and Mrs. Tillotson about our veterinary services. My partner and I do indeed work long hours, as you mentioned, but it is basically because of a love for animals and particularly our four-footed patients. They all have such colorful and completely different personalities that no one could ever be bored working with them, no matter how long or at what hours.

We'll look forward to seeing Blackie when you go on your trip. He is one of our favorite boarders and our young assistants all love him.

Thanks again for your thoughtfulness.

Cordially,

Free Service Call

Dear Mr. Parmett:

We appreciated your business last fall and were delighted to be able to serve you and upgrade your water filtration system. We like to follow through after about six months and make sure our installations are functioning at top capacity. Consequently, I have asked our installer technician, Bob Hawke, to call you within a few days to see when he might check things at your plant.

Incidentally, we have just received a shipment of a brand-new type of disposable filter insert. Bob will give you a complimentary supply when he makes his rounds.

Sincerely,

Repair Problem—Offering Discount

Dear Mrs. Fairweather:

We were distressed to learn that a faulty connection had resulted in a leakage in your water filtration system and are happy we could adjust this before there was any damage to your facilities. Even though you have had the equipment for six years, there should be no problems of this nature.

When our design engineer inspected the piping circuit, he noted that your use of water has almost doubled since the initial installation. He strongly suggests that you let us add one more holding tank and subfilter to accommodate this increased flow.

Because you are a valued customer, we can give you a 20% discount on the upgrading cost.

Sincerely,

GIVEAWAY OFFERS

One vital point: Make sure the "giveaway" or "offer" is something of value to the recipient. If you offer a piece of junk, you lower yourself to the "junk mail" category.

Stimulating Sales with a Giveaway—Food Products

This writer has generated repeat business by using the following gimmick in his correspondence with a dozen or so of the company's largest customers.

August 2, 1991

Dear Arnold:

As you may recall, we like to commemorate birthdays—just for fun—by tying in the corporate with the personal in our usual gimmicky fashion. Your birthday, August 2, is just 96 days away from the company's anniversary on November 6. Therefore, you are eligible to receive 96 jars of Mrs. Jack's Juicy Jams, compliments of the house.

They will reach you on November 6, suitably boxed in cartons of six, colorfully assorted and tied with rainbow ribbons. Nice litle gifts for Christmas. Or eat 'em all up yourself.

Happy Birthday!

Stimulation of Sales with a Giveaway—Household Equipment

Dear Mrs. Corrigan:

We are writing to a selected list of people who have purchased, and been satisfied with, our household products in the past, to announce a brand-new service.

Starting on March 1, we will have a display in the front of our store of the most common household and kitchen equipment we carry. Next to each item will be a sample of the cleaning or polishing product we have found—through testing and research—to be the best on the market for that purpose. Visitors like you can have a field day experimenting with these liquids, lotions, creams, and sprays to decide which ones work best for their specific purposes.

Best of all, with each piece of equipment you buy for $5.00 or more, we will provide a container of the recommended cleaning product—with our compliments.

We want you not only to have the best products on the market, but the cleanest and brightest.

Sincerely,

Special Offer to "Qualify" Customers

Dear Paul and Martha Danielson:

Commemorating our 15th year in business, Mapmakers, Inc., has just published a magnificent full-color catalog, THE WORLD IN PRINT, describing our complete line of maps, charts, and global guides. Because of the production cost and mailing expenses, we want to send copies only to people who are very much interested in the contents and not likely to toss the catalog into the wastebasket, along with all the unwanted publications that arrive in the average daily mail.

We're hoping for a positive reply from the Danielsons.

If our catalog would really be of interest to you, simply return the enclosed postcard. It is already stamped and imprinted with your name and address. There is no charge.

If you are not interested, but have friends who might be, please pass this information along to them.

Yours for a better world,

CREATIVE FORM LETTERS

Form letters have been discussed earlier in this chapter and represented by a number of model letters. However, there is another offshoot of this kind of communication that might more correctly be referred to as the creative form letter. This is one devised by the writer to be sent to many people at the same time, but which contains an imaginative twist, style, or approach that sets it apart from the routine. Such letters can be used for the same reasons as conventional form letters for such purposes as announcing a change of address, developing cooperative programs with many people at once, sending a seasonal message, and so on.

The following model letters offer a few examples.

Announcing a Change of Address

Knowing that recipients of address changes tend to ignore them, forget them, or confuse them, the writer took this offbeat approach to make an impression.

Dear XPYRTQZ:

So I spelled your name wrong!

So I forgot to add the Zip!

So it took a little longer to reach you and irked you that liberties were taken with your title!

Well, maybe you'll do the same with me. But if you are a stickler for accuracy, like to keep the record straight, or just plain want to reach me with a message, a bill, or a birthday card, please note:

MY NEW ADDRESS AND PHONE NUMBER ARE ABOVE.

Thanks, in advance,

Promoting Consulting Service—A Seasonal Message

Happy Thanksgiving!

What's wrong with this communication?
Quite a few things.

- It's sent at the wrong season of the year.
- The message doesn't make sense
- Right now, a robin would be more appropriate than a turkey
- It ignores Memorial Day.

But there is one thing *right* about it. The card reminds you that you can't communicate effectively without keeping in mind your recipient's calendar, schedules, and interests. You'll just be out of step.

Which is one way of suggesting that you call our firm, ABC Retailing Consultants, to help you plan ahead so that your promotional efforts pay off at the right time to the right people in the right place.

And a joyful New Year too!

Selling a Service to Marketing

Dear Mr. Clary:

You know the old saying that "one picture is worth a thousand words." But sometimes ten words have more impact than one thousand pictures. How would these words grab you?

"You have just won the $50,000 jackpot!"
"You are slated for an IRS tax review Monday."
"Your biopsy shows no sign of cancer."
"Received your proposal. Sure I'll marry you."

I have composed a ten-word sentence that could bring your firm a major contract from at least half of the prospects to whom you send this message.

Would you like to see it?

Sincerely,

Selling a Service—Collection Agency

Dear Mrs. Peterson:

If you are like most small businesses, trying to collect past-due accounts involves more in time, money, effort, phone calls, postage, and paperwork than the results are worth.

But there is a realistic solution: now you can benefit from a collection service that promises results—and for far less than you spend doing it yourself. You can't lose since we *guarantee* that we will do just that. How can we? Because we are specialists in collecting past-due accounts. That is our one and only business.

What about our fee? There is no charge for our service. We take a small percentage on amounts that we collect.

Take a big load off your shoulders. Try us. For full details, give me a ring at your convenience.

Sincerely,

Transmittal Letter—Catalog

Dear Mrs. McKenzie:

Wait just a minute—don't throw this catalog out until you've seen what kind of prize may be in it for you.

Pages 12, 26, 42, and 51 contain names that refer to products but are also the names of American Presidents. You can win a gift certificate worth $20 for purchases in this catalog just by looking at those four pages and correctly identifying the names. It won't cost you a cent either because you can mail your answers in the postpaid envelope attached to page 2. And your gift certificate will go off to you right away, by return mail.

Over and beyond that kind of unique gift, you'll find this catalog filled with bargains almost too good to believe. Take a look and you'll see what I mean.

With the best of luck,

S ALES AND ADVERTISING STAFFS AND OUTSIDE VENDORS

When you correspond with your sales and advertising staffs, keep in mind that the recipients of your letters and memos are people who are accustomed to words and phrases that are forceful and promotional. They are likely to react well to descriptions that use positive, persuasive, and compelling statements. Here are a few examples of vigorous, expressive language:

- stunning success
- significant achievements
- positive goals
- aggressive action
- commanding lead
- assertive discussions
- authoritative forecasting
- professional standing
- dynamic leadership
- emphatic rebuttal
- electrifying statements

When communicating with people who are involved with selling, advertising, promoting, marketing, and similar fields of activity, don't be afraid to speak out in strong terms. And at all times, avoid meaningless phrases. Some of the worst offenders are phrases like these:

I want to thank you...

After due consideration...
As one who has always been known for...
You may wonder why I am taking the time...

BASIC PREPARATIONS

Many letter writers find that it helps to compose a good letter if they jot down notes first on a piece of paper to indicate the point(s) they want to make and the reaction they hope to get from the recipient. If they have difficulty deciding what they want to say, then perhaps it is better not to write the letter at all. There is always an exception. One famous letter began, "I am writing to tell you I have nothing to tell you...." In effect, he did have something to convey: that all was going well and that the recipient should be assured that he was not beset by any immediate problems.

Be specific. We are all only too familiar with long letters that ramble on and on and leave us wondering just why they were ever sent or what we are expected to do, or how we should react. Unfortunately, we usually react by (1) shoving them in a drawer with miscellaneous papers, (2) giving them to someone else to handle, or (3) tossing them in the wastebasket (File 13).

One small-business owner who has to write ten or more letters a day to sales and advertising staff members and outside vendors finds that it helps him to save examples of letters he has received that, like the ones in this book, have proven to be effective. But he also keeps a file of letters he considers to be "no-no's," examples of what *not* to say when you write a letter.

THE VALUE OF BREVITY

In this age of electronic communications equipment when personalized letters can be dispatched by the dozens, and even hundreds, people welcome letters that are necessary, to the point, and brief. How do you avoid sending out letters that are plodding and overwritten? Try the following steps:

1. Limit each letter you send to just one topic. It is better to send three letters on three topics (at well-spaced intervals) than try to cram everything into one missive.

2. Write a preliminary draft and review it carefully.

3. Cut everything that is repetitious.

4. Condense every sentence that seems lengthy.

5. Avoid side comments about nonrelevant matters.

6. Substitute short words for long ones.

7. Limit your entire message (salutation and closing included) to one page.

8. Use note-size paper for very brief messages.
9. Consider sending a postcard where the message is very brief and the subject is not confidential—neatly typed and properly spaced.

WHAT TO DO WHEN YOU CANNOT BE BRIEF

Occasionally, when you write salespeople, advertising colleagues, and vendors, brevity is almost impossible. You may have to describe new products, explain changes in service, or discuss needs for new kinds of supplies and equipment. Since experience demonstrates that very few small-business owners and managers are skilled enough to write a letter that is more than two pages of single-spaced type, the odds are against your doing a good job. What's the alternative?

When describing a product or service that is specialized or highly technical and requires a detailed summary, it is usually best to make the primary letter short and to the point and enclose an insert. As noted earlier, an attractive, well-designed envelope stuffer, printed by the supplier, is generally more convincing than a typewritten description in the body of a letter.

OBJECTIVES

You can avoid being long-winded and repetitive if you jot down one brief sentence or phrase as the key to what you are going to write. What is the *purpose* of the letter? Some typical objectives are

1. To provide timely information
2. To express a pertinent opinion
3. To generate empathy or consideration
4. To motivate action
5. To stimulate a favorable response to a business decision
6. To improve coordination or cooperation
7. To anticipate forthcoming events

HOW TO DO IT

1. Address your message to the right person(s).
2. Schedule it so the message arrives at the most propitious time.
3. Use words and phrases that are active, forceful, and even provocative.
4. Focus on one fundamental topic or issue.
5. Make it clear that you want a response—what, when, where, and how.

MOTIVATING THE SALES TEAM

Think of yourself as the coach of a team. You see the players as a group of individuals who are constantly changing in their outlooks and degrees of enthusiasm. One day, some of them are really up, having concluded substantial sales. The next day, they may be discouraged and need encouragement to get them going again. This kind of situation tells you four things:

1. You are needed as a motivator to generate a positive force.
2. You constantly have to be informed about what is going on and who most needs motivation.
3. Timing is all important and you have to strike while the iron is hot to be most effective.
4. You must have something constructive to suggest that will stimulate individuals to follow a decisive course of action.

You can tackle negative situations, as some of the following letters do. Never be hesitant about acknowledging that a real problem exists and airing the details. But you must sharpen your pencil and create positive suggestions.

If you are unclear about the problem, ask questions before you set pencil to paper.

Better Follow-up

Dear Parker:

Last month, we lost a large travel booking by Motorist's Mutual, which has used our Charleston office for its annual sales conference tour for the past four years. In part, this was due to the aggressive sales techniques used by AllWay Travel, whose high-pressure methods may backfire in the long run. But in greater part, I have for some time felt that we are losing repeat business because of a lack of communications and follow-up. We see evidence of this just in our own internal letters and memos—or I should say a certain *lack* of written reports and proposals to keep us all informed and make sure business does not fall between the cracks.

The purpose of *this* letter, therefore, is to inaugurate a procedure so that we keep each other apprised of activity on all past and current accounts. We will also circulate copies of correspondence on new business and potential business with the objective of making suggestions that will be productive. To start with, I'd like to see an interoffice routing file of *all* written communications (other than forms and billings). Later, we can streamline the folder and pare away the nonessentials.

If you and your associates have any questions or suggestions, let's discuss them at our monthly meeting.

Cordially,

Keep Up with the Competition

Dear Sandra:

Recently, the Arnold Agency beat us out in securing the two-state Madison Motels account, despite the fact that we offered more services, and at slightly lower cost. After scouting around, I discovered why. It was all quite simple. In its presentation, Arnold simulated newspaper ads and counter-top literature by using computer graphics and desktop printing. We, unfortunately, followed the presentation formula that has always been effective in the past, displaying art department layouts and sketches. The Madison executives were impressed by ads that looked just like the real thing. And they wanted—and got—samples they could take back with them to their staff members as almost finished products.

In light of this, we are going to make full-scale use of our computer systems from now on, using *simulation* formats, typography, and graphics wherever possible, instead of hand-rendered art. To that end, please set up an indoctrination program to make sure that everyone concerned knows exactly what can and cannot be expected of our computers. I would also like your recommendations about new hardware and software we should consider purchasing to achieve these objectives.

Sincerely,

Sales Forecast

Dear Monica:

The prophets of doom and gloom are everywhere. Hardly a day goes by that we do not read newspaper editorials trying to define whether we are in a "recession," "decline," "slump," or something equally sinister. Unfortunately, many of us tend to react by doing nothing and deciding to sit back and wait and see what happens.

Right now, however, is when we should be putting our time to good use, lining up contacts that could pay off in the future and making inspections of available properties with which we should be more familiar. The market is sure to turn around—it always has in past times like these. And the salespeople who are on "Go!" are the ones who are going to benefit, while those who are on Hold" are going to be scurrying around wishing they had been more alert.

Cordially,

Declining Sales—Change in Strategy

Dear Lola:

We all know how conscientiously you have been striving to boost sales of our health care products in Orange County, and I appreciated your realistic and frank report evaluating the tough economic situation in your region. We are behind you 100% and will supply whatever promotional materials and ad support you need. You know that.

After examining your statistics and financial data, however, I suspect that the problem is not so much an economic as it is a psychological one. You have been promoting the health angle for our products and all but ignoring the cosmetic benefits. Don and I suggest strongly that you reverse the emphasis and feature *good looks* rather than skin care. At least, try it for a month and see what happens.

As always, we're ready to help any way we can.

With best wishes,

Building Company's Image

Dear Sherman:

You asked me what the firm can do to improve its "image", now that you have a public relations director (me) at last and a small p.r. staff.

To tell you the truth, the greatest image problem you have is a *lack* of image. What we have to do now is to get out and sell ourselves. Sell our name. Sell our people. Sell our goals.

We in public relations can help you. But first, you have to train everyone in the organization to be a salesperson. I suggest that you form a Sales Committee, made up of people who are experienced in selling, and start a practical orientation program.

With best wishes,

Communicating with Customers

Dear Bart:

It is the nature of our duties as sales representatives that we often have to communicate by letter with prospective customers in order to stay ahead of our competition. Yet form letters turn many people off because they are so distant and cold and give the impression that the sender is too "busy" to provide the kind of personal attention customers want when they buy products and services. A very successful salesman told me he uses the following technique: He types all the information he wants a prospect to know about in the form of a newspaper release. Then he sends copies to the people on his list with a personal note on his letterhead, to this effect:

Dear Mr. Jones:

Our public relations manager has just sent the following release to local editors. Since you and I have had discussions about water purity, I thought you'd be interested in the information covering the latest state-of-the-art news about our water filters. Please give me a ring soon and I'll answer any questions you have.

Thanks,

PS: To assist you in composing other form letters that can be effective, I enclose four letters to use as models. I'd be happy to send others or assist in any way I can if you feel that you are not using the mails to best advantage in your sales programs.

Suggestions for Improved Teamwork

Dear Kenny:

The sales manager and I have been discussing the subject of teamwork and how we can coordinate our sales and promotional activities better and interest more people in buying Crystal Pure Pools and the equipment and accessories we carry for them. It occurs to us that we have an excellent corps of "salespersons" whom we are not using for product promotion: the mechanics, electricians, and technicians who go to our customers when maintenance or repairs are needed. There is no reason why we cannot train them to seize opportunities that come up to sell customers on additional products they may not even know we carry or in some cases to suggest replacements rather than repairs. This kind of teamwork could pay off—for you and your crews, as well as for the company.

Please give the matter some thought, and let's discuss ways in which we can coordinate these activities.

With best regards,

Present and Future Plans

Dear Esther:

October is not usually a busy month for you in Dallas, but this year may be different. At the urging of several of our account executives, the Planning Committee put its joint heads together and decided that the firm should celebrate its 25th anniversary. Since the first office was opened in Dallas, we all agreed that is the location on which we should focus and where any commemorative event(s) should take place.

Now we are not so naive as to expect that a birthday party will have any special meaning to clients or any impact on the management community. But we would like to use this occasion to pinpoint some of the firm's accomplishments and to tie our name in with those of well-known clients. Therefore, a first order of business is to ask you use your well-recognized innovative skills and come up with initial suggestions.

Expectantly,

INTERNAL SALES POLICIES

Sales and advertising staff members tend to follow established procedures that are already known and with which they are familiar. It is important for you to consider two facets of communication regarding company policies and related procedures: First, if the important policies remain unchanged, simply reaffirm them from time to time in letters, memos, or other media. Second, if a change is imminent, communicate this at your earliest opportunity and in the most decisive manner. If there is any doubt about sales and advertising procedures and functions that hinge on these policies, reaffirm them as needed and when it is timely to do so.

Customer Complaints

Dear Susan:

From time to time, we receive complaints from wholesale customers that they have received shipments containing batches of products that were defective in one way or another. As you know, our policy has always been to take them back without the slightest question, replace them immediately, and also refund any money the customer may have lost in the transaction, whether for shipping costs or lost sales. About 99% of the time, the customers' claims have proven to be erroneous or exaggerated, based on examinations by our independent testing laboratory.

So why would some customers make gripes that have no foundation in fact? I have reviewed past complaints and our resultant reports and have come up with the following reasons, which it might be helpful for you to bear in mind:

• To get even with a salesperson they do not like in general or who had made unflattering remarks in particular

• To renege on an order when an opportunity unexpectedly arises to purchase similar types of flavorings from a competitor at substantial discounts

• To lure us into offering the "defective" goods at a big discount

• To make an occasional noise to emphasize that the customer is always right and the supplier is at his beck and call

As you can see, it is largely psychological. But we should continue business in a professional manner, do our job as we always have, and not be worried about who is Right or Mr. Big.

Sincerely,

To Sales Representative—Discount Policy

Dear Eileen:

Please do not take this letter to be anything more than a statement of policy and procedure, necessary for the proper implementation of our business. One of our regular customers phoned me the other day to say that you had offered her a discount on our line of kitchen and laundry detergents. In effect, she was scolding me because this was the first time she had "learned that we discounted our prices" and she had always paid the full amount in the past. I was taken aback, but managed to hedge and say that "discount" was the wrong word and that we had simply lowered the price on certain items.

It is totally against policy—which, of course, you did not realize—to undercut a price in any way, make "two-for-one" offers, or otherwise lessen the stated price. Please note the procedure on page 16 of your sales representative's handbook.

Sincerely,

To Employees—Product Testing

TO: Front Office Staff Members
FROM: Processing Manager
RE: Product Testing

One of the side benefits of working for Mrs. Plum's Country Jams is that, from time to time, you receive free jars of our products, like the one enclosed. These are full-sized jars, pulled at random from cartons destined for our retail outlets. For this small courtesy, you are asked to evaluate these products and report briefly on them. Simply tear off the questionnaire below and return it to me when you have sampled the product. Use the reverse side if you need more space.

Name of product (as labeled) _____

Quality of flavor _____

Consistency _____

Color _____

Fragrance _____

Fairness of retail price (as marked) _____

Attractiveness of packaging _____

Comparison with any competitive products with which you may be familiar _____

_____

_____ .

To Salesperson—Warning About Bad Financial Risks

Dear Gloria:

We have been delighted with the way you and your staff members have exceeded the sales quotas in your territory way beyond what anyone had expected. We do, however, have to come to grips with a recurring problem: the above-average number of overdue accounts on your books, some of which may never be collectible. Reviewing the accounts and judging from past experience, we think the problem lies in the number of new salespersons you have had to recruit, many of them who are apparently unfamiliar with procedures for checking a firm's solvency and financial track record before delivering large orders on credit. If it's all right with you, I'm going to ask our comptroller, Gus Wheaton, to set up an appointment to drive down and give your people a session—two hours or so—on practical economics. He's very good at spelling out the details, and I think everyone will profit from the seminar.

With best regards,

To Regional Sales Managers—Explanation of Sales and Marketing Incentives

Dear Arlen:

Although the economic aspects of our business are very complicated and difficult to explain clearly to laypersons, there are three points you might make at the sales meeting you are planning. As you have already explained to me, the younger members of the sales team are likely to be receptive to the environmental advantages our products have over others, whereas the old-timers are going to be swayed more by the profit motives. So try these on for size:

1. All our products can be recycled. So when our salespersons buy back used cartons and bags, they help the environment, but they also amass "playback" credits which in part determine their year-end bonuses.

2. A good sales talk can convince at least 75 % of the purchasing agents that they should spend a little more for materials that are going to prevent a lot of pollution. The higher prices naturally result in commissions that are higher for our reps than for those of our competitors.

3. When sales reps place large orders for recycled materials, they are really selling something that has already been sold once before (maybe two or three times before) and thus makes a substantial profit for the company. That profit, in turn, greatly enhances year-end bonus and incentive figures.

What you are saying overall is that a sound ecological policy builds sound economical strength and is financially, as well as environmentally, beneficial to all of us.

With best regards,

Commissions Arrangements—Salespersons

Dear Luther:

Your campaign to obtain larger commissions for men and women who have served long and hard as our best representatives throughout the Northwest has finally paid off! You will be most happy to learn from this letter that Parker Publishing has upped the commission rate from 6% to 7% on basic sales and to 8% on all contracts that gross $120,000 or more. The only restriction is that the commission increases apply only to representatives who have been with the company on a full-time basis for a minimum of one year. That clause was instituted to rule out cases in which unscrupulous promoters join the company with no idea of permanence and oversell a huge order. They then take their commissions and run, only to have half the order bounce back when the customer realizes he or she has been talked into far too large a stock.

Sincerely,

Expense Accounts—Salespersons

Dear Henderson:

Your inquiry about business expenses worries me because it indicated that your salespersons are not keeping adequate records and could be challenged by both the IRS and the state tax collection agency. Investigations could result in penalties and interest assessments for past years as well as for the current year.
Please impress on your sales employees the following key points:

1. They must be able to prove that expenses were related to selling and promotional activities for specific products and/or services and to existing customers or logical prospects. General "field trips" to explore markets or see what competitors are doing can be reported, but should be kept to a minimum and could easily be rejected by the IRS.
2. They can deduct costs for training programs, technical courses, textbooks, and on-site educational costs if they are authorized by you or the company.

3. They must keep accurate records of meals, accommodations, auto mileage, and other expenses and be ready to document them if necessary.

4. They should request that the company—not themselves—purchase supplies, equipment, clothing, or other products necessary to their job. This procedure eliminates personal bookkeeping and makes such purchases more acceptable to tax agents.

5. They should submit memos to you or another company officer and get a written approval if they feel it would be productive to entertain a customer or prospect for anything more than a regular lunch, coffee, or an occasional drink.

6. They should submit to me a draft of any tax return (or portion of it) they are preparing if they are worried that it may not be acceptable. A quick glance by me could save them hours of work and possible unnecessary headaches and assessments.

Enclosed is an IRS guideline on expense accounts, which should answer any other questions you have.

With best regards,

To Sales Managers—Control Expenses

Dear Reed:

Reviewing our marketing distribution and orders for the next three months, I see nothing but a dark picture where I was hoping we would have a bright forecast. Part of it is due to the general national economy. But the crux of the problem is really the downtrend in building starts in our own region.

Unfortunately, our expenses have to follow the trend: down, down, down. So I am asking everyone in merchandising and sales to pinch pennies, at least until further notice. I leave it up to your discretion as to how you put the brakes on with your own sales force. But if you have any questions or knotty problems, I'm always ready to assist.

Regards,

MOTIVATING DISTRIBUTORS

When communicating with distributors, be consistent and relay the same messages to them that you do to your salespersons, whenever appropriate. In many instances, owners and managers of small businesses do not have as much contact with, or control over, their distributors as they do with sales and advertising staff members. In such cases, their letters should lean a little more heavily on themes of teamwork, cooperation, and coordination for the benefit of all involved.

Holiday Mailing Piece

Dear Belva:

Last year, you told the advertising evaluation committee that its concept of a promotional mailing piece was off target. And you were proven right when the response turned out to be slow, spotty, and very expensive in the long run on a per sale count. So it is understandable that you should have doubts about this year's plans for our holiday mailing piece. Before making any final judgment, though, please bear in mind the following differences between last year's mailer and the one now proposed. The new mailer:

1. Will go to a selected list of known purchasers of our products or similar products

2. Will be inexpensive, about half the cost of last year's

3. Will have a strong endorsement, in print, from the president of Rotary

4. Will also contain an excerpt from the highly favorable article in the *Denver Post* about our business

5. Will be announced in a tie-in newspaper ad scheduled for the day the mailer is likely to be seen by most recipients

With so much new riding in its favor, the new mailer deserves your support and participation in its distribution. I hope you will feel so inclined.

With best regards,

Error in a Company Advertisement

Dear Calvin:

When we make a blooper, we really manage to pull out all the stops!

No one around here—let alone the undersigned—knows how we could have featured in boldface in the *Herald* a price of $76.50 for the "Fall Foliage Fashion" party dress when the figure should have been $92.40. However, since we did, we are asking you and our other outlets to honor the published price in the ad. And we will reimburse you for every order on which you lose $15.90.

In the meantime, we'll rerun the ad with a correction and hope we don't have too much red ink. Thanks in advance for your patience and understanding.

As ever,

Defective Product

Dear Mr. Capabolo:

Please give this your urgent attention because we want to alert all distributors and retailers who handle our line of Super-Flo™ water filters as soon as possible. Please examine the electrical surge circuit breakers you have in stock. If any of these have serial numbers that start with H-1, *they should be taken off the market right away.* During a test just concluded, it was found that, although a utility power surge is readily absorbed, the protection is not sufficient in cases where a nearby power line is struck by lightning.

We will replace all "H-1" surge protectors with newer "H-2" models that have checked out properly on all counts, regardless of the source of the power surge.

With my best regards,

Manufacturer's Guidelines to Retail Outlets

Dear Mr. Goodman:

We appreciate your continuing interest in HealthLine™ products and look forward to a long and mutually rewarding relationship in our business. Ms. Colson told me about your increasing concerns and how to deal with customers who, in effect, are hoping you can act as some kind of medical or clinical adviser. On the one hand, you want to stimulate their interest in buying products from your shelves. But, on the other hand, you certainly do not want to risk censure for letting your clerks offer professional counsel that they are not qualified to give.

We have studied this problem and feel that you can do best by taking a leaf, as it were, from the pharmacist's book. When a customer asks whether a certain product will "prevent constipation," provide the "right balance of vitamins," or even—as is cited so often—"reduce the risks of cancer," simply do two things: (1) ask the customer to please read the label, which is as specific as you can get, and (2) recommend that the customer consult with his or her physician or nutritionist.

If pressed, and if a customer is someone you definitely do not want to lose, you can always provide my phone number and suggest a call for "professional" advice. We are accustomed to fielding tough questions, and several of our staff members are trained nutritionists who *are* qualified to provide this kind of information.

Thanks again for your business and rest assured that we stand behind you and our product lines in every way possible.

Sincerely,

LETTERS TO ADVERTISING AGENCIES AND THE MEDIA

When writing to individuals in these outside groups, try to imagine yourself in their position as recipients of whatever information or suggestions you are hoping to impart. You have to walk something of a tightrope here, in that you want to make sure they know about your programs and plans, but you want to avoid trying to stuff a lot of data down their throats. One of the best means of doing this is to state your purpose in a brief letter and enclose a publication or other informative material for their review, should they desire to know more.

Stating Goals to Ad Agency

Dear Sheldon:

Going back to the very beginnings of our company, my late wife, Agnes, and I researched, tested, created, and produced our original line of flavorings, condiments, and extracts because we wanted to improve the *quality* and *efficacy* of products available for enhancing foods. Later, we hired a scientific consultant who helped our small company to improve the *durability* of each product—that is, the capacity for retaining freshness and basic characteristics.

Everyone who writes copy for our lines, whether for advertising, public relations releases, sales letters, booklets, speeches, or annual reports, should keep those three basics in mind. I do not want to drift into such matters as discounts, cuffs at competitors, packaging, "specials," or the like.

Keep the three basics always at the forefront: *quality*, *efficacy*, and *durability*.

Sincerely,

Telemarketing Plans

Dear Mary Louise:

When we met for lunch two days ago, I expressed the opinion that we were not at all satisfied with the results of our spring ad campaign in newspapers and regional magazines. The public response was poor and sales slumped. That is, of course, a *negative* opinion.

To take a *positive* look, I feel strongly that we can expect greater results, with the same-size budget, by trying the TV route. Telemarketing would give us an opportunity to generate the kind of instant phone inquiries we want. Our products are such that women buy them on impulse. They will see the full-color image of the product. They will have a phone number. They will call. And we will have a sale.

We made the mistake in our print campaign of assuming that prospective buyers would clip the ads and later buy the product. They may have clipped the ads, but if so there must be piles of clippings scattered around that were forgotten or ignored.

I'll look forward to seeing a draft of your telemarketing presentation next week and will plan on having you show it to our president and sales VP in about ten days.

Cordially,

Presenting Advertising Goals to the Media

Dear Mr. Ingram:

As a designer and manufacturer of residential fences, both decorative and utilitarian, our firm has an annual budget of $750,000 for advertising. We have elected to concentrate on print media in the five states in which we market our products for two reasons: (1) to provide a quick, visual image of our fences in their natural surroundings and (2) to make it easy for prospective purchasers to clip ads to consider different styles and prices.

Our objective is largely to reach new purchasers, since repeat business, though sometimes substantial, is generally secondary to initial orders. Therefore, we are interested in media which can provide the following:

- An ad section close to editorial matter that stimulates interest in home exteriors.

- Tie-in media promotions that are related to local residential home developments

- A referral service that puts callers quickly in touch with the appropriate advertisers

- A media seal of approval or similar symbol that can be displayed with products that pass certain standards of quality and good design.

We would appreciate knowing what *The Independent Record* offers advertisers like us that would upgrade the consumer response to our advertising.

Sincerely,

Direct-Mail Form Letter

Dear Messrs. Brunson and Halliday:

In the past, we have not asked that you submit final copy for our direct-mail letters to our ad agency for their review and suggestions. Now, however, my partners and I feel this would be advisable. The direct-mail letter that was sent last week to our catalog list is a case in point. It very definitely should have been reviewed before printing and mailing.

Why? Because the review would have revealed that the list should have been edited and condensed; that a competitor had already mailed a similar type of letter; and that the timing was all wrong for the products mentioned and promoted.

While it is true that this kind of reviewing is time consuming and involves extra expense, it is worth it. The answer to the first objection is to start earlier. As for the second point, a small initial cost is much preferable to us than the expense of an ineffective mailing.

Sincerely,

CREDIT, COLLECTION, AND OTHER BILLING PROBLEMS

Letters relating to credit, collection, and billing problems are among the most difficult for a businessperson or professional to write because there is a decided conflict of purpose here. On the one hand, the writers of such letters are taking specific steps to try to keep credit situations in line, collect payments that have been owed them for too long, or tackle ticklish billing controversies. On the other hand, the writers do not want to discourage future business and income, especially from customers and patrons who may have made honest mistakes or suffered temporary financial setbacks, yet could be active and responsible purchasers of goods or services in the future.

Looking at the situation in reverse, it is equally trying for people who have to write creditors explaining delays in payment or to request extensions of time. In between are the myriad other circumstances that are embarrassing, if not threatening, to one or both parties.

The most vital elements in letters of this kind are likely to be (not necessarily in order of priority):

1. The person selected to receive the letter, especially if it is going to an organization, rather than a specific individual

2. The opening sentence, making the situation and reason for the letter perfectly clear

3. The language and tone

4. The timing

5. Identification of any past business necessary for the recipient to refer to before responding

6. The closing sentence, specifying what is expected of the recipient

7. The authority or position of the person writing and signing the letter

WHO, WHERE, AND WHAT?

One of the most prevalent weaknesses of letters that concern credit, collection, and other billing matters is that they initially reach the wrong person. In many instances, the recipient is a clerical employee too far down the line to take any positive action. In other instances, letters simply arrive on the wrong desk and the recipients may or may not forward them to the right persons. If you are not sure whom your addressee should be, it is sometimes worth a phone call to find out even *before* writing the letter.

Only after this personal identity is established is it possible to determine what language and tone should be used and how aggressive the approach should be—particularly if there is a substantial sum of money or business at stake. Letters that make blunt claims or imply unethical procedures can easily backfire. It is not uncommon for angered recipients to tear up such letters or at the very least stuff them into a dead file. In a few cases, unsubstantiated claims or false inferences can lead to legal action. Generally speaking, the writer can expect a more favorable reaction and more positive response by using a low-key approach than an aggressive one. If you feel that you have to unleash your emotions and spill them onto paper in order to get action, do so. But then either let the letter sit for a day or two and review it in a calmer mood or else have an associate (preferably one with no axe to grind) read it and make suggestions. Overreacting can play havoc with effective communications.

LOGICAL SEQUENCES

Many situations that necessitate the writing of this sort of letter develop because the people responsible for making payments, clarifying financial matters, or taking action are slow to respond, delinquent, or defiant for real or imagined reasons. Don't let yourself get trapped into the same mode. Be businesslike, stick to the point, and keep your cool. This does not mean that you should be namby-pamby in your approach. When more than one letter is necessary to achieve an objective, the sequence is conventionally like this.

1. The first letter states the facts clearly and precisely, and requests a timely response.

2. When a response is lacking after a reasonable time, the second letter refers to the first and again states the facts and requests proper action. It may add an additional item of identification in case the addressee is having difficulty locating proper data.

3. The third letter should include a carbon or photocopy of the previous letter. It should be brief, express surprise or bewilderment at the addressee's silence, and again ask for a response.

4. In place of a letter, the fourth attempt to establish communication might be more effective as a phone call and reference to three attempts to achieve satisfaction.

5. Failing to reach the recipient by phone, the fourth letter often refers to third-party action, for example, a collection agency in the case of an unpaid bill; an attorney when a credit agreement or a financial contract is the problem, or some other professional consultant. Should you take this approach, be prepared to take the action within the time specified in your letter if the problem is not resolved.

HOW TO DO IT

1. Clarify the problem as you see it.
2. Suggest a solution or alternative.
3. Be firm and precise.
4. Avoid being emotional.
5. Make it clear what response you expect from the recipient of your letter.

CREDIT

The subject of credit is one many small-business executives approach with doubt and misgivings—whether they are asking for credit, rejecting it for customers, or trying to determine the pros and cons. The letters that follow cover a range of issues and methods of approach. A perusal of these examples and model letters will provide some practical guidelines, as well as put your mind at ease that you are not alone in having to deal with this sometimes sensitive topic.

Establishing Credit

Dear Ms. O'Grady:

You may recall that my firm, Management Impact, Ltd., used Greenwood's Executive Star Suite for our May 26 seminar and awards dinner, which was most successful. My partners and I were delighted with both the environment and the service and, in fact, wrote a note of commendation to your director at the time.

We hold these seminars on a quarterly basis, host an annual dinner dance for staff members and spouses, and several times each month entertain clients and prospective clients at lunch or dinner meetings. For this reason, we would like to open a charge plan, both for convenience and to avoid any uncertainty that we are hosting these occasions. My three partners and I are the only ones for whom I seek authorization, and the firm itself would bear full responsibility. I enclose background data on MI, along with profiles of the partners, and would appreciate whatever applications are necessary to obtain the desired credit.

Sincerely,

Application for Credit—a New Company

Dear Mrs. Parsons:

Your name has been given to us by Adam Garner, who knows me, as well as two of my partners, as holders of personal checking and savings accounts in his bank, the Third Federal of Rochester.

We have recently formed a small partnership in Rochester to act as consultants in matters related to water storage, use, and conservation. Our firm is described in the enclosed flyer, which we have been mailing to prospective clients. Now, in order to be more competitive with larger firms in our field, we intend to establish a water testing laboratory. At first, we had intended to finance this by applying for a loan. However, should we line up enough clients, we might be able to handle the expense through advance billing contracts and thus would need only modest, fluctuating amounts until our business stabilizes itself.

We understand that a "Stretch Credit" business checking account would be ideal for this purpose. If so, and if we'd qualify, we would appreciate information and an application.

Sincerely,

Establishing Relationship with Credit Bureau

Dear Ms. Susskind:

Your name was given to me by Roger Aimsley at Greenville National Bank, where my firm has an account. We would like information about credit ratings and related matters to answer the following kinds of questions in our business:

1. When contracting to supply building materials to Contractor A, how do we determine his rating if we intend to let him purchase on credit?
2. How do we ourselves establish a credit rating to use in obtaining large orders on credit?
3. How often are credit ratings updated?
4. If an individual has a bad personal credit rating, does this reflect unfavorably on the rating given to a firm he or she has incorporated?

5.. Is there such a thing as credit-rating insurance to cover any losses that might occur from inaccurate data?

6. What are the charges for using credit rating services and what do they cover?

Any information or suggestions you have would be much appreciated.

Sincerely yours,

Requesting Credit Information

Dear Mr. Hartley:

We appreciate your recent order for 280 units of our ornamental brick for your current construction project and are happy to welcome you as a new customer.

Although we approved the order and have already scheduled the shipment for next week, we would appreciate it if you would complete the enclosed credit information form for our files. This will enable us to handle future orders in a routine fashion.

We look forward to serving you again.

Sincerely,

Enclosure

Requesting Discount on Credit Purchases

Dear Warner:

After having purchased thousands upon thousands of products from Barnes Medical over the years, I was astonished—in fact, shocked—to learn from your accounting office that discounts do not apply on credit charges. As you can only too readily understand, this puts small independents like us at a tremendous, and very unfair, disadvantage by comparison with the big chains. I can threaten to take our business elsewhere, to one of your competitors. But that is a laugh and a half, in view of the fact that our business must look like an anthill next to a mountain when you size up our order next to that of an Eckerd or Grant's.

So I appeal to you, person to person, to amend your policy. We always pay our bills on time. We never complain, and we seldom return merchandise. Don't we deserve those discounts?

With best regards,

Acknowledging a Credit Installment Agreement

Dear Rev. Thurston:

This letter confirms our agreement by which we will supply the church, parsonage, and retreat cottages with weekly linen supplies on a rotating installment plan. The monthly charge will be $50, half of which will be credited to your parish account for the purchase of linens and cleaning supplies.

The basic installment can be increased or decreased as long as you give us two weeks' notice. Also, should you later decide that you do not want to continue the accumulative credit arrangement, we can lower the installments so they reflect rental charges only.

Thank you for letting us serve you.

Sincerely,

Arranging Automatic Payments

Dear Ms. Truman:

This will instruct HH District #3 to change our water account from a mail-receipt status to automatic billing. You are hereby authorized to deduct the full amount owed, on a quarterly basis, from our High Valley Inn checking account at Southern National, No. 45-7890-R. For your records, I enclose sample check #0350, signed by me and marked VOID.

As I understand it, your automatic deductions will commence with the second quarter of the year.

Sincerely,

Refusing Request for Personal Charge Account

Dear Mr. and Mrs. LeClare:

We welcome your patronage and are glad to see you taking advantage of our regular discounts. We wish we could also establish a personal charge account for you, but frankly we've had to abandon this age-old institution for two reasons: (1) With the kinds of discounts we offer and special sales we hold, our margin of profit is too narrow to permit the increased cost of maintaining personal accounts, and (2) we've had so much difficulty hiring a competent bookkeeper that we'd just be burdened with the extra job of trying to keep books ourselves. So we reluctantly made the decision last year to continue to honor those customers who already had regular charge accounts but open up no new ones. We do, however, honor all major credit cards, should you care to use one.

Thanks for your interest in Kelly's Hardware.

Sincerely,

Notifying Customer Credit Card Approval Denied

Dear Mr. Avalon:

We are writing this letter because you have been a valued customer of ours for almost ten years and we hope to be able to continue to serve you in the future.

It is with regret, therefore, that I have to inform you that we cannot fulfill your current order using the credit card number you indicated on the order form. According to the card's issuer, your balance is higher than the credit ceiling allowed. We call this to your attention in the event you are not aware of this, or of the limit.

If you still want to place the order, we would be pleased to accept your personal check or a money order. Just drop us a note or phone our "800" number above and ask for our "Orders on Hold" clerk.

Sincerely,

Apology for Mistakenly Rejecting Credit Application

Dear Ms. Peterson:

If the tables had been turned, I would have been annoyed, indignant, and probably insulted. So I can well appreciate your distress when you received a form letter from our accounting department saying we would not extend credit to your firm for fabrics ordered from us on spec for selection by your clients.

The error here was so stupid it is beyond explanation. Needless to say, we certainly give you carte blanche to display our materials and decorating products at no cost until an order is firmed up.

Although I am sorry, on the one hand, that we caused a problem, if not an embarrassment, I am delighted, on the other, to take this small opportunity to tell you we have received nothing but compliments about the elegant ambience you created here when you decorated our new office. It is a showplace of which you can be proud.

Cordially,

Explaining Credit Policies to Employees

TO: All Salespersons
FROM: Art Raybeck
RE: Unsuitable Credit Policies

The Appliance Ark was founded three years ago on the principle that, as we say in our ads, "Your Credit Is Our Business." We encourage people to buy on credit because it has been proven in studies that people tend to buy more when they can go home with something they desire without having to put down any cash.

From a business viewpoint, however, we want to sell on credit *only* when we are reasonably assured that the credit payments will be made on time. Last year, we lost an average of $1,000 per month because of charges that were accepted that never should have been. Please verify the validity and currency of all credit cards and charge accounts before finalizing any sale. If you are not sure, contact the floor manager.

Use of Credit Cards Versus Cash Payments

Dear Rodney:

I know that you have been operating your stations in an effective and profitable manner and would like to continue pretty much as in the past. However, there is one aspect of our business I'd like to see changed. If we can stimulate more *cash payments* for gasoline and services, in place of the very extensive use of credit cards that exists, we can function more independently and with a greater share of profits. It is tough to try to change old habits, but I intend to run newspaper ads and erect on-site posters announcing substantial discounts for cash payments on the spot. We'll also institute a "Bonus-Buck" plan whereby cash purchasers will get greenbacks worth cash for later purchasers.

I'll discuss details next time we get together.

With best regards,

COLLECTION

Composing collection letters often tests the skills of even the most accomplished writers. They have to effect a balance that is somewhat delicate and that satisfies the following essentials:

- Stating the obligation that exists
- Taking a firm stand, yet not antagonizing a customer who, though delinquent, might represent future sales
- Offering an alternate method of payment if it seems justified

Standard Collection Letter

Dear Ms. Lloyd:

Our records show that your account remains unpaid in the amount of $127.89, of which $67.00 was for purchases made more than 60 days ago.

We would greatly appreciate your payment since we have already paid our suppliers for the goods in question.

Sincerely,

Series of Collection Letters

Letter 1

Dear Mr. Guillard:

Since our billing over the last two months may have gone astray, I enclose a duplicate for the balance, $82.46.

Also enclosed is a self-addressed stamped envelope for your convenience.

Sincerely,

Letter 2

Dear Mr. Guillard:

We do not like to press customers for payments overdue if there is some reason why a bill has not been paid. If that is the case with your account, please let me know what the problem is and we will do everything possible to cooperate.

If there is no problem, naturally we'd appreciate your check for $82.46.

Sincerely,

Letter 3

Dear Mr. Guillard:

Since four months have gone by with no response from you about your seriously past-due bill, we cannot understand why you have avoided this responsibility. Perhaps you do not realize that we had to pay our wholesaler almost that long ago for the merchandise we provided you with.

At a time when more and more small businesses like ours are facing bankruptcy because of situations like this, we urge you to make a payment—even a lesser one if $82.46 is beyond your current means.

Sincerely,

Letter 4

Dear Mr. Guillard:

When we resort to using a collection agency to try to collect greatly overdue bills, we do so reluctantly because we know that it means the end of what we had hoped would be a satisfying and continuing customer-store relationship. This step is also costly and hard on our kind of family-community business.

Won't you please, therefore, help us to avoid a step that is embarrassing—and we think unnecessary—for all concerned. Your check for $82.46, if received before the first of next month, will avoid our having to turn your account over to a collection agency.

Sincerely,

Letter 5

Dear Mr. Guillard:

Since our repeated efforts during the past five months have failed to get any payment—or even a response—from you, we must resort to a step we dislike: turning your account over to a collection agency ten days from this date.

As you know, this will reflect badly on your credit rating.

Sincerely,

Series of Collection Postcards

Postcard 1

Dear Customer:

Because of the rising costs of extending credit to people who use our convenient charge account service, we have been forced to apply interest on all bills that have been unpaid for longer than one month.

Although most local businesses and financial institutions have been engaging in this practice for a long time, it is a step we have been trying to avoid. But the economic situation has finally caught up to us. Starting March first, there will be an interest charge of 1% per month for all charges remaining unpaid for 30 days or more.

Sincerely,

Postcard 2

Dear Customer:

Many of our customers have expressed an interest in leasing our equipment for periods up to one year with an option to buy as a means of avoiding initial bills or large installment payments. Therefore, we have established a plan whereby you can rent any of our machines at a modest monthly charge, 50% of which will be credited should you later decide to purchase the equipment outright. Thus, if you are paying a monthly rental of, say, $42, you will be credited with $21 toward the purchase price. Remember, too, that all our purchase prices have a 20% discount for our regular customers.

For further information, call Jenny on ext. 346.

Sincerely,

Postcard 3

Dear Valued Customer:

Please be advised that we are discontinuing all charge accounts as of *December 31*. The cost of bookkeeping and the increase in delinquent payments have made it impossible for us to handle the financial burden of charge accounts. Having been in business for more than ten years and having added many valued regular customers to our list, we take this step with the greatest regret. We hope you will understand and continue to look to us for some of the finest merchandise and best values in town.

Very truly yours,

Postcard 4

Although this information has been distributed in more detail in the past, our clients are reminded that the firm of Holly and Baron has instituted a new billing procedure, to be effective at the beginning of next month. Starting on October 1, you will receive bills on a bimonthly basis, instead of monthly. This will reduce our paperwork, cut postage costs, and in the end result in slightly lower costs for our clients, as well as for us. If, for any reason, you prefer to receive bills on the same timetable as in the past, we will be happy to oblige you. Just let us know as soon as possible.

Collecting a Debt from a Personal Friend

Dear Adrian:

Do you remember the story about the elderly lady who was always overspending and could not keep up with her bills? Each month, she would throw her bills into a hat, pick out ten or a dozen at random, pay them, and cram the rest back into her desk.

Whenever creditors dunned her, she would tell them about this selective procedure and end up with the threat, "If you don't stop nagging me about your bill, next month I won't even put it into the hat!"

Well, you may not be using the same method, but for some reason the payment owed on your account never seems to reach our bookkeeper.

Won't you give her a pleasant surprise and send in the overdue $67.42. We'd all be thankful.

Regards,

Requesting Prompt Payment

Dear Mr. Brookhaven:

When you experienced the plumbing leak in your second-floor bathroom, we dispatched our emergency truck and were able to effect repairs before any damage was done to the walls or ceiling. We were happy to perform this assistance as part of our professional service.

Since we fulfilled our part of the bargain promptly and effectively, we would greatly appreciate it if you could make your payment, now 30 days overdue, so we can take it off our books.

Sincerely,

Reducing Charge for Prompt Payment

Dear Mr. Barnard:

As we discussed on the phone, we did everything possible at this end to keep the repairs to your car at a minimum, in part by using reconditioned parts rather than new ones. Emergency engine repairs always come as a shock since they are seldom in anyone's budget, so I certainly sympathize with your lateness in paying the bill.

I'm hoping to clear up the books here and would like to make you an offer. If you can send me a flat payment of $130 by the end of the week, we'll reduce the bill from the $178 for which you were billed. We are losing money, but you have been a long-term customer, and we hope this will make the financial situation a little easier for you.

Sincerely,

Proposing a Payment Plan

Dear Mr. and Mrs. Delgado:

We received your letter explaining why you have been unable to pay us the $460 that has been long overdue on your account. Had we understood the circumstances earlier, we would not have placed the matter in the hands of a collection agency, despite the fact that such delinquencies cause serious problems in our firm's own economic health.

We suggest that you make payments amounting to 25% of your bill—or $115— each month, so that the entire matter will be resolved some four months from now. If you can stay on schedule with these payments, we will waive our usual interest charge on delinquent accounts.

We sympathize with the financial problems you have had to face and trust that these terms will be satisfactory to you.

Sincerely,

Suggesting Installment Loan to Cover Payments

Dear Ms. Hollingsworth:

When our accountant talked with you three weeks ago about your bill for $482, which is almost 90 days overdue, she had the impression that you were going to pay half of it that week and the balance by the end of the month. Since both of these deadlines have come and gone, we are concerned about the situation. If you are having financial difficulties of any kind, I suggest that you consider a loan arrangement that would permit payment by installments. We have in the past worked out such arrangements through the Finance Guild, Inc., and would be happy to provide you with an application form and information about interest rates.

Of course, if you prefer to send us one-half of the payment now, as you had originally intended, and one-half within the next three weeks, that would be appreciated.

Sincerely,

Interest Charge for Late Payments

Dear Ms. Raynor:

As you mentioned in the note you attached to your last payment, the amount of interest we charge for accounts that are 60 or more days in arrears does indeed negate the discounts we offered on the products in question. We regret having to add these charges, but the fact is that we have to pay our suppliers within 30 days and they in turn charge us if we are late. We also have to pay our nursery employees weekly, so delays in payments from customers have to be compensated for out of funds that otherwise would be earning interest for us in the bank.

As a graduate landscape architect, I entered the nursery field because I love nature. I, too, dislike paperwork and bookkeeping. But, unfortunately, that's all part of the business—if we want to keep from going under.

Sincerely,

Freezing Charge Account

Dear Mrs. Spielvogel:

As manager of the Appliance Ark, I regret that your request to purchase a microwave oven on your ArkAccount charge card was turned down by our floor manager last Thursday. I hope that she was gracious in dealing with you and did not cause you any embarrassment. Our policy is to freeze the charge privileges on any account that is 60 days or more in arrears. We don't like to do so, but we simply have to if we are to stay in business and offer appliances at the substantial discounts for which Appliance Ark has become noted.

Your charge account will most certainly be honored as soon as it is current. In the meantime, you might want to consider our Layaway Plan, which makes it possible for our customers to bank payments in advance and later profit from the discounts built into the Plan.

Believe me, Mrs. Spielvogel, we value your business and sincerely hope you'll find our prices the best in town.

Cordially yours,

Threatening Legal Action—Bad Check

Dear Mr. Arthur:

You have repeatedly refused to respond to our request for payment of the $342 which you owe for merchandise purchased at our Pineville outlet. To make matters worse, you paid our collection agent with a bad check and later excused it over the phone on the grounds that it was an "honest mistake" and "on the part of the bank" at that.

When we investigated, we found out, that this was not the case. If we do not receive our payment before April 12, we will turn the matter over to our attorney.

Sincerely,

Apology for Slow Payment

Dear Ms. Replogle:

The evidence is staring me right in the face as I look through the bills on my desk. We are in arrears to Brockton's Office Furniture Depot for $1,239.76 for purchases made a little more than two months ago. You have been very patient in not dunning me, and I am writing to ask you to extend that patience just a little bit longer. The bankruptcy of one of our major customers has left us with a rash of canceled orders which all but demolished our profits for this quarter.

We are taking active steps to secure new business, as well as holding a discount sale on the overloaded inventory caused by this unfavorable turn of events. So you can expect our full payment within 45 days.

With thanks,

Requesting Permission to Skip Payment

Dear Ms. Burberry:

You may recall that you approved our $25,000 business loan to launch the Bailey Company six months ago, on which we are making monthly payments of $1,500, and have been for the past 120 days.

Because of an unexpected commercial property assessment, recently approved by the town council, we find that our budget is badly squeezed for November. As I recall, there are certain circumstances that make it possible to skip a loan payment on occasion, paying only the interest and not the capital.

Is this possible in our case? If so, what would be the minimum we'd have to pay for November?

Sincerely,

Refusing to Make Payment—Poor Workmanship

Dear Mr. Quigley:

Your bill for $1,670 is nothing more than a testimonial to incompetence, delay, and excuses. I have conferred with our purchasing agent, and we agree, as does our controller, that we should not pay this bill—or any part thereof—until you can live up to your promises. After you installed the marquee over the entrance to our main office last spring, we reported on three separate occasions that the canopy was not level or parallel to the pavement.

We have even sent you photographs to document this problem, but our complaints have been ignored. We expect this situation to be corrected within ten days. Otherwise, we are not only going to refuse to pay your bill, but are going to demand that our initial advance of $1,000 be refunded.

Sincerely,

Establishing Relationships with Collection Service

Dear Mr. McCall:

Your name was given to me by a mutual friend, Pat Bray, who described your approach to collections as "tactful, understanding, and friendly, as well as effective."

As you can understand, our business attracts a lot of young people, many of whom are overly optimistic about their salary potential and who tend to overspend in matters relating to physical fitness and health. While we certainly want to receive our payments regularly and in full, we do understand the problems, and we would hate to be too harsh on young people who are not really deadbeats or goldbricks. Therefore, I'd be interested in knowing just how you function with clients and how you approach those with overdue accounts.

Sincerely,

Thank You for Overdue Payment

A thank you letter once payment has been made, helps restore the customer's goodwill.

Dear Mr. Keane:

Your final payment of $83.49 for the CD player was greatly appreciated. I hope that the sound system is living up to your fullest expectations. But if, at any time, you have problems feel free to get in touch with us at our toll-free number, above.

Incidentally, we are expecting a shipment of brand-new CD titles and are having a preaudition sale on Saturday. So, come on down and hear what we think will be the best music ever recorded.

Sincerely,

OTHER BILLING PROBLEMS

Check in the Mail

Dear Mr. Nigrone:

Re: Locater #45-890-H

Please be advised that, although the amount in arrears that you mentioned, $174.00, was correct, I had already mailed a check for the full amount two days before receipt of your letter.

I trust that this has brought my account to a "current" status and will require no further action.

Sincerely,

Tracing Lost Payment

Dear Jarvis:

We have been upending the department trying to locate the check for $5,675 which your controller mailed to us on May 30 in payment for last month's services. We know that it arrived safely because we have the statement, the letter of transmittal, and the postmarked envelope.

Rather than have you issue us a new check and request a "Stop Payment" on the original one at this time, we would like to continue the search for a few more days at least. It is important that we find out what happened and why, if we can possibly do so, and to correct any flawed procedure we may have in the accounting department and prevent a recurrence of the situation.

Sincerely,

Requesting a Replacement Check

Dear Ms. Torrence:

We appreciated your letter of January 22 in which you explained that you had returned the work order to our production department, along with a check for $369.50

to pay for the work to be done in your shop. We have found the work order, intact in the very envelope you addressed to us, but with no sign of any check.

We would appreciate it if you would (1) contact your bank to make sure the said check was never processed; (2) put a "Stop Payment" order on it, if the reply is negative; and (3) send us a replacement for the like amount. That will make it possible for our contractor to proceed with the job.

Naturally, should the original check turn up in our office at any time, we'll return it to you immediately.

Sincerely,

Explaining a Bounced Check

Dear Ms. Gisser:

It was something of a shock to get your letter this morning, attached to our controller's check for $543.78, which was marked "insufficient funds." I have just come from his office, where we had placed a phone call to our banker at First Trust. I am not exactly jubilant that it was the banker's face that was red and not ours. But, apparently, a trainee in the processing department had confused our firm name with that of another company which recently went out of business. Hence the embarrassing mixup.

Enclosed is a freshly drawn check for the above amount, made out to your company.

By now, you have probably received a phone call from our bank, apologizing for the error and offering restitution in case you had to pay any overdraft fee in your account.

Sincerely,

Making Charge for Bounced Check

Dear Mr. Pombard:

The check for $87.60 which you mailed us has been returned by your bank for "Insufficient Funds." Because of the costs involved in reprocessing returned payments, our management has had to add a $12.00 surcharge in such instances. Therefore, we are sending you a new invoice, for $99.60, which includes the surcharge.

We would appreciate payment of that amount. If there has been an error on the bank's part, however, please let me know, and we'll be happy to make the necessary adjustment.

Sincerely,

Enclosure

Billing Discrepancy

Dear Dr. Bowsley:

I'm writing on behalf of Stanley Ames, a metalworker who has medical insurance under our group plan. As your records will show, Mr. Ames was treated at your clinic for cuts and abrasions on two separate occasions in June and was referred by you to Memorial Hospital for X rays after the second visit. The first visit and the X rays were approved for insurance, but the second visit was disapproved because of a discrepancy in the billing, as documented by your clinic. Either the code number or the diagnosis was improperly listed.

I enclose herewith the form letter from the insurance agent and would appreciate it if you would fill in the blanks and return the document to me, with a corrected billing statement.

With my thanks,

Enclosure

Apology for Billing Error

Dear Hank:

In response to the phone call from your production manager, I have just dispatched six dozen shelf brackets, as described in the enclosed shipping advice. These should reach your warehouse within the week.

I apologize for the billing error that overcharged your account, and left you short of the desired items. We have been having some problems lately recruiting experienced clerical employees in this area, and, unfortunately, your erroneous billing is not the only such example that has come across my desk this month. But I think we have the situation under control now and should cause you no further grievance.

Thanks for your patience.

Sincerely,

Enclosure

Apology for Oversight

Dear Mr. and Mrs. Burdick:

You made a large purchase at our Glendale Shopping Center outlet back in January, and we were delighted to be able to give you fast delivery, a whopping discount, and ready access to our home decorating service.

But, on top of all those fine things, we really goofed! We overlooked the fact that you had made your final installment payment. And then, to add insult to injury, we dunned you for $44.50. I'd like to be able to blame it all on the computer, a handy excuse these days. But the fact is that we made a human error, and I apologize for it. You are fully paid up now on our records.

You are a valued customer. So, to show you how much we care, I have authorized the bookkeeper to issue you a gift certificate worth $20 on your next purchase at any of our six warehouses.

With every good wish,

Overcharge for Service

Dear Ms. Kurian:

We try hard, but sometimes things go awry. You have every reason to be outraged by the bill you received last week. The account books make it quite clear that you had mailed us the payment in question more than a month ago. So please forgive us, because we value your patronage and would like you to know that the accounting department offers its sincere apologies. Under separate cover, we are sending you a small gift, which we hope you will enjoy, with our compliments.

Very truly yours,

Duplication of Charges

Dear Russ:

We could blame it on the computer. We could blame it on the new employee in the accounting department. Or we might even be brash and say our service was so great we decided to bill you double for the good things we did for you. But this time I'll be perfectly honest and say I was the one who goofed. Since I personally sent you the report, which included the duplicate statement, I should have spotted the error.

Anyway, it won't happen again. And we may even give you a discount for the insult.

With best regards,

Apology for Billing Error—Computer Malfunction

Sometimes an error affecting many clients occurs. To minimize the damage to goodwill, a form letter explaining the problem and the steps being taken to rectify it will save the day.

Dear Client:

For reasons that have yet to be determined, our usually reliable computerized billing machines have been issuing data that are erroneous. Typically, statements rendered have claimed more billboard placements than were actually made, obviously tipping the scales in our favor.

We are making adjustments that should eliminate further errors and make life easier for all of us when the phones start ringing and indignant voices assert their rights. However, if you should spot any errors or suspect any billings for billboard placements not made, please call our office at once. We have established a *Hotline* for complaints, as listed on the letterhead above. But we hope no further action will be needed.

My apologies to any of you who have been inconvenienced.

Sincerely,

Complaint—Repeated Dunning Letters

Dear Mrs. Neptor:

A check in payment of the March bill for $2,345.89 is enclosed herewith.

Please note that it is our policy to pay for supplies no sooner than 30 days after receipt of statements. We do so because we, in turn, have to face delays of payments from our roofing customers, and it is perfectly reasonable to hold to this kind of schedule. We do not care to be dunned repeatedly by mail as soon as 10 or 12 days have passed from receipt of delivery. If you cannot adjust to our schedule, which we do not feel is out of line, let me know and we'll solicit another roofing supplier.

Sincerely,

Complaint—Billing Procedures

Dear Mr. Tompkins:

We have enough paperwork around here to require about one quarter of our office space just to accommodate the masses of records. In an effort to reduce unnecessary input, we have reviewed billing procedures by our suppliers. In your case, may we suggest that you bill us once at the end of each month rather than biweekly. Also, we'd appreciate it if the bills could be classified alphabetically by the names of the clients for whom we have prepared mailings. These names are clearly printed at the head of each project.

If you can follow this system, we'd have fewer pieces of paper to begin with. And we could simply transfer the items to our alphabetical records without having to reclassify them.

Thanks for your cooperation.

Sincerely,

Continual Billing Errors

Dear Ronald:

Please.
Please.
Please.

Ask your accounting clerks (or whoever is responsible) to check their specification sheets, as well as arithmetic, before they calculate your discounts and bonuses and submit their statements. Paperwork is annoying enough without having it doubled because of billing errors.

If the problems just seem insurmountable, I'll gladly lend you one of our accountants for a day or two, to try to get the bugs out of your system.

Thanking you in advance,

Refusing to Cancel Order

The recipient of the following letter has a reputation for making commitments and not honoring them. Therefore, the tone of this letter is much more severe than it would have been had an honest mistake been made.

Dear Mr. Colbertson:

It came as a great surprise to me to learn that you had asked our milling department to cancel your special order for 38 dozen "L" brackets, 7 inches long with a 1-inch lap. As you well know, your request was made more than 24 hours after we had phoned your shop to say that the shipment was ready for pickup by your trucker. As you are also aware, the size you specified is not standard and the brackets are not marketable elsewhere, even at a reduced rate.

Therefore, we have no alternative but to bill you in full for the order under the original stipulation, a confirming copy of which was mailed to you the day after your telephone order was received.

Our statement is enclosed.

Sincerely,

C H A P T E R   6

$\mathcal{E}$MPLOYMENT

Although the focus in this chapter is mainly on hiring, firing, and related matters, the model letters also provide insight into other aspects of organizing and strengthening the internal staffing of a company. The reactions of employees to letters, memos, and other communications depend upon a number of vital factors:

- The timing of arrival
- The manner of address
- The title and role of the sender
- The choice of words and phrases
- The clarity of the message
- The tone of the communication
- The ring of honesty and authenticity
- The credibility of the message
- The objective
- The nature of the action or response desired

Whether a letter involves hiring, firing, or personnel matters of almost any kind, the message often touches on highly sensitive subjects that have to be handled with delicacy and tact, avoiding too much emotional involvement, yet at the same time evidencing the right amount of compassion and interest. Some of the most delicate subjects employers have to address themselves to in letters are terminating employment, placing an employee on probation, cautioning against unethical actions, answering charges of racial or sexual discrimination, refusing a request for promotion or salary increase, warning about job-related misdemeanors, correcting misinformation, quashing rumors, and refusing to make personal recommendations.

In addition to covering these topics, this chapter also provides model letters for the following subjects, and many others:

- Announcing salary increases
- Making statements of performance
- Specifying requirements for job duties
- Outlining responsibilities
- Stating company policies regarding employees
- Encouraging pride in the company
- Providing information about training seminars
- Making awards for accomplishments
- Commending employees for outstanding work

WHY WRITE A LETTER?

It has often been said that effective managers are ones who communicate well face to face and who are themselves always on the firing line or in the thick of things. The managers who can be *seen* in action are the ones who are likely to command the most loyalty and generate the most cooperation from their associates and employees at all levels. Do these people really have to sit down and write letters to people who may be just down the hall?

The answer is *yes*. In fact, many business leaders who communicate well in dialog, person to person and one on one, are the best and most frequent users of the written word. For one thing, an effective letter is precise enough to avoid misunderstandings or blanks that often weaken the spoken word. Equally important, a typewritten letter (or even a handwritten note) confirms what has been said, or says what has been left unsaid. In some cases, a letter not only explains something, but substitutes successfully for an action that cannot be taken or a venture that cannot be undertaken. There are actual cases, for example, when a letter has proven more satisfactory than a pay raise.

Letter writing is usually called for, too, when there is (or could be) some kind of legal or regulatory element related to the subject and the best interests of the recipient. A good letter will serve as a specific record from the employer or manager in such matters as equal employment opportunities, antidiscrimination policies, job responsibilities, safety practices, or insurance claims. No matter how detailed and precise *verbal* instructions and information may be, they will not hold up under challenges from someone who disagrees. But a written letter, particularly one that has been placed in a formal file and perhaps sent in copies to other parties, will usually carry its intended weight.

YOU, WE, BUT NOT ME

When writing letters that directly involve the recipient, writers make a serious mistake if they place too much emphasis on themselves and their interests, rather than on the interests of those to whom they are addressing their message. The focus should be on *you*, or at the very least on *we*, as a team. Such letters will not only be better received and understood, but are likely to generate more positive action. Even a letter rejecting a job applicant or turning down an employee suggestion can be more successful if it places the emphasis on the recipient. For example,

> • Your resume and personal endorsements were most impressive. So it is with great reluctance that we have to turn down your application to join our production group. You...

> • You were very thoughtful to make suggestions about using the far end of the parking lot for employees who would like to hold a rollerblade meet next month. Your idea shows great imagination. However, our legal department...

> • Your job resume suggests that you were aiming too low when you applied to our processing division for a position. You have much stronger qualifications for a company with greater technological needs than ours and...

> • While your recent suggestion about the library expansion is too costly for this year's budget, we appreciated your sense of teamwork and your ability to come up with positive and productive ideas. Your approach suggests...

You will find this same kind of theme and emphasis in many of the model letters in this chapter.

HOW TO DO IT

1. Know the employee you are writing to as accurately and specifically as possible.
2. Take a firm, nonemotional position if the situation is a sensitive one.
3. Confine your letter to one subject.
4. Be businesslike, not personal.
5. Make your position clear.

6. Make it clear what you expect the employee to do upon receipt of the message.

RECRUITING NEW EMPLOYEES

Recruitment letter writing requires a substantial amount of homework, especially if this is an activity that is currently important to your business. You want to reach the right prospects, yet at the same time discourage a flood of inquiries from people who are not eligible. The sample letters provided here suggest ways of reaching some primary sources and presenting your case. Be as specific as you can about the nature of the positions that are open, the qualifications that are essential, and the timing.

College Campus Recruiting

Dear Dean Collingwood:

Kellogg Search, Inc., is an executive recruiting firm I founded five years ago that maintains offices in three cities, as described in the enclosed pamphlet. Interestingly enough, we are now seeking staff members for a new branch we'll be opening in June, and I hope you'll communicate our needs to those of your students who will be receiving their MBA degrees in May. Our salaries and benefits are competitive with those of other professional firms our size.

We are especially seeking young men and women who are knowledgeable about current executive and professional needs for employment in the small- to medium-sized companies who are our most predominant clients. One of our offices specializes in firms in the high-tech field and another in the publishing and printing industries.

As you can imagine, we have quite a high turnover because of the number of staff members who eventually accept positions with the clients we serve.

Any of your graduates who would like to explore a career with us should get in touch with me whenever convenient.

Sincerely,

Soliciting Fulltime Employees—College Recruiting

Dear Provost Henley:

The recruitment literature you requested is enclosed. You may be surprised to learn, however, that the text for *Your Successful Career* was not written by either our own company or our agency. It was composed in its entirety by three members of the graduating class at Duke's Fuqua School of Business. Thus it reflects the thinking of students whose ages and goals mirror those of students in your own classes at Berkeley.

It is our corporate policy at Bennett Investment Services, Inc., to let young people like these to take the reins whenever appropriate. I think the readers of the *Career* booklet will particularly appreciate the challenge.

Sincerely yours,

Soliciting Employees—College Recruitment Seminars

Dear Professor Goldwaite:

One of the problems faced by small corporations like ours, and sometimes those in the medium range, is that we annually face substantial executive recruitment problems. Part of the difficulty lies in the fact that our industry has very little glamor to attract young people, without high salaries to compensate for the so-so image. But much of the problem stems from the hodgepodge nature of on-campus recruitment, particularly in Florida where we have located a number of our middle and upper executives. The system is anything but scientific and is about as chancy as a bingo game. When I visit Campus A to recruit, I find there is no resemblance to the procedures at Campus B, while Campus C will introduce a whole new kettle of fish.

All of which leads me to propose that the University of Florida take the lead in establishing a seminar on recruitment practices. The system could be studied from three different viewpoints: that of industry, that of the educational institution, and that of the student. I can assure you that you would have a wealth of case studies to draw upon for classroom discussion.

If you are interested, I'd be happy to send you an outline and draft of the kind of seminar I have in mind. Or I could meet with you the next time I visit the UF campus, which will be in about four weeks.

Sincerely,

High School Campus Recruiting

Dear Dr. Bragden:

You are probably familiar with Marshland Nurseries, if only because of the sight of our green-and-white trucks used for delivering nursery stocks to our customers throughout town and in other parts of the Tri-City area. My three brothers and I are landscape architects and contractors; two of us hold degrees from Adelphi in horticulture; and I am the author of *The Garden Guide*, published last year by Green Thumb, Inc. We take pride in the fact that our firm is not just a "garden center," selling plants, mulches, soils, and tools. Rather, we are full-scale nurserymen, conservationists, and ecologists at heart, who have made extensive studies of our region and are at the forefront of improving our environment.

In this spirit, we encourage young people to seek part-time jobs in our company during vacation periods and weekends. Our salaries are competitive with those of other firms offering student employment. More important, we provide an excellent opportunity to perform a public service and at the same time become well acquainted with a field that has offered many young people a rewarding and satisfying career.

Enclosed is a brief description of Marshland Nurseries, including our pay scales and hours. I'd appreciate it if you would call us to the attention of any students interested in meaningful part-time jobs.

Sincerely,

Engineer

Dear Harrison:

Two years ago it was only a dream.

Last year, it was only on paper.

But this year, it is a reality, officially on the books as Foundation Research Associates, Ltd. We will specialize in an engineering field that is all too unknown and yet vital to safe and economical construction in the southeastern coastal areas where water tables are a problem and soils variable and commonly unstable.

We are looking for a core of four specialists who are experienced in foundation engineering and who can develop plans with clients whose needs will range from small office buildings to complex industrial plants. I think of you as an ideal candidate because (1) you have had 15 years of solid experience in this field and (2) you know the waters and landforms of the Southeast better than most cartographers.

The bad news is that FRA (as we hope to become widely known) can offer these four initial staff members nothing but a partnership compact and commissions based on contractual arrangements with new clients. The good news, though, is that conventional salaries would probably pale by comparison with the recompense attainable—and in very short order—through productive client contracts.

This is a real challenge, Harrison, and could be an exciting turning point in your career. Are you game?

With best regards,

Sales Representative

Dear Lowell:

Because of your track record in sales and your desire to maintain your own independence and work at your own pace, you could not do better than to join Amboy. You would be entirely your own master, planning your own schedules and lining up your own prospects. Yet you would have very solid backing from Amboy every step of the way and would see your products advertised in national magazines, on television, and in the company's own consumer magazine. The magazine is mailed once each month to present and former purchasers of Amboy products, and the copies in our region would bear your name and address as the authorized distributor.

You already know about the incentive plan that helps you recruit your own salespersons to assist you, increasing in numbers and benefits as you build your business. But you may not yet be familiar with the Pep Premium offers that stimulate regular customers to buy more and more Amboy products in order to earn discounts and cents-off credits. I'll tell you about this the next time we get together. In the meantime, believe me when I say that I have been associated with six other major sales organizations in the United States in my long career and all of them put together would not equal Amboy in the matter of merchandising incentives and sales-boosting premium plans.

Yours for a bright future,

HIRING

When writing to prospective employees—perhaps after inaugurating a recruiting program—your letter should be short and businesslike, yet include pertinent details, such as

- Specific job description
- Company department or division
- Salary or range
- Starting date
- Fundamental employee benefits
- Expectations from applicant, such as a resume, character references, financial references, and samples of work.

Acknowledging Resume—Description of Job Requirements

Dear Mr. Zachary:

We appreciate your interest in joining Acme as a sales representative. The resume you sent us seems to be compatible with our needs. However, we consider ourselves unique in our field and want to make it clear that our marketing and selling functions are guided by the following policies and concepts:

1. Regardless of previous experience, personnel new to our sales force must wait 30 days, during a period of company indoctrination, before being eligible for commissions.

2. Customer representatives will receive training to enable them to understand fully the Acme policy of low-key, courteous, and attentive service that has made the company what it is today.

3. A performance and salary review will be given 90 days after arriving on the job.

4. Expenses for a home office will be paid for at the end of this 90-day period and will include a desk, chair, two file cabinets, on-line computer with printer, minicopier, fax machine, and telephone with a separate business number. These will, however, remain company property.

5. Each representative will be assigned to a district sales manager, whose judgment will determine such matters as territory, exclusive options, and changes in commission, where applicable.

6. Representatives are required to sign a waiver at the end of the 30-day indoctrination period, warranting that they will not join a competitive sales force in the region for one year after leaving Acme, whether retiring, resigning, or being terminated for cause.

If you feel that these policies and concepts are fair and in accord with your best interests, we would be happy to set up an interview with our vice president of sales at a mutually convenient date and time.

Sincerely,

Postponing a Job Interview

Dear Ms. Pressly:

As you will recall, we met last month at the alumni placement meeting, at which time you expressed interest in advertising and your desire to move from a large agency where you are doing clerical work to a small, specialized agency like ours where you might be able more easily to assist with copywriting assignments and exercise your creative talents.

I did not get back in touch with you right away because we are presently reorganizing our copy and art departments, and I wanted to review our situation, explore the potential for the future, and determine how many new people we will be hiring. If you have not already made other commitments, I hope you will keep Batten, Barton, and Barnsmith in mind and get in touch with me around the end of this month. The timing will be better, and we'll be able to talk more specifically about possible openings and how you might fit in with our plans.

Believe me, we were impressed with your educational background and qualifications, even though you have not yet held a professional copywriting position.

Sincerely,

Describing Products to Prospective Employee

Dear Ms. Chandler:

We appreciate your interest in representing our firm in Texas and Oklahoma. At the moment, that territory is available to a qualified person with a good track record in consumer sales and services. Judging by the brief resume you sent me, you might be such a person. As you can well understand, it is essential that people who represent us be confirmed believers in, and users of, our products.

As you will note from the enclosed booklet, we carry a full line of health foods, natural vitamins, organic foods, salt- and sugar-free foods, macrobiotic products, and dried fruits and nuts, among others. It is imperative for those who represent us to know the specifications of all these products and be able to converse professionally about them with the retailers and wholesalers with whom we do business. We avoid fads and controversial dietary products. We never make claims that cannot be fully substantiated and documented. And we maintain prices at reasonable competitive levels, almost never engaging in discount battles or "bonus" plans.

If you are still interested, please contact the district manager whom you spoke to in Oklahoma City, Charles Rigby, and he will answer any questions you have.

Sincerely,

Explanation of Job-related Benefits—to Prospective Employee

Dear Hubert Protley:

Our CEO asked me to write you an informal letter about our company, since four years ago I was in almost the same position as you are today. I was trying to decide whether to opt for the small, personal firm where advances and internal transfers are limited or to head for the sprawling corporate giant where, on the one hand, the opportunities are limitless but where, on the other hand, people can get swallowed up in anonymity. As you can see, I chose the little guy. And I have never regretted it. The job-related benefits are not as clear cut and formalized as in a large corporation. The numbers aren't always defined. But you will find things that really matter, such as encouragement to try things your way and do some research without having to go to a committee for approval; stopping by someone's desk for interchanges of ideas, without risking censure for going "over the boss's head", knowing you'll have sympathetic ears in times of trouble; and being able to work long hours when you are meeting a research challenge and then taking some time off on your own without treading on any toes.

I could go on at more length in the same vein. But in the end, you can only judge by what you see and hear in a relatively short—too short—time. I urge you to talk to a couple of other people here also—and as soon as you can—in an informal, forthright way.

In any case, good luck in your choice and

Best wishes,

Pre-employment Test

Dear Dr. Samanders:

As you know, we have been in touch with a number of communications specialists to determine whom we should select to teach our staff members how to write better letters. We liked your presentation and ask just one more favor to help us make a final choice.

Enclosed you will find four letters that were recently personalized and sent to a list of some 90 prospective clients. We don't expect you to devote a great deal of time or go into detail, but please select *just one letter* and tell us how the writer could have improved the message to assure a better chance of convincing the recipient to use our services.

I think this step will help us to reach a decision.

Sincerely,

Enclosures

Offering Employment

Dear Ms. Schildauer:

You have been accepted for the job for which you applied, and it is my great pleasure to be the one to tell you so.

To be perfectly frank, I have to admit that there were other applicants who had more experience, whose references were more weighty, and whose salary demands were lower. But what my associates and I were most impressed with was the amount of homework you obviously undertook to evaluate our company and our industry and the way in which you see yourself as being involved. And we are genuinely enthusiastic about the fine suggestions you have already made about future growth and the expansion of our business.

We will hold you to it, firmly believing that with staff members like you the future will hold more than mere promise.

Welcome!

Rejecting an Applicant—Overqualified

Dear Ms. Moran:

I can't tell you how narrowly you missed acceptance for a position here in the financial analysis section of Proctor & Proctor. I seldom make it a practice of explaining the reasons to any applicant we turn down, but in your case I'd like you to know so you can benefit by our opinions in your search for the right employer.

The fact is that you are *overqualified* for even the top assignment in the department. We could not, in good conscience, hire you to fill a position that leads nowhere and where future salary increases would be small and far between. I suggest that you apply to several of the other financial firms in our area that are two or three times our size and would be more likely to have the right spot for you.

Sincerely,

Declining Employment—Company

Dear Robert:

I was sorry to hear that Albertson Electronics has gone bankrupt and you are consequently out of work. But, despite Albertson's demise, the electronics field is strong and steady and I have no doubt you'll land a good job—probably better than the one that folded. I wish we could offer you the sales position here that was advertised in the *Sentinel*. But our board instituted a very firm policy five years ago that we would not knowingly hire relatives and close friends of any of our managers. So if I were to break that rule, as CEO of the company, I'd face a rebellion by all the other managers who wanted to hire relatives and friends. I won't go into the details, but the policy has helped avoid some internal problems ever since it went into effect.

Enclosed is a copy of the current issue of *Electronics*. It has a classified career section that might provide leads.

With very best wishes,

Welcoming New Employees

Letter 1

Dear Cordelia:

We particularly welcome you this day to our small, but growing, company "family" and hope you will be happy here.

We have fine facilities. We have good products. And we feel that we have the greatest bunch of employees in town. That is one reason why we selected you and three other people out of dozens of applicants to join our production staff—because we like what you have to offer in the way of background, experience, diligence, and personality.

We hope you will feel as highly about us as we do about you and that together we will continue to build our company and make it an ever better place in which to work.

Welcome!

Letter 2

Dear Helene:

Welcome to the San Remo Oil and Gas family.

We don't like to be clannish, but we do take great pride in the people who work here and always try to foster feelings of mutual admiration and respect.

As you'll come to believe, we have the most loyal group of employees in San Remo. That is partly because we believe in one another, and partly because we are engaged in work that is beneficial to the community and the nation. And we aren't just being flattering when we say that is one reason why we voted to have you join are ranks. You're our kind of person.

Welcome.

With best wishes,

Letter 3

Dear Mrs. Rumford:

It is a pleasure to welcome you to our company, and particularly so since this is our fifth anniversary year and we look back clearly to the time when we were all new on the job. You will find that working here is an enjoyable and rewarding experience, since it is our policy to encourage our colleagues to use their own initiative and have a voice in what is going on, to the greatest degree possible.

Within the next week or so, you will be invited to attend a luncheon hosted by your department to introduce you and two other new employees to your coworkers. We hope you can attend. If you have questions about any phase of your work or company programs, please feel free to speak up.

With our best wishes,

Company Information for New Employees

Letter 1

Dear Hazel:

In welcoming you to the *Journal*, we take pride in the kind of professionalism you will find at all our editorial desks, as well as in the printing plant, the circulation department, and other areas of publishing. Internally, we are a finely organized team, and although we do not always function with the clockwork efficiency we try to achieve, we have a pretty good track record, going back almost 25 years since the day the paper was founded.

Outside, however, we are not always so successful, a situation we can sometimes brush off with that lame old excuse: "factors beyond our control." The purpose of this letter is to assert that we should dedicate our journalistic efforts (when outside our hallowed halls) to eliminating such factors, particularly when we are interviewing people to obtain facts for a story. I urge all reporters to keep the following precepts in mind when soliciting information from individuals and groups on the street or in other public places:

1. Do your homework to whatever extent is possible in light of the time, the place, and the situation. The more you know beforehand, the better equipped you will be to ask intelligent questions.

2. Double-check names, numbers, dates, and other statistical data.

3. Request sources that can confirm or complement information that seems incomplete or questionable.

4. Be firm in insisting on details, as a professional journalist with a duty and responsibility

5. Be polite and patient, ignoring slurs, lack of cooperation, and bad-mouthing about the press.

6. Give thanks and appreciation for cooperative efforts on the part of the person(s) interviewed.

7. Leave your card as a contact for any person who might later want to get in touch with additional information.

Most important, remember that you are not infringing, intruding, or being solicitous, even when interviewing someone wracked by tragedy. It is your *duty* to be factual.

Sincerely,

Letter 2

Dear Dr. and Mrs. Rodale:

Welcome to Hanover!

We don't know how familiar you already may be with our community, but we go along with the idea that the more you know the more delighted you are likely to be with the people, the facilities, and the environment. Even the old-timers say they are always discovering something about the place that is either new or they didn't realize was true. At any rate, the enclosed map, guidebook, and descriptions will be a fitting introduction.

To make your arrival more eventful, we have given the hospital's Hospitality House your new address and telephone number. After you are settled in, one of the hostesses will call for a visit, at which time she'll present you with free samples, several small gifts from local retailers, and a coupon book that will entitle you to discounts worth more than $200 at restaurants, stores, and various consumer service organizations. These can be used at any time, up to a period of six months after your arrival.

It goes without saying that if I can be of service to you at any time, now or in the future, I would be delighted to help. Just give me a ring, or leave a message.

With our warmest welcome,

Enclosures

Recommending a New Position to Chief Information Officer

The letter writer is the major stockholder in a high-tech corporation. The recipient is one of the board members whom he knows well.

Dear Henley:

It is time for the corporation to keep pace with the Space Age. Your board should take immediate steps to select a well-qualified manager, whether from inside or outside the company, to serve as the chief information officer (CIO), a position now badly lacking in your ranks.

The title is a relatively new one—so new, in fact, that only 2 top executives out of 19 that I talked to had ever heard of a CIO, let alone could describe the duties and responsibilities that go with the office. Fundamentally, a chief information officer is one who has to be skilled at compiling and assimilating information about both the company and the industry. He (or she) has to be able to evaluate the facts and figures, rank issues and elements by priority, and release the right data at the right time and in the right order when, and as, they are needed.

I suggest that the board confer with Franklin Williamson of Aurora Industries, one of the most adept CIOs I know, and handy because his office is just down the street from ours. He can quickly describe the qualifications you should look for, as well as the duties expected.

                                    Sincerely,

RAISES, PROMOTIONS, AND AWARDS

The most important letters in this classification are the ones that anticipate accurately not only what is going to occur in an employee's immediate career, but what he or she is likely to inquire about in the near future. It is better, for example, to alert employees that promotions and raises are not going to be likely than to wait until they bring up the subject themselves. When promotions, raises, and awards are imminent, notify employees personally by mail or memo yourself rather than risk letting them hear about it from another source.

Announcement of Promotion

Dear Cecilia:

YOUR FIRST PROMOTION!
Congratulations for getting it and deserving it.
Place this letter in your calendar file so that six months from now you can review it and ask yourself, "What about my *second* promotion? Am I living up to expectations?"
With that spirit in mind, I'm sure you will be eligible in proper time for a second. And a third. And etc.
We have enjoyed working with you.

                                    With very best wishes,

Denying a Promotion

Dear Nate:

You and I had both hoped that by now you would have climbed the ladder and be favorably considered as an assistant sales manager in my department. I did, in fact, include your name on the list I submitted last week to Herm Sachs, pointing out that you had been instrumental in securing the Continental Foods container business last fall. The problem was that your gross sales record was eclipsed by three people on Dick Culp's list. So that not only leaves you out in the cold this time around, but finds me with no new ASM in my own department.
That sounds like bad news. But the good news is that I have every confidence in

you as a salesman and I am positive this will be borne out, now that we have two promising new accounts to develop during the next few months.

With best wishes for the future,

Denying Request for a Raise

Dear Macy:

You had every right and reason to request a raise, now that you have been with the company for 18 months and have been commended for your performance on the job. So it is with real regret that we have to turn down your request. More accurately, I should say, we have to *postpone* it. As you and our other employees know, for the past year, we have been fighting a commercial tax increase that we felt was unfairly assessed and we have just been notified that we have lost our case. So the financial picture is momentarily bleak.

On the positive side, we expect some new business within the next three or four months, which will put us right back in the black. I have made a note to review your request at that time and would most assuredly like to see you get a well-deserved raise.

Sincerely,

Special Salary Increase

Dear Amelia:

My personnel management job is made all the more pleasant on those happy occasions when I can inform an employee about a special salary increase. This is particularly true when—as in your case—the increase reflects a substantial promotion as well as more income.

As of January 1, your salary will be increased to $33,000, with a proportionate rise in your profit sharing in the company. Along with this news goes our heartfelt thanks for the contributions you have made in the research department and the field.

With my best wishes,

Announcement of Bonus

TO: All Account Representatives
FROM: Jerry Faldo
RE: Bonuses for 1991

It is with both pleasure and optimism that I report the board's decision to award a 5% bonus to all staff members who are full-time account representatives, as well as a general 2% bonus to all other employees. The bonus represents the increase in business that we enjoyed for the 1991 calendar year. And the increase in business results—we are delighted to report—largely from the referral program that we instituted in 1990.

May your bonus checks remind you that you can expect even greater rewards in 1992 if you continue to make promising contacts with prospective clients and attract new business on the continuing scale evidenced last year.

With appreciation,

Award for Special Service

Dear Mrs. Vanamee:

Please accept the enclosed Gold Heart locket on our behalf for your contribution to the company safety program. We are publishing an acknowledgment in the *Rockdale Record* to this effect:

Awarded: A Gold Heart award to Jane Marietta Vanamee for her creative safety program. Mrs. Vanamee, who studied mechanical engineering in her spare time, devised a system whereby power to the paperboard assembly line is cut off automatically whenever a container that is ripped, wet, or otherwise defective passes over a signal device. Mrs. Vanamee first thought of the idea while in a supermarket line. If items could be checked by a pricing device, why couldn't a similar instrument be used to warn of defective merchandise on an assembly line and take corrective action?

It may interest you to know that you are the 20th recipient of a Gold Heart, which we have been awarding to worthy employees since 1984.

Good luck and good health!

Sincerely,

RESIGNATIONS

When employees resign, for whatever reason, be gracious enough to wish them, in writing, a happy and rewarding future. This step is good public relations, if nothing else.

Announcing Resignation of an Executive

Dear Mr. Thurgood:

It is with regret that we announce the resignation of Charles Banson, who had been assigned by us to handle your account as one of our new clients. Mr. Banson did not inform us of his plans until yesterday, when he told us that he is going to move at the end of the month and then establish his own firm.

Please be assured that we will place your account in the hands of one of our senior executives and will discuss the selection with you, as soon as we have had a chance to review the situation more explicitly and at greater length.

Sincerely,

Announcing Resignation of a Partner

Dear Ms. Holloway:

My secretary has just informed me that you had scheduled an appointment with our training director and junior partner, Dr. Hardly. I am sorry to report that Dr. Hardly has resigned without much advance notice and is no longer with Benson and Associates. If it would be of any help to you to meet with one of our other associates, we would be happy to reschedule an appointment. Just call Ms. Fries and she will make suitable arrangements. If you would prefer to get back in touch with Dr. Hardly directly, she can give you his home address. As I understand it, he will return there in about two weeks.

Sincerely,

Accepting a Resignation

Dear Elise:

I am devastated that you have decided to resign.

The members of the Plans Board are in a stew because you will no longer be on hand to guide them away from disastrous decisions.

The comptroller is aghast at the amount of profit sharing you are taking away with you.

The personnel director is undone by the challenge of trying to find someone to take your place.

In other words, the company is ruined!

I guess the only solution is to start a new company.

Well, I've had my laugh. I really am sorry about your leaving. But maybe I can talk you into a new plan of action. Our Prexy, in his infinite wisdom, confided to me last week that he has plans afoot to launch a new venture next year that will make our present enterprise look like an earthworm farm by comparison. With your track record as an entrepreneur, you might just be interested. I'll tell you more—next month.

Hopefully,

Request to Reconsider Decision to Resign

Dear Lamar:

When Trav told me you were planning to pull up stakes and go to the Big City, I thought he was pulling my leg. When you joined us in Cheyenne eight years ago, you were obviously fed up with the struggles of the Windy City. And I thought you had become as addicted as I am to the Big Sky country and the open spaces. I suspect that you are feeling the political itch, having accomplished so much in the state senate for two years and finding new challenges on the Governor's Civil Rights Commission. If that is so, why not bypass Chicago and go all the way to Washington, D.C.? We could use some representation on Capitol Hill and might even open up a lobbying office on Pennsylvania Avenue.

Well, if I can't convince you, at least you know you can always come back to Wyoming when you find how badly you miss the fresh air and the saddle.

With best wishes,

Invitation to a Retirement Party

Dear Mr. and Mrs. Sussman:

You are cordially invited to a buffet to be given in honor of your neighbor, Henry Maniford, who is retiring from our firm after 32 years of service.

Since this is to be a surprise to him, we ask that you keep the affair in confidence.

The buffet will be held at the Harbor Club on March 7, at 6:30 P.M. The club asks that gentlemen wear jackets and ties and that the ladies dress accordingly.

Please R.S.V.P. to my secretary, Joan Goren, at the number on the above letterhead.

Sincerely,

PS: Bring a card, if you like, but, please, no gifts.

WARNINGS AND PROBATIONS

One of the most unpleasant writing assignments is most certainly the letter telling the recipient that he or she has not "cut the mustard" or has been deliberately unscrupulous. The three MUSTs are that the letter (1) must be written immediately upon learning about a delinquency, (2) must be blunt and to the point without being emotional or indicating that the writer is overreacting, and (3) must specify what steps are to be taken to avoid further unpleasantness.

Absenteeism

Dear Ms. Leach:

I have been informed by your department supervisor that you have been repeatedly arriving at work late, leaving early, and in a few instances being absent without any adequate excuse. Her admonishments to you have apparently gone unheeded. Please be advised that you cannot continue in this manner if you intend to remain an employee of this company. If there is any basic reason why you have problems, I would be happy to talk with you and your supervisor about them at any time.

Sincerely,

Inadequate Job Performance

Dear Mr. Morino:

Last week one of our customers returned 12 cartons containing our miniature toy vans because they had not been tooled properly and had sharp edges that could injure a child. These cartons all contained your inspection number and gave evidence that you have either been handling your tools improperly or not paying close enough attention to your work. This letter will serve as a reprimand and a warning that further failure on your part to do the job expected could result in dismissal.

Sincerely,

Safety Violations

TO: All Warehouse Employees
FROM: The Management
RE: Fire Safety and Violations

When the fire department made its monthly inspection last week, it gave our warehouse bad marks for storing flammable chemicals too close to the pumping station, which on occasion generates excessive pressure and heat. Regrettably, this is the second time our company has been cautioned about this potentially hazardous practice.

Despite previous warnings by the company to supervisors and employees in general, the message seems not to have registered. If we are subject to fines—and that may be imminent—we intend to deduct proportionate amounts from the salaries of all employees involved in fire violations.

Warning—Safety Violations

Dear Mr. Tomasaki

When you signed up as a rights-holder with Five-Star Oil and Gas, you agreed to abide by the specifications relating to safety precautions on premises, as well as the policies of the company in regard to pricing, marketing, and sales. We have no quarrel with your business methods, bookkeeping, or promotion and advertising programs. But we are greatly concerned about your capacity to implement what we feel are straightforward and simple rules to minimize the dangers of fire, explosion, or injury in the day-to-day handling of volatile materials.

You have been verbally cautioned on three occasions not to permit smoking in the pumping islands. While this restriction is sometimes difficult to enforce with customers, who often conceal the fact that they have lighted cigarettes in hand, there is no excuse for violation on the part of employees, as has been observed at your station. If this continues, the management of Five-Star Oil will have no alternative but to judge your contract broken for cause and rendered null and void.

Sincerely,

Personal Appearance

Dear Stanley:

It has not been the practice of our company to try to enforce codes of dress on our employees, at any level. We have always felt that pride in achievement and dedication to the job were the most important factors, and so we have not stressed the visual appearance of our people. However, there has to be a limit, and I feel it has been reached when employees arrive for work looking as though they had just emerged from a train wreck. If the managers of golf courses, tennis courts, and fine restaurants can suggest proper dress, I think we are entitled to the same respect.

Therefore, would you please inform the members of your transportation group, who unfortunately seem to be the worst offenders, that the following are not acceptable:

- Cut-off jeans
- Sleeveless undershirts with no tops
- Shabby sneakers with holes in the toes
- T-shirts with tacky slogans
- Badly ripped sweaters
- Gaudy fluorescent caps

Thanks,

Misdemeanor

TO: Ray Ventura
FROM: The Dispatcher's Office
RE: Misdemeanor

On July 25, you called in sick at 7:30 A.M., and we had to spend time and effort locating a driver at the last minute to take over your Pondfield Avenue route.

On July 25, at 11:55 A.M., you were seen by an official in the maintenance office coming off the 18th green at the Municipal Golf Club, as he was arriving at the club to inspect the shuttle bus, which had broken down in the parking lot.

On July 26, you reported for work and told your supervisor you "felt better." There is nothing like a round of 18 holes to cure what ails a person! Your supervisor's response was to suspend you for three days without pay. Henceforth, and for the next six months, you will present a doctor's written confirmation of any illness that prevents your strict attention to your scheduled work.

As you know, falsification of an illness is a dereliction of duty. It is not condoned by the union. It will not be tolerated by us.

Yours truly,

Inappropriate Public Remarks

The writer has already conveyed the message in person; the purpose of the letter is to transmit a copy of it to the client in question.

Dear Owen:

Jerry Pratt phoned me yesterday to emphasize the fact that he was not happy with the comments you made about water pollution in your speech to the Wentworth Rotary Club. He reminded me that his firm has pioneered in the prevention of oil spills and the perfection of the double-link natural gas piping system that has never yet had a joint-leakage or rupture problem. I assured him that your critique was directed—as you explained—at the Mexican cartel, which has twice been admonished for slipshod practices, and not at any company or group in the United States.

As you suggested, I am passing along your comments to the editor of the Rotary *Newsletter* so that the issue can be clarified in the minds of members who were in attendance at the Wentworth meeting.

With kind regards,

Recommending Additional Training

Dear Jeff:

When we brought you into the media department last year from your former ad agency, you and I discussed at considerable length the goals and prospects for increasing our new client accounts by about 25%. It has been discouraging to see that the trend has been downward rather than upward during the past six months, and we can easily blame it on the national economy in general and the financial setbacks in the Northeast in particular. But neither you nor I are the kind of people who are content to sit back and make excuses. I am establishing a new business program for myself, which I'll outline in detail later. And, on a parallel basis, I propose a course of action that could pay off for you, as well as the agency.

The Harvard Business School is conducting a six-week seminar on advertising, media relations, and the psychological elements in agency-client relationships. Normally, a program of this nature is open only to MBA students. However, since the AAAA is contributing several guest speakers, temporary participation is available to a limited number of professionals from local ad agencies. I have taken the liberty of enrolling you for the seminar, which starts January 21. Let's discuss the scope and nature of the program and how it can benefit you—and all of us—the most.

With best regards,

Proposing Professional Seminars and Programs

Dear Chris:

Now that you have been with the company for 14 months, you have been recommended for attendance at a Performance Evaluation Seminar being conducted in May by the National Management Association. The program requires two weeks of attendance, during which time you will be given a leave of absence, with full salary and benefits. The company will, of course, pay tuition and travel expenses.

The purpose of this seminar is to help executives—particularly those who are younger or less experienced—to evaluate their skills, objectives, and procedures as a means of improving performance and enhancing their career potentials. As you may know, several of our managers have attended PES in the past and found the results beneficial.

The enclosed leaflet describes the seminar, the locale, the facilities, and the faculty at PES. Please complete the information requested in the inset. As you will note, each attendee is asked to provide personal information about such matters as goals, future objectives, and self-image and an analysis of recent participation in corporate business ventures and decision making. These matters are to be used solely by the seminar director as an aid in the evaluation process. They are *confidential*, will not be seen by our management, and are to be given only to the director upon your arrival at the seminar itself.

Let's sit down for about ten minutes within the next few days and discuss the program. I'm available almost any time.

Sincerely,

Placing Employee on Probation

Dear Ms. Sanders-Reed:

I was informed last week by your supervisor, Susan Smith, that you have been repeatedly coming to work late, leaving early, and in a few instances failing to show up at all. As she explained it, she pleaded with you on several occasions to get yourself under control, but now feels the problem is beyond her ability to solve.

You would normally have been dismissed for cause. But we sympathize with the situation we understand you are in, coping with a drug-addicted dependent. You must seek outside help. We suggest you try Family Consultation Service, which has successfully assisted several of our employees. Of course, we cannot force you to do so, but if you cannot find some way of bringing the situation under control, we will have no choice but to terminate your employment.

With sympathy,

LAYOFFS AND TERMINATIONS

The least wanted letter-writing assignment for a small-business executive (or any other for that matter) is the one terminating an employee, whether for cause or an unfortunate decline in the company's fortunes. There is no alternative but to get to the task and announce the sad fact of the matter. The more promptly you do so, the less painful this experience will be. Letters of layoff and termination should be brief, to the point, and authoritative. State your regrets, if you like, but avoid getting involved in explanations and condolences.

Terminating for Cause

Dear Maxwell:

As the old Truman saying goes, the buck stops here and I am the one who has to tell you that your job with our firm will be terminated three weeks from this date.

This decision should come as no surprise to you, since you and I have discussed, with increasing frequency, your inability to fill the sales quotas established at the start of the year.

If we were a larger company, I would be the first to suggest transferring you to a department not concerned with sales, since you have obvious talents in a number of other fields. My suggestion is that you look for employment in some organization where you can put your artistic talents to good use—perhaps in advertising or design.

Let's discuss the possibilities so that we may at least part with mutual respect and understanding.

Regretfully,

Terminating—Economic Slump

Dear Sheila:

It is my sad duty to inform you that your job with Marston Metals will be terminated on March 31, two weeks from the time you receive this letter. I hasten to add that the move in no way reflects on your ability or your performance. Rather, it is an economic necessity, forced on the company by the recent cutback in our state government contracts.

You will receive an extra week's pay for each of the three years that you have been with MM, Inc., and continuation of your company medical and health policy for six months. We will also provide assistance, if you like, in helping you find new employment and will provide favorable references concerning your career with the company.

I extend management's regret that we have no alternative and the wish that you will find a new position quickly.

Sincerely,

Seasonal Layoff

Dear Ms. Trippett:

The part-time position you are now holding three days a week will be discontinued on September 15. We regret that this is necessary, but, as we discussed last year when you applied for the job, the seasonal nature of our business causes employment fluctuations beyond our control.

Unless you intend to look for full-time employment, we suggest that you keep us in mind for a possible opening next April. As you know, our business traditionally increases in the spring, and we anticipate a new hiring schedule. Should you come back with us, you would receive credit for the time you have already spent on the job, which would be reflected in benefits and a possible salary increase.

With our best wishes,

Plant Closing

Dear Sherman:

At your earliest opportunity, will you please inform all personnel at the Riverhead plant that this facility will be shut down, effective two months from now, on May 1. Those employees who desire to remain with the company can apply for openings at any of our three other plants, and we will do our best to find appropriate positions for them. Please make it clear, however, that such transfers will depend upon (1) the qualifications and experience of the applicants, (2) the number of positions that will be vacant in May, and (3) the number of employees who elect to apply for transfer.

Employees who decide to resign from the company and seek employment elsewhere will be remunerated with one week's salary for every year of service.

Sincerely,

Unexpected Layoffs

TO: All Supervisors
FROM: The Human Relations Office
SUBJECT: Layoffs

Because yesterday's layoffs occurred more quickly and unexpectedly than anticipated, you are requested to inform employees in your department about the facts before unfounded rumors can be circulated to everyone's disadvantage. The following may be helpful to you in communicating the situation to your people. These statements are based on comments that have already started to surface.

Rumor: The company is financially shaky and is starting to "trim the fat."

Fact: The company is economically sound and has no intention of other cutbacks in personnel.

Rumor: A dozen people were suddenly let go because they expressed opposition to the projected merger with a competitor.

Fact: Only nine people were laid off—all of them aware that they were hired for temporary service to assist with a new government contract.

Rumor: The employees were ruthlessly fired, without prior warning.

Fact: All nine were informed at least 45 days ago that the government was not going to renew the contract.

Rumor: The company has demonstrated a lack of humanity.

Fact: A corporate program was underway more than two months ago to line up appropriate jobs for any who might be laid off under these circumstances.

If you foresee any problems or have any questions, please contact the Human Relations Office at once.

Sincerely,

REFERENCES AND RECOMMENDATIONS

Requesting Reference

Dear Dr. Alshall:

This is to request information about Alva Smithers, who has applied for a position in the firm I have recently started. We distribute medical supplies, and I understand that Ms. Smithers worked in your clinic as a supply clerk and is familiar with medical equipment and terminology.

Any nonconfidential information you care to give me would be greatly appreciated.

Sincerely,

Declining Request for a Reference

Dear Mr. Sommers:

Your associate asked me if I would write a letter of recommendation for Mrs. Allen Browne, who was temporarily employed with our firm. While I found her very personable and apparently enthusiastic about her work, I regret that I am not the right person to evaluate her professional capabilities. She was assigned to another division, working in the accounting department, whose operations I am not at all familiar with.

To be fair to Mrs. Browne, I suggest that you get in touch with her supervisor who would of course be familiar with her experience and skills. I am told that Ms. Emily Bowen would be the proper person for you to contact.

Sincerely,

Refusal to Provide Recommendation

Dear Mrs. Raymond:

It caught me by surprise that Kenneth Smith had given my name and my firm as a reference when he applied for a job with you. I have known relatives of this young man for several years, but have neither met him personally nor been shown his credentials. Much as I would like to oblige you and see him placed in a position he obviously desires, I would be less than honest if I tried to provide any kind of commendation at this point. I suggest that you ask the other people on his list if they could provide more information about prospective references, in addition to their own.

I look forward to lunching with you and your staff again one of these days and hope your business is prospering.

Sincerely,

Recommending a Former Employee

Dear Captain Hartzell:

You will shortly be hearing from one of my former business associates, Margaret Mattheson, who is just now moving to Phoenix and will be seeking employment. She has had to move from the Northeast to the Southwest because of her husband's declining health and his physician's advice that he move to a warmer climate.

Mrs. Mattheson worked for our firm for more than ten years, much of the time in my department. She is a superb programmer, and I cannot say enough for her sense of loyalty and commitment. Over and beyond that, she always has a positive outlook and contributes a great deal to the workplace, as well as the home. I suggested that she contact you, as well as two or three other companies that were suggested. She realizes full well that you may not happen to have an opening, no matter how well received she may be. But I thought it worth looking into.

Sincerely,

Recommending a Specialist

Dear Reverend McMasters:

Your letter requesting our opinion of Ms. Sommer's talents as a programmer has been referred to me, since she was for two years a member of my department. I'd be delighted to recommend her at any time. She was not only skilled in her work but was always pleasant and responsive and willing to work overtime whenever the need arose. She required very little supervision on the job because she was goal oriented and very conscientious about obtaining the best possible results in her assignments.

As you may know, she was widowed last spring and shortly thereafter left our firm of her own volition so she could move to your community and be closer to her daughter. Since she was always involved in church affairs here and took on a number of volunteer jobs, I am convinced she would make an excellent addition to your office staff, as well as to your congregation membership.

If you need further information, please call or write me at any time.

Sincerely,

Introduction and Recommendation

Dear Dr. Wharton:

This is a letter of introduction for Mary Ridgeway, who has ably served as my assistant for almost ten years and is moving to your area because of her husband's recent job transfer. You will note that she is academically well qualified for a management staff position in a school system, what with her Bachelor of Arts degree in Psychology and her Master's in Education. What you will not see on paper, however, are the intangibles that have made her one of the most valuable members of our school family here: loyalty, devotion to learning, dedication, and the willingness to sacrifice personal interests for the betterment of others.

She would be ideal as the assistant to one of your principals, as a person who is not only fully supportive but has the initiative and strength to take over during periods when her superior might be ill, on vacation, or out of town on business. Should there be no such openings, I recommend that Mrs. Ridgeway be considered for any management position calling for a combination of educational know-how and executive skills. I would be more than happy to elaborate on this at any time.

Trite though it may be to say that "my loss is your gain," I feel this to be one time when the truth is even more potent than the platitude.

Sincerely,

Recommendation—Former Secretary

Dear Thurman:

I understand that you are looking for a secretary/receptionist who not only has the professional skills but is personable, can answer questions intelligently, and will make a favorable impression on your clients and others who visit your office. With these capabilities in mind, I recommend very strongly that you put on your "prime candidate" list the name of my former secretary, Julia Borchard, whose resume is enclosed herewith. Ms. Borchard has a pleasant, sympathetic personality, but she can also say "no" when the occasion warrants. She is enthusiastic and responsive, without ever being gushy, and is quick to grasp unfamiliar concepts and circumstances. You could probably turn her into an effective paralegal in no time. I wish I could keep her myself, but, as you may know, I am moving to the West Coast and she has no desire to change her residence or location.

With best regards,

Best Wishes—New Job

Dear Alton:

Our loss is somebody else's gain, and we all wish you well in your new venture. The shop won't be quite the same without your repertoire of stories and your uncanny ability to forecast power problems and the consequent need for emergency electrical service. But we'll be thinking about you and hope your new electrical engineering research project will prove to be satisfying and rewarding.

Give my best to Suzie and the girls.

And do come back and see us occasionally.

With best wishes,

Statement of Organization's Objectives

Dear Beth-Anne:

When you interview workers who want to serve in our organization on a part-time basis, we feel it is important that you use descriptions similar to the following:

"Our mission is to improve the quality of life for nursing home and boarding home residents and to ensure that consumers in general, regardless of age, have a voice in the long-term care system. Consumer action groups around the country, supported by us, are encouraged to work on behalf of older people and persons with disabilities who may be totally institutionalized. We also conduct seminars on nursing home issues, recruit sponsors, and run a speaker's bureau, and we serve as a clearinghouse of current information on nursing home care."

Feel free to rephrase the wording if you like.

Sincerely,

Company Policy—Hiring Relatives of Employees

TO: All Employees
FROM: Personnel Office
RE: Hiring Relatives of Employees

The question has arisen a number of times about the practice of hiring relatives of employees who might work together in the same department or office.

While some organizations have discouraged the practice of permitting husbands and wives or parents and children from being employed under the same roof, our company has no such outlook. In fact, our attitude is that we like to be thought of as something of a "family" to begin with. So if parents or spouses or cousins or other relatives of present employees have the necessary skills and goals, we see no reason why they should not apply for a job here rather than down the street.

This does not mean that we tolerate nepotism, that is, favoritism shown on the basis of family relationship, whether by blood or marriage. Yet, neither do we permit any kind of advantage based on whom you know or are indebted to.

We have a job to do and we can pitch in as friends, relatives, colleagues, or even strangers.

Company Policy—Job Skills Testing

Dear Ms. Terrell:

Your supervisor has informed me that you are reluctant to take the job skills test now being administered by an outside personnel management agency.

Let me assure you that the testing will be to your benefit and that you have been selected only because we think your potential will be improved and your employment category upgraded. In no way are these tests designed to pinpoint an employee's shortcomings or lack of knowledge. Rather, they have been prepared by occupational professionals to help us plan for future promotions and salary increases for employees whom we feel have the ability to move upward in our company.

Should you elect not to take the tests, your career here will in no way be jeopardized. But I did want you to know that the program will be beneficial to most of the people who participate in it.

Sincerely,

$\mathcal{P}$ERSONNEL MATTERS

Familiarity with recipients is an essential requirement of letters addressed to employees and other personnel who are involved—or might be involved—with the writers' interests and organizations. It is almost better not to communicate at all than to write letters to "faceless" correspondents. As this chapter points out, you must make every effort to learn about the persons to whom you are writing, if you do not already know the individuals or have basic data about them and circumstances relating to the subject under discussion. Quite obviously, this is most essential in letters, memoranda, and other communications where the issues are sensitive.

The chapter provides guidelines for addressing many of the common subjects and situations, internal and external, that come under the heading of "personnel." When a person gets a letter or memo from you, he or she also gets a distinct impression that may be favorable or unfavorable—regardless of whether the subject is one that is welcome or disagreeable. Improbable though it may seem, you can write a letter to an employee to announce a promotion or to several employees describing their relocation to larger offices and leave a bad taste in their mouths. How? As is quite common, by using a condescending tone. Or by making the message sound as though it begrudged the extra expense. Or by being formal when the topic calls for a more casual, friendly approach.

QUESTIONS TO ASK YOURSELF BEFORE WRITING

1. Do I know the employee well? a little? barely?
2. What is the purpose of the message?

3. Should it really come from me or someone else?

4. Is the timing right?

5. Will the same message go to others, who might compare notes?

6. Is the medium right—letter, memo, note, or other vehicle?

7. Are the style and format right for the message, whether typed, printed, handwritten, or otherwise?

8. Should a copy be filed and/or sent to anyone else?

HOW TO DO IT

1. Try to be natural in your opening sentence and the approach to the matter at hand.

2. Stick to the point and don't be too chatty in an effort to seem casual.

3. Keep the message brief.

4. Be firm and authoritative, as needed, but not imperious or overbearing.

5. Use teamwork as a theme, when appropriate, but avoid pressing an employee's loyalty.

6. Make it clear what you expect the recipient to think or do.

7. Make sure your closing is in keeping with the salutation and the tone of the message.

Employee communications should be cultivated by the owners and managers of small businesses as a direct, effective, and inexpensive method of achieving numerous organizational goals. These range from welcomes and dismissals to praise for jobs well done, congratulations on promotions and salary increases, interoffice instructions, policy guidances, personal news reports, cautions about problem areas, quashing rumors, announcements of forthcoming events, and introductions to newcomers on the scene.

Letters can be excellent morale builders, when well timed, intelligently composed, and solidly presented. Many successful companies make it a policy to send written expressions of appreciation for accomplishments or participation on the firm's behalf over and beyond the call of duty. Consistency is an important criterion, because expected messages that are *not* received can backfire—if employees have seen fellow workers on a project commended when they are not. Managers should always keep in mind that their organizations can be the settings for infighting, jealousies, and cliquishness, but good employee communications can often help avert controversies, or, at least, smooth over some of the personnel (and personal) problems.

COMMENDATIONS

In the course of day-to-day operations, many small-business owners and executives classify complimentary letters as low priority, not so much because they think them less important but because of the pressures of attending to more critical mail. Yet thank you notes and the recognition of personal achievements can be excellent morale boosters within the company and public relations steps outside. When writing a letter of commendation, be sincere and avoid any hint of sheer flattery or ulterior motives. The rewards can be more than you might anticipate.

On-the-Job Accomplishment

Dear Dr. Chiyoda:

For the past five years, we have been badgered by the Pure Air Coalition, which has claimed that our vinyl adhesive refining process contributes to air pollution, despite the installation of multilayer filters. Now you have abolished PAC's arguments forever. Your wet-process formulation for refining the adhesive cannot be referred to in any way as suspect. Moreover, since the formulations are used over and over, there is no waste discharge to account for and hence no chance that PAC will switch its focus from the air to the water.

We can all take pride in this accomplishment.

Sincerely,

Thank You for Cooperation

Dear Elsie:

The long hours and hard work you have committed to the company's first-aid program has earned the respect and deep appreciation of your colleagues and all of us in the front office. In recognition of your achievements, we invite you and your husband to attend a luncheon at the Community Center on Tuesday, the 17th, at noon.

Whatever we can say or do by way of thanking you for your participation pales by comparison with the record of accomplishment already documented. I have been told by your supervisor that you have recruited more than 20 employees to volunteer for first-aid work and that you and they have already administered aid to more than 100 people who had become ill or suffered injuries.

Keep up the good work!

Respectfully,

Personal Achievement

Dear Theresa:

It was with considerable pride that we read in the *News* about your selection to represent the county in the Political Debating Contest this year. We always knew you were a good speaker, judging by your ability to make successful marketing presentations to our clients. But now we are even more aware of your abilities in front of audiences, large and small.

Congratulations, and good luck in the forthcoming debates!

With every good wish,

Morale-boosting Memo

TO: Production and Assembly Departments
FROM: A. L. Gilbert
RE: Notable Achievements

In the course of our daily work, which often appears on the surface to be humdrum and routine, we often forget the fact that your company is recognized in scientific circles as one of the prime makers of precision instruments in the United States, as well as several countries abroad.

The public relations manager recently sent me a folder with newspaper and magazine clippings that have mentioned Gilbert & Gilbert instruments, and I was fascinated to see how often we have played a part in significant, often historic, events. Consider the following examples that were documented by the press:

- Our AH-34 meteorological instruments helped to predict the course of Hurricane *Hugo*, saving many lives.

- Our U-series heat detectors prevented the overheating of engines in tanks during Desert Storm operations.

- Our radar-ranging device spotted wreckage from at least six marine sinkings off American coasts, making it possible for Coast Guard units to reach survivors in time.

- Our home smoke detectors have alerted hundreds of residents to life-threatening fires when they were asleep or otherwise unaware of danger.

- Our commercial smoke detectors made it possible for firefighters, by remote control, to trace the course of the fatal fire in the Los Angeles Center and deploy units to the right places when visual surveillance was impossible.

Drop by the p.r. office sometime during a coffee break or lunch hour and browse thorough the clipping folder yourself. You'll be amazed at what your work has been accomplishing!

So the next time you think of your job on the line as routine or unexciting, think about what the product in your hands may do to save lives, prevent damage, or simply enhance our life-styles.

With my best personal wishes,

Job Well Done

Dear Kathleen:

Congratulations on your new *Stakeholders Report*!

Sending a newsletter to people who own stock in the company is a fine idea and a way to strengthen our internal and external ties. But I particularly like your theme of promoting an active "stake" in our operations rather than simply referring to the rather passive ownership of stock.

You asked everyone on your circulation list to submit comments, factual matter, and ideas. Those of us in management will certainly be sending you continuing suggestions. In the meantime, keep up the good work!

Sincerely,

"Special" Bonus

Dear Truman:

Along with many other small businesses, we long ago had to abandon the idea of giving Christmas bonuses to valued, long-time employees. It has discouraged me that we have not been able to provide some kind of tangible recognition to those who have helped our business to grow. So, this year, we have come up with a plan whereby we can offer a different kind of "bonus" to six of you who have brought in the most new business during the past 12 months.

We are opening up our vacation house in Sarasota, Florida, for 60 days, and are offering it to each of you for ten days. The dates will be drawn by lot. You can then exchange with any of the other recipients, if you like. You are also free to invite up to five others to share the time period with you, since the house accommodates six. Utilities and local phone calls are on the house. Equally important, the period will not be classified as vacation time, but will be over and beyond your regular vacation.

Enjoy!

Sincerely,

EMPLOYEE SUGGESTIONS

Responding positively to an employee suggestion is an easy writing assignment, and one that provides much personal satisfaction. But what do you do about rejecting such a suggestion and at the same time show your appreciation for the expression of interest? Two of the following four letters typify acceptance of ideas and two indicate how you can turn down ideas yet encourage the recipient.

Approving an Employee's Proposal

Dear Mrs. Woodwick:

It gives me great pleasure to report that we have considered and approved the innovative proposal you made to the production supervisor about a method of eliminating waste on the packing and crating line. Our accountant has determined that your method will save us more than $4,000 annually, and for that we are very grateful. More important, we are delighted to know that there are loyal employees like you who have the interests of their coworkers and the company in mind. You have contributed to our betterment, and we, in turn, would like to contribute to yours. You can expect a 10% increase in your paycheck, effective at the beginning of next month.

With appreciation,

Commendation for Suggestion

Dear Ms. Piner:

Thank you for filling out one of our suggestion slips and coming up with what we think is a fine idea. Those of us who plan the meals and the ordering procedures are always looking for ways to speed up the process without in any way reducing the service or the quality of the meals. So we think it would accomplish our objectives to follow your suggestion and have people on even-numbered floors arrive for the 12:00 lunch seating and those on the odd-numbered floors come to the 12:30 seating.

Got any more useful ideas?

Thanks,

Rejection of Suggestion—Management Rotation

Dear Monica:

We greatly appreciated your proposal to rotate office managers for one-week stints at each of the seven agencies in our Travel A Conference. As you so wisely pointed out, that would not only give them a chance to become better acquainted with all agents, but would stimulate the cross-fertilization of ideas and improve our overall effectiveness as a group.

I have discussed this idea with the board, and we regret that we have to say "no" to your suggestion. The problems lies not with your proposal, which everyone felt was innovative and positive, but with the covenants governing our professional licencing contract. I don't profess to have any legal skills, but the covenants apparently require that, though we can be affiliated as a group, we have to maintain each agency as an independent entity, the objective being to foster competition for the benefit of the traveling public. Rotating managers, even temporarily, would apparently conflict with the letter—if not the spirit—of the law.

But don't be discouraged. If you can come up with good ideas like this one, let's hear some others.

With our appreciation,

Rejection of Suggestion—Tax Return Assistance

Dear Terence:

Sure, we could assist employees of CB Forms, Inc., at any level and at any time in the preparation of their IRS and state income tax returns. Heaven knows, it is tough to keep up with the game these days—even for the pros—and our people do deserve some help. But I personally, as well as professionally, would be very nervous about what could be both an invasion of privacy and a conflict of interest. We are too much of a "family" concern where employees know each other personally and many spend their entire careers without ever moving to another company. It would be very difficult to guarantee that we could keep personal information confidential at all times. A safer way would be to pick up the tab for an outside CPA whom employees in need could visit in privacy.

Sincerely,

BENEFITS

Although routine, letters and memos informing employees of the benefits that come from working for your company are of great importance. Be matter-of-fact in describing benefits—never conciliating—and impart the news in a timely manner.

Announcing Supplemental Medical and Health Plans

Dear Tracy:

Effective January 1, we are offering our flight crews and ground personnel a new supplement to the standard medical and health policies already available. This is a long-range plan for health and hospital insurance called FuturePlus^{TM}, which does not increase the coverage, but accumulates credits. These credits can be used in two ways: (1) as dollar values toward group insurance if an employee leaves the airline two years or more after joining the program or (2) as credit toward coverage after retirement at the age of 60 or older.

We have just made arrangements with the underwriter of the policies to enlarge the program and extend it to any of our subsidiaries or suppliers who want to join. However, action must be taken within 30 days. Let me know if you're interested, and I'll send you the prospectus right away.

Sincerely,

Announcing Increased Vacation Time

Dear Claudia:

It is always a pleasure to dispense good news.

In this case, the tidings are that employees of the company with more than five years of service are being given increased vacation time, with pay. The amount depends upon the number of years of active service. In your case, our records show that you have worked for ComProgramming Ltd. for seven years and eight months. Therefore, based on a half day for each year of service, you are now eligible for an additional four days of vacation. This extra time is in no way affected by official holidays or time off for specific reasons, such as recuperation from an illness or family distress.

Enjoy, enjoy!

Cordially,

Offering Cholesterol and Blood-pressure Tests

TO: All Employees
FROM: Ruth Peters, RN, Nurse's Office
RE: Medical Tests

The company has arranged with a local medical clinic to provide free medical tests for employees from time to time. The first of these will be cholesterol and blood-pressure checks, to be given on May 4 and 5 between the hours of 9:00 A.M.

and 1:00 P.M. A shuttle bus will be available in the east parking lot on a first-come, first-served basis, leaving every hour on the hour and returning on the half-hour.

We urge you to take advantage of this complimentary health-protecting benefit, and on others we plan for the future.

Announcing Employee Assistance Program

Dear Stan:

Following through on our past discussions, I have been increasingly concerned about recent problems that have arisen as a result of drug abuse and drinking alcoholic beverages while on the job. You have done a commendable job with posters, newsletters, and orientation sessions. But there is little you can do to help those employees who are confirmed alcoholics or drug addicts. Our only realistic solution is to establish an EAP—Employee Assistance Program.

I am about to do just that and have already set the wheels in motion. As a first step, I am asking you and all the other company division and department managers to attend a meeting on Tuesday at 6:15 P.M. in the cafeteria to meet two professionals from Memorial Hospital who will explain how they will set up an EAP in our company. They will explain how other companies have succeeded and will answer all questions.

Sincerely,

Stock Options

TO: All Employees
FROM: The Treasurer
RE: Stock Options

Although information has been distributed from time to time in letters and reports to employees, this is a good opportunity to emphasize the value of the company program. Our over-the-counter stock has steadily been rising and was most recently mentioned in the monthly newsletter, *Your Investment.* Employees who participate are eligible to purchase shares through monthly payroll deductions of as much as 4% of their salaries. The company will match these deductions, up to 2% of the salary of participants.

For further information, see Ms. Snelling in the Treasurer's office to obtain a reprint of the newsletter item and a flyer on the company program.

Explaining Bonus Program

Dear Chandler:

You asked about the ground rules for our revised policy governing the issuance of company bonuses. Fundamentally, the program will pertain to all representatives who have been with the marketing group for one full year. The amounts will be determined by their length of service, as well as their sales record for the year. We have devised a chart, using the length of service, sales record, and other factors for calibration, so that it will be easy for anyone who qualifies for a bonus to determine the amount due at year's end.

These charts will be issued to all qualifiers within the next 30 days.

Sincerely,

Organizing a Car Pool

Dear Marianne:

The most disruptive factor in trying to maintain hospital shift schedules without absences and late arrivals seems to be the High Plains mass transportation system. Despite its relative newness and the politicians who have touted its efficiency, the network of bus and train services seem to be deteriorating, not improving (or even holding their own). Therefore, I have asked, and received permission from, the High Plains Hospital Board to investigate and report on the feasibility of a comprehensive car pool system, which could operate on a 24-hour timetable, not simply on a nine-to-five schedule. The purpose of this memo is to ask each of the 76 people to whom it is being sent is to ask the following questions:

1. Are you interested in car pooling?
2. If so, at what hours and days coming to work?
3. At what hours and days going home?
4. What is your home destination?
5. Are you interested in, and capable of, taking turns at driving?

If we have enough participants, the hospital will lease five or six eight-passenger vans on a trial basis. The model selected is comfortable, attractive looking, and easy to drive. The monthly cost per passenger would be moderate, probably less than individuals now pay for mass transportation or driving their own cars.

Please let me have your answers (and any comments) by Monday, the 30th, so we can determine how to proceed.

Thanks,

Explaining Advantages/Disadvantages of Early Retirement

Dear Curtis:

If I were in your shoes, with 25 years of service to the company behind me and a sizable chunk of profit-sharing investment on the books, I'd certainly give early retirement some positive thought. Yet, you have to consider two factors that I feel are critical. First, you are only two years away from regular retirement, which assures full benefits and no cutbacks or restrictions. Second, if you take early retirement now, you will be doing so at a time when the marine engine market is in a shambles, our stock is low, and we have not yet formalized the retiree medical and health plan, which will be approved in approximately 16 months from now. Your pension would be only 65% of the conventional retiree benefit. And, in the end, you would lose a substantial amount in order to gain two additional years of retirement freedom. But maybe it's worth it, what with all the hassles and stresses today.

With very best wishes,

Policies—Early Retirement

Dear Sidney:

Like the fictional mugwump who sits on the fence with his mug on one side and his "wump" on the other, we have no inflexible policy—pro or con—about early retirement. My personal outlook is that we hope our people find the environment pleasant enough and their jobs stimulating enough so they will continue at the firm until the traditional retirement age of 65. That viewpoint is flexible enough, however, to accept the fact that circumstances often color the retirement picture one way or another.

In your own case, you have to consider whether the drop in pension income is worth the increase in personal freedom to come and go as you desire. You should also ask yourself how well you would adapt to a life-style in which you have to set your own daily schedules and objectives. Even with no financial worries, many people find it difficult to know what to do with themselves, unless they have an avocation, active hobbies, a real love of sports, or a continuing desire to travel.

One alternative is to take a sabbatical and test that vast, unknown world of retirement. We are not at all averse to granting such leaves of absence to people who seriously want to test changes in life-style. You might want to consider this alternative, and I would be happy to discuss the idea with you at any time.

Cordially,

Announcing Seminar Program

TO: All Technical Field Specialists
FROM: Dan Morgan, Engineering
RE: Update Seminars

A series of ten 2-hour seminars has been programmed for the months of May and June, the objective being to provide information about latest technical developments in the energy field, particularly as they relate to utilities and customer services. These will be conducted entirely during regular work hours, so there will be no question of overtime or any rescheduling of normal on-the-job hours for those who want to participate. Four separate schedules have been set up to provide greater flexibility.

While the seminars are in no way compulsory, I heartily recommend them to employees who are engaged in technical work and are interested in upgrading their knowledge and skills. For further information, stop by the Training Program Office at any time.

Notice of Special Event—Company Picnic

TO: All Staff Members
FROM: B. J. Pierce
RE: 20th Anniversary Picnic

Since September 10 marks the 20th anniversary of the founding of Gaulden Brothers & Co., a special committee has been formed to propose and consider a number of commemorative plans for early fall. The first to be approved is the *Big-20 Picnic* which will be held on September 20 at Winnetonka, a summer camp on Mulberry Lake whose grounds and facilities have been leased by the company for the occasion.

You are invited, along with all members of your family, from 9.00 A.M., when swimming and boating contests will start, until 9:00 P.M., when the day will be concluded with a group songfest, following a cookout and awarding of prizes.

Keep your eye on this bulletin board space, which will be reserved for *Big-20* notices.

COMPANY POLICIES

Employee attitudes and behavior are based to a large extent on what they know about a company and its objectives. Therefore, it is important that you routinely keep them informed about company policies through letters, memos, and other media. Three factors are essential: first, provide the information as soon as a new policy goes into effect or an old policy is revised; second, make sure the policy is clear, but do not go into lengthy explanations about the reasoning behind it; and third, keep the door open for all who want more information or are not clear about how the policy specifically applies to them and their jobs.

Personal Telephone Calls

TO: Department Heads
FROM: The Business Manager
SUBJECT: Excessive Phone Calls

It came as something of a shock when we took an accounting to discover that our phone bill has climbed 75% over what it was at this time last year. I'd like to say it was because we enjoy a large increase in clients and accounts. But that aspect of the business has risen only 12%. Could it be the rise in the phone rates? I ask myself. But no, we have maintained a steady rate level because of our multiple-usage discounts. What then?

The fact of the matter is that many employees have gotten into the habit of making personal phone calls—even expensive, long-distance ones—from our office instead of their homes. Helps the household budget, you know.

How can we discourage, or limit, the practice? I plan to send a monthly printout of telephone charges to each of you. This will be a sampling of charges actually listed by Southern Bell on our corporate bill. Although no names will be printed alongside numbers called, I think a lot of people will get the idea, once they see how much money we spend.

If that doesn't work, we'll try another tack.

Employee Expense Accounts

TO: Members of the Purchasing Department
FROM: The Treasurer
RE: Expense Accounts

It is recognized that personnel assigned to the Purchasing Department must incur transportation costs while engaged in evaluating merchandise being considered for purchase for our three retail shops. In order to reduce the mounting costs of doing business, however, the company is establishing a new policy regarding expenses for meals, as follows:

1. No meals are to be listed on expense accounts when the total time out of the office is three hours or less.

2. Lunch may be considered an expense if the time requirement is more than three hours or if the purchaser is attending a trade exhibit requiring his or her presence between the hours of noon and 2:00 P.M.

3. Dinner will be approved as an expense item only if the time away from the office is more than seven hours, or if attendance is required during the evening.

Revisions in On-the-Job Safety Rules

TO: Annie Gruber, Personnel
FROM: Ralph Jenks, Research
SUBJECT: Fitness for Research Laboratory Assignments

Consider this memo an informal proposal that your department revise its list of qualifications for hiring new research personnel or transferring current employees to jobs in the new product labs. We have experienced a plethora of absences during the past year or so because of asthmatic attacks, skin diseases, and other disorders—to such an extent that we hired an outside medical consultant to review and evaluate our testing procedures. It was discovered that the patients were, for the most part, people with histories of asthma, allergies, or other physiological conditions adversely affected by unfamiliar chemical substances in the atmosphere. We suggest that you reject any candidates for lab work who fit this category.

On-the-Job Fund Raising

TO: Employees in the Hanford Office
FROM: Judy Lennon, Assistant Business Manager
SUBJECT: Contributions and Canvassing

We have many outstanding charitable institutions in Westlake, and it is heartening to know that so many of our own employees give their time and efforts so generously to causes that are worthy and in need of help, such as Community Care, the Scouts, and the Center for the Elderly. We all know, without a doubt, that financial aid is crucial to their effectiveness in serving the needy and, indirectly, the entire community, and that volunteers must work as fund raisers.

With these facts in mind, it is distressing for management to have to issue an edict that employees are hereby forbidden to canvass on company premises at any time. But the fact is that we are forbidden by the county supervisor of taxes to permit any kind of financial soliciting without first filing a nonprofit voucher for each and every institution involved and applying for a solicitation license for each volunteer participating. As can easily be imagined, such actions would tax our personnel and bookkeeping resources and would be almost impossible to police. Furthermore, the individuals involved, as well as our company, would be liable to fines and penalties for any violations confirmed by the tax supervisor's department.

Code of Ethics

TO: The Sales Staff
FROM: The Chairman of the Board
RE: Ethical Conduct

All of us who have a vested interest in selling our products and who regularly—or even occasionally—make contacts with prospective purchasers of uniforms, must be clearly familiar with, and uphold, the rules of ethical conduct. These include

- Offering our products only at published prices and discounts
- Avoiding any entertaining of people in purchasing capacities, for anything more than a light lunch
- Refraining from giving gifts of any kind to any customers, prospects, or their representatives
- Providing samples only as basically required for comparative testing or decision making.
- Using respectful and restrained language when discussing competitors

It goes without saying that we should not, under any circumstances, put any purchasing official in a position where he feels obligated to us and pressured into making decisions in our favor.

If there is any question at any time about ethical behavior, sales procedures, developing contacts, or conducting business, please call me at once.

Sincerely,

Use of Company Vehicle

TO: All Employees
FROM: Bert Odell
RE: Company Van

Since as far back as I can recall, I have been getting requests from employees and others who do business with our firm to borrow the company van for personal use, usually to assist in transporting bulky purchases or furniture.

Since this has also seemed like a reasonable request, in the past we have complied in some cases. At other times, however, job priorities have necessitated refusals, causing discontent and in at least two instances protests that we were "playing favorites."

After reviewing the pros and cons, I regret that we have to say "no" to any and all such requests for the van. My decision is based largely on the opinion of our casualty agent who informs me that multiple use of the vehicle in this manner might jeopardize our insurance in the event of an accident and would in any case increase the rate of our premium.

With your personal interests in mind, I have completed arrangements with XYZ Van Rental, Inc., to provide vans and pickups to our employees and friends at a 20% discount.

I hope that this meets with your favor and that you will understand our position.

With appreciation,

Statement of Equal Employment Opportunity Policies

Dear Mr. Legere:

In response to your inquiry about equal employment opportunities, here is the way we have phrased our policies and practices in a memorandum that we circulate to all our employees:

Our company subscribes fully to a policy of equal employment opportunity in which we judge individuals on the basis of performance without record to race, color, sex, faith, or ethnic background. We take this stand in the belief that it attracts productive employees and retains them long term. We believe furthermore that this kind of non discrimination should not only be our professional policy but should be practiced by all employees as well.

It is our fundamental objective to make certain that all employees have equal opportunities to progress within the company in accordance with their abilities. Our program thus focuses on continuing efforts to uphold employment practices that are fair and just for minorities, women, veterans, and the handicapped, among others. To that end, we appoint monitors to determine where flaws and weaknesses, if any, may be evident. This is not an invasive system that threatens personal privacy, but rather a positive overview of the human environment.

We also encourage employees to speak out if they sense any abuse of policy or if they have suggestions about ways in which the program can be improved. Thus far, we have been proud of our record and determined to keep it intact.

I hope this answers your inquiry in the manner you anticipated. However, if you have any further questions, please call me at the toll-free number on this letterhead.

Thank you for your interest.

Sincerely yours,

Voting Privileges

TO: All Employees
FROM: Your Management
RER: Voting Privileges

You are reminded that it is important for all citizens who are qualified to go to the polls and cast their votes for the persons and issues of their choices. If you are newcomers to our community, check to make sure that you, along with any other family members who are of age, are registered.

If you need help in determining your voting status or want to know where to go to vote, stop by the personnel office any time to get whatever you need. If you are not certain about candidates and issues, you can get reliable, objective information from the League of Women Voters. These printed LWV materials are also available at the personnel office.

Remember, each employee is permitted to take up to two hours on Election Day in order to vote. Voting schedules should be coordinated with your supervisor.

Getting Out the Voters

TO: All Employees
FROM: Cy Baldwin
SUBJECT: Voting

Next Tuesday is Election Day.
Do you know which candidates you want to vote for?
Are you familiar with the legislative issues being voted for?
Most important, are you properly registered?
It is vital that we all get out on Tuesday and exercise our rights as citizens. There are so many places in the world where the inhabitants can't do that. Or where their vote is meaningless. So don't throw your rights away.

Every employee has a minimum of three hours on Tuesday to go to the polls. More if you need to travel any distance, or take more time, to vote.

SAFETY AND SECURITY

A vital part of your management responsibility is (1) to establish procedures and regulations regarding safety and security and (2) to communicate that information to your employees as well as to outsiders who frequent your premises on business. Promptness of communication and clarity of presentation are the most important essentials. If necessary, letters and memos can often be supplemented by visual aids, such as maps, floor plans, or diagrams.

Preparing an Evacuation Plan—Flood

Dear Roger:

Because our Palmetto Dunes outlet is in a low-lying coastal area, subject to flooding in the event of offshore storms or torrential rains, we need to anticipate that we might have a dangerous situation at some future date. So I'd like you to confer with the Island Meteorological Service and draw up an evacuation plan for employees and customers alike in case of this eventuality.

The plan might well be in two parts: one as standard procedure for employees and the second to be designed as a poster for customers. We should then follow through with some on-site orientation drills, perhaps with an evacuation chart and advice for people caught in flooded areas anywhere in our vicinity.

With best regards,

Preparing an Evacuation Plan—Earthquake

Dear Jerry:

In case you missed the enclosed prediction about earthquakes, please note that our Redlands store is right smack on the fault mentioned by the geologist who is quoted. It really astonished me to learn that we can expect a major tremor at any time during the next three decades. I don't want to start a panic, but would you talk to Dr. Hedley, chairman of the geology department at Carlton State, and get whatever details you can. He knows us because we have contributed to the university's research endowment within the last two years and will surely be very cooperative.

Then start drawing up a realistic evacuation plan in two parts: one as standard procedure for employees and the second to be designed as a poster for customers. The clipping contains some graphic advice for people who might get caught in an earthquake, whether at work, at home, or on the road. That's a good place to start. I'd like to put this project on my agenda as soon as I return, as a top-priority item for discussion and implementation.

With best regards,

Announcing Emergency Evacuation Plan to Tenants

Dear Mr. Snyder:

Now that we have completed the planned office buildings in our executive park and leased most of them to firms like yours, we are making this important recommendation:

Please review all passageways, entrances, and exits carefully and prepare an evacuation plan in the event of fire, explosion, or natural calamity. A copy should be sent to us for consideration and for transmittal to the Fire and Police departments in our municipal zone. Once approved, the plan should be published and distributed to all your employees. If you need assistance in preparing the instructions or sketching a route map, we can provide everything you need.

Sincerely,

Notifying Employees of Potential Hazard

TO: All Employees
FROM: The Vice President, Production
RE: Existing Hazards Caused by Damaging Blaze

While most of us are relieved that the plant fire on Friday was brought under control quickly and with only a few minor injuries to firefighters and our own personnel, we must insist that you avoid the following areas until further notice:

1. The boiler room where the fire occurred and which is being intensely examined to determine the cause.
2. The floor above the boiler room, since there is evidence of structural weakness.
3. The parking lot at that end of the building, which has slick spots from an oil leak caused by the heat.

Only those few who are authorized to help with the investigation and repairs will be permitted in these areas.
By order of the Safety Committee,

Recommending First-Aid Program

Dear Norman:

Now that our company roster has grown to more than 100 people, I recommend strongly that we recruit employees, provide an orientation program, and launch a first-aid program. Just consider these examples of what first-aid orientation meant last year to another company about our size and just down the road from us in Commercial Park:

• Three laboratory technicians were spared critical burn defacement during a gas explosion because a fourth technician knew what emergency procedures to follow.

- A woman's finger was able to be saved after being severed because her assembly-line companion has been informed about emergency aid.
- Three people were saved from possibly choking to death by employees who had been made familiar with the Heimlich maneuver to dislodge food stuck in their throats.
- Four cases of heart attack were alleviated, possibly with the saving of lives.
- Four people were given first aid at car accident sites before the arrival of police or ambulance attendants.
- More than 100 cuts, bruises, and other minor injuries were successfully treated, in some cases preventing more serious aftermaths or side effects.

These are just some of the examples of what can be accomplished when employees are properly trained in first aid. I think we should follow suit.

With best regards,

After-Hours Security

Dear Mr. Schleman:

My position as chief security officer for Paragon Park, West, is sometimes like that of a tightrope walker who has to stay in the middle and not risk a fall to the right or left. Thus, we have established a policy for our patrol officers that they are to be courteous and congenial with employees at all levels and at all hours of the day or night, yet err on the side of being too tough if they spot any weakness in the security system or suspect any kind of suspicious action. That was apparently what happened when Officer Parkerson apprehended your van driver parked next to a pickup truck in a remote section of your parking lot at 8:45 Tuesday evening, long after your usual business hours.

As Parkerson reported the incident, he could not help but suspect that some kind of illegal transaction was taking place, possibly the receipt or transfer of stolen goods. The time, the location, and the seeming stealthiness all contributed to his evaluation of the activity. Therefore, his superior officer and I feel that he was perfectly right to demand that the two drivers accompany him to security headquarters. I am sorry that the incident cause any embarrassment to your employees, after learning the reasons for the truck operations. But I want you to understand that the action taken by our patrol officer was motivated by a clear-cut security policy and not any rash conclusions on his part.

Our aim is always to protect your company and the other organizations in the Park.

Sincerely,

CORPORATE ISSUES

Announcing Merger

Dear Harry:

By this time, you have probably heard numerous rumors to the effect that our firm is "going out of business" or "being sold." I'm sorry you had to get the news secondhand, but we have not been at liberty to make an official announcement until today. What is true is that we are merging and, as of January first, will become a wholly owned subsidiary of the Regal Stationery Company, headquartered in Cleveland.

Both the chairman and president of Regal have assured us that it is their intention to let us operate our subsidiary as an autonomous division and to retain all managers and other employees currently on our payroll.

Please inform all those who work with you that we will hold an orientation meeting next week at an hour and date to be announced. At that time you will learn more about Interstate and will understand why we are so wholeheartedly enthusiastic about the merger and what it means to your future.

Sincerely,

Encouraging Pride in the Company

Dear Associates:

If you'll go into the conference room and look out the window and across the baseball field you'll see a new flag pole in front of the high school. It was dedicated yesterday, along with a replacement for the tattered American flag that had long since seen its day, as a gift from our sales force for having exceeded the past year's quota by 28%.

We could have put the money we spent on behalf of the school into bonuses for all of you. Or an improved intercom system. Or embossed bags for the bowlers and gloves for the softball team. Or a bang-up company party at the King's Inn.

But the salespeople had a different idea. They foresaw something symbolic and meaningful. They wanted to extend their good fortune into the community.

So the school has a handsome new flagpole with an appropriate bronze plaque. And a weatherproofed Old Glory.

And we have something just as important, which we can see all year long in good weather and bad: An emblem that stands for Our Country, Our Young People, and the vitality of Free Enterprise.

Thanks to all of you,

ᚵINANCIAL CORRESPONDENCE

One of the mistakes many business and professional people make has to do with writing letters about financial matters. Such letters are too often classed as "routine" and are assigned to employees on the lower rungs. However, many of these letters can have substantial impact on your business and should be written with care. Some of these matters have been covered in Chapter 6, Collection, Credit, and Other Billing Problems. This chapter will focus on more general financial matters, such as correspondence with stockholders, evaluating the financial health of a business, applying for loans, price increases, monetary transactions, royalties, contracts, bad risks, franchise operations, accounting, joint ventures, and much more.

As the model letters in this chapter effectively demonstrate much of this correspondence can be positive and productive—not only achieving the immediate purpose but improving public relations, expanding sales potential, and opening doors to other areas of endeavor. That is not to imply that financial letters should be bogged down with irrelevant topics and asides. Rather, they can be counted on to perform these secondary, "between-the-lines" tasks when they

1. Are addressed to the proper person
2. Use correct titles and complete addresses
3. Use clear, direct language
4. Are assertive, yet with constraint
5. Establish a firm, assured tone
6. Provide precise, accurate data
7. Come to the point quickly

8. State unmistakably what action is desired

9. Are signed by a person with authority

If you have more than one financial subject to cover, consider the alternative of writing two or more letters instead of one. A letter that requests some form of financial aid and then adds a paragraph about an irrelevant business transaction is like painting a room half one color and half another. At best, it leads to confusion; at worst, it can negate the writer's real objective. No matter how well you know the person being addressed, quash the temptation to infuse a bit of friendly chatter—about golf, the change in the weather, or your forthcoming vacation trip.

HOW TO DO IT

1. Determine the primary objective of the letter.

2. Make a checklist of all points that have to be covered to achieve this objective.

3. Make certain all data and figures are correct—do not just assume that they are.

4. State the purpose clearly in a first draft.

5. If the subject has been discussed orally with the addressee, make sure you have not said one thing and are now presenting a different picture.

6. Create an attitude of cooperation or understanding.

7. State clearly what you expect from the recipient.

Financial letters are in a class by themselves in a number of ways. Unlike general letters you may write to customers, clients, sales personnel, the media, or government officials, they are likely to be addressed to people who have specific areas of operation and responsibility. Such recipients include, for example, loan officers in banks, certified public accountants, treasurers, controllers, contract negotiators, financial analysts, trust officers, and brokers. Your target is, in effect, much more narrow and precise. So your letter must take more careful aim, depending upon where you have set your sight. Frequently, financial letters reflect (or *should* reflect) an existing relationship of mutual respect and trust between the owner or manager of a small business and a nearby financial institution. Hence, when the subject of a letter is of considerable consequence to the business, it is all the more important that the signer of the letter be a person of substance and not a lesser employee.

If the very nature of a letter demands a wealth of detail, it is usually more effective to keep the letter itself as brief and simple as possible and put the details in an insert or attachment. This would be true, for example, in a request for a commercial loan or a complex business transaction in which many facts and figures have to be included. In certain instances, a *progression* of letters might be called for. For example, following topics were pinpointed in each letter of a series of five:

1. Announcement that the company is taking on a new line of products to market
2. Note with a release stating that the company has purchased an adjoining plot of land on which to build a small assembly plant
3. Annual statement showing a decisive rise in sales and profits
4. Request for information from a banker about commercial loans for expansion
5. Application for a commercial loan to build the assembly plant mentioned in letter 2

Progressive letters can be effective when a small business is unknown to an organization from which it hopes to obtain some form of financial assistance or with which it might hope to merge or affiliate. The first letter establishes the name and nature of the company. Intervening letters provide facts of a promotional, or image-building, nature. And the final letter makes a direct plea for assistance.

Financial letters are often the most demanding to write since their expectations are high. The model letters that follow will ease the burden.

BANKING

Letters to banks and other financial institutions are usually written in a strictly routine way, the subjects being conventional business matters. However, aggressive managers can often use this medium for putting in a little extra plug for the company or helping to cement relationships with key banking officials who might be helpful to the business in the future. You should never clutter up a financial letter with other, non relevant topics, but the addition of a mere line or so can sometimes accomplish this mission.

Applying for a Commercial Checking Account

Dear Ms. Greska:

After I spoke with you on the phone last week about a commercial checking account for our firm, you sent me several documents to fill out and sign. These have been completed and are returned herewith. We also enclose a copy of our Transfer of Business certificate, which authorizes the conveyance of our business from the State of North Dakota to Alabama. It is our understanding that the TB certificate makes it possible for us to transfer our credit rating from our former bank to yours at the same level.

The three officers of our firm have signed the signature cards you sent me, along with the Corporate Resolution. We also enclose a bank draft for $6,500 to open our new account and are looking forward to doing business with you.

Sincerely,

Stop Payment Order

TO: Checking Account Manager
FROM: Geneva Motors, Inc.
RE: Stop Payment Order

You are hereby authorized to stop payment on the following check when it is presented for payment:

Name of Payee: Solar Tire Company
Date of Check: April 2, 1992
Check Number: 2982

Charges for this action should be deducted from our commercial checking account, ' 345678.

Authorized by

Samuel S. Smith
Treasurer

Supplying Data for a Mortgage

Dear Mr. Bunker:

Thank you for your promptness in sending us the commercial real estate mortgage application for processing through your branch of the First United Bank. You were correct in your belief that we would like this to be secured by a first deed of trust on the property. To acquaint you further with our firm and holdings, I enclose a copy of our descriptive brochure, which contains profiles of the two owners.

Also enclosed is the loan application, completed and notarized, as requested. We are ready to conclude negotiations whenever the papers have been approved.

Sincerely,

Series of Letters Introducing a Business and Requesting a Loan

There are occasions when a request by a small company to obtain financial assistance from an institution will fail without a preliminary introduction and buildup to "soften" the lender and make the financial proposition seem more realistic and feasible. The following five letters illustrate an effective sequence. All are written by the owner of the company to the chief loan officer at the bank.

Letter 1

Dear Mr. Newsome:

Since we recently opened a commercial checking account in your bank, we would appreciate it if you would maintain an active file on our business for reference use in the future. As the enclosed leaflet informs you, we are wholesale marketers of hardware supplies. Among our customers are several retail stores in the community. Recently, we made a management decision to fabricate a new type of garden hose nozzle that is difficult to obtain from conventional sources, but that should be very popular in this area where so many people are active in gardening.

It is quite possible that this venture may open up new business opportunities in town. So, with your permission, I'll keep you apprised of further developments.

Sincerely

Enclosure

Letter 2

Dear Mr. Newsome:

Just a note to follow through on my first letter to you, describing our company and business plans for the near future. The enclosed release, just distributed to local business editors, was sent to inform them about a commercial development that could be of interest to the business and financial community. We have just purchased a three-acre plot of land next to our office and warehouse. This will be used for the construction of a small assembly plant to produce the new garden hose nozzles I mentioned to you earlier.

I'd appreciate your adding this to your files relating to our checking account.

Sincerely,

Enclosure

Letter 3

Dear Mr. Newsome:

Please add the enclosed annual statement to our company reference files. As you'll note, we are enjoying a 26% increase in sales over last year. Our biggest deficit was the cost of the property on which we intend to build our assembly plant. Even so, we are establishing a firm financial standing in the community.

Sincerely,

Enclosure

Letter 4

Dear Mr. Newsome:

At your convenience, would you please send me pertinent information and the necessary forms and data sheets for an application for a commercial loan. As I've mentioned in earlier correspondence, our company is growing steadily and expanding its product lines. As we evaluate the situation, the market has excellent potential, and we are ready to plan construction for our new hose nozzle assembly plant. Originally, we had intended to phase into this at a later date. But there has been so much interest among our customers that we would like to introduce this new line of products in time for the spring gardening season.

Sincerely,

Letter 5

Dear Mr. Newsome:

Thank you for supplying us with the necessary forms and instructions for applying for a commercial loan. We have completed these in full and have supplied an active list of business references, as you suggested. We have also included, for your information, the names of our outside attorney and our accountant.

We do hope the loan can be expedited as quickly as you anticipated, since we are all anxious to see construction get underway so we can make our plans for introducing the new products in the early spring.

Thank you for your interest and assistance.

Sincerely,

Enclosures

Applying for a Loan After Rejections from Other Lenders

Dear Ms. Tanager:

Birkwell Foods is a medium-sized retail shop specializing in health foods. We have been in the community for more than five years and have grown from a "Mom & Pop" operation to a much larger business employing seven clerks and a manager on a full-time basis. We intend to double our sales and our profits within the next ten months and during the same period move into larger quarters. To do so, however, we require additional funds and have determined that we need a business loan of $25,000, to be repaid on a monthly basis for a period of two years. This is a realistic investment, and we have floor plans, an artist's sketch, and marketing data to show how we propose to enlarge our physical capacity and our retail sales.

Now comes the hurdle. We have made loan applications to two of your competitors, First Parkway and Beaufort National, and have been turned down. Why? Because the mall where we are located has a dismal history of bankruptcies and failures. We know that and one of our objectives is to move to another mall where the consumer traffic flow is much greater and the lighting is designed to stimulate evening, as well as daytime, purchases.

We'd like a chance to get together with you, or whomever you designate, to present our case and to show you realistic evidence that the economic climate is extremely favorable for a business like ours. Our products—particularly our new lines of low-cholesterol foods—are at the forefront of a nutritional health trend that is more than a mere fad. And our plan to move to a select site, now available, is well timed.

May we set up an appointment to that effect?

Sincerely,

PS: Enclosed is a leaflet describing our specialities

Filing Additional Data for a Loan

Dear Ms. Trudeau:

As you requested, we are complementing the statistics we gave you with documentation concerning our potential as a new business. I enclose the following for informational purposes: A copy of the booklet describing our educational consulting service, a tear sheet from the *Gazette's* editorial section that mentions our new firm, and a report from the New Jersey Department of Education that contains three quotes from state educators about the qualifications of my partners and our professional expertize and experience.

These enclosures should provide all the additional data you need.

Sincerely,

Analysis of the Financial Health of an Industry

Dear Mr. Forsythe:

When you asked me for an evaluation of our industry, I interpret that to mean that you are primarily interested in the financial solidarity of firms located in the southern states in which your bank is a prominent lending institution. The Water Filtration Society of the Southeast, of which our firm is a member, has grown rapidly in membership during the past five years, has more than doubled its active programs and seminars, and has had to implement its headquarters staff by almost 50%.

That may seem like an evasive answer to your inquiry, but it is not. What our association's growth evidences is the fact that the need for purer, more potable water has escalated enormously, particularly in regions along the southern Atlantic and Gulf of Mexico where available water sources contain more undesirable elements and traces than might be found, say, in the Northeast or the Midwest. Consequently, many new water filtration firms have sprung into being, while existing ones like ours have grown steadily, sometimes dramatically.

Of course, we both know full well that growth of this kind does not always go hand in hand with economic stability. In fact, sometimes the reverse is true, and we see many cases of rapid growth in an industry accompanied by economic confusion, overdevelopment, and a proliferation of inexperienced people eager to join the gold rush. Happily, this has not occurred in our industry and I can say quite honestly that, were I an officer at a bank, I would tend to encourage applications for loans or credit from firms in the south engaged in water filtration, purification, and related operations.

Very truly yours,

Analysis of Financial Health of a Business Firm

Dear Mrs. Petrie:

Your letter to Alvin Keffler, our business manager, has been turned over to me to reply. Regarding the request for a loan made by Allied Dyes, Inc., you indicated to Mr. Keffler that you would have to turn down the application unless he could provide statistics and forecasts showing a favorable uptrend in the printing processes which have called for the major delivery of our products in the past.

What you really need, however, is documentation that we are at the forefront of a completely new trend that will bring about a substantial demand for our dyes. And I am the one best qualified here to assure you that such is the case. For the past four years, my research department has pioneered in the perfection of metallic "sensing" dyes, which are revolutionary and will create an enormous demand. We hold five patents on what we call "guidance" pigments. The potential applications are limitless. Commercially, they can be used to paint aircraft which can then be located much more clearly by radar, as well as by short-range instruments that will prevent midair collisions.

Militarily, they can be applied to missiles to assist in tracking and guiding them. And they can make a truly great impact in NASA's programs, again as an economical and reliable method of tracking hardware in outer space.

I have asked the editor of *Dye and Pigment Digest* to send you three copies of the January issue for you and your loan committee to review. It contains an article on this new breakthrough in our business and mentions Allied in a highly favorable light. This prognosis, rather than the forecast and figures you requested, should give you a very positive feeling about Allied's future development and growth.

Sincerely,

SOLICITING INVESTMENT

Letters that solicit financial investments in a small business should not be confused with those that solicit funds for charitable purposes. When properly written, the former leave readers with the impression that they are recipients, not donors, and that their investment of time, money, and sometimes talent will pay off handsomely. Letters in this category must clearly avoid the implication that the suggested financing or professional involvement is for the purpose of resuscitating an ailing business. Start on a high note and end on an up beat.

Financial Partnership

Dear Mr. Simpson:

As a patient of ours for the past six years, you are familiar with our services and the degree of experience we bring to our joint practice here. We have steadily enlarged our list of regular patients and now feel that we must ease the work load by employing two more technicians. We also have plans for upgrading the quality of service by replacing about half of our technical equipment with new models and types. Such a move obviously calls for expenditures and financing. My two partners and I have discussed the feasibility of paying out of pocket. However, since we all have growing families, we do not think this is realistic at this time.

It occurred to me that one solution would be to attract an outside investor who is not a dentist. Our accountant feels that such an investment could be quite beneficial, based on the current and past performance of the clinic and the anticipated growth. Knowing from our past conversations that you had previously invested in medical and health institutions, I thought it worth tossing the idea in your direction to see how the idea strikes you. As for the amount, we are thinking in terms of $50–75,000. Our accountant, who also works for a Wall Street firm, has worked up some figures to show the financial potential and tabulate the risks. I'd be happy to show this to you, should you be interested in pursuing the proposal.

Sincerely,

New Venture

Dear Gracia:

When we left New York City to move permanently to what we knew as one of the loveliest towns in the Carolinas, we entered a new world so compatible and so naturally endowed that we did not hesitate a moment to leave behind some vital amenities we had come to think of as important to the quality of life as we knew it. These included concerts, the theater, music, great works of art, and other cultural marvels.

Now it is quite possible that we can enjoy the best of both worlds, glorifying this setting of beauty and healthful relaxation with a Cultural Center of our own, which would bring to our doorstep many of those same refinements we thought we had been forced to sacrifice when we moved. This letter is a first step toward that goal—a goal we think is realistic, attainable, and affordable. Within a week, you will receive an artist's rendering of the Cultural Center we are founding as an active commercial venture, along with information about its location, size, capacity, and the kinds of performing arts programs and exhibits that would be scheduled regularly.

Since we cannot launch this venture at the start without advance subscriptions, we are approaching people like you who would be likely "angels," much the same as theatrical production companies do when bringing a new play to Broadway. Along with my three partners in the enterprise, I extend our fond hope that you will join us.

Sincerely,

Proposing a Joint Venture

Dear Henri:

Since we were once business associates and always worked well together on projects—the more challenging, the better—I have a proposal to make. It would utilize the experience and capabilities of both of our companies to our mutual advantage and would result in a product that would be badly needed and highly marketable. What I have in mind is a miniature cassette unit that will translate words and phrases instantly from one language to another. It would be useful for tourists who may have taken a stab at familiarizing themselves with a foreign language, but suddenly find themselves tongue-tied when they get into a tricky situation and cannot remember what little they learned. And it would be indispensable for business executives dealing with foreigners, at home or abroad.

We have experimented with a mockup model, but really need input from someone who is (1) an expert programer and (2) a skilled linguist. Since you fill the bill perfectly in both departments, it seems natural for me to propose a joint venture of this kind.

Let's put our heads together and see what we can come up with. Nothing ventured, nothing gained. Or, as our machine might say in Latin, *ad astra per aspera*—"to the stars despite the difficulties."

With kindest regards,

Suggesting a New Business Opportunity

The author's research has tuned up the names of wealthy retirees who have in the past invested in new business ventures. Here is his initial proposal for collaboration.

Dear Mr. Smathers:

By way of introduction, I am an electronics engineer whose career has spanned three decades of research work with blue-chip companies, during which time I perfected high-tech instruments and devices that have had widespread applications. I also hold more than two dozen patents in my own name, seven of which relate to a new type of sensor that could revolutionize residential fire and security alarm systems.

So convinced am I of the accuracy, dependability, and longevity of these sensors and the marketability of products using them that I have resigned from my last company, General Electronics, to launch my own business. This letter is, quite honestly, a proposal that we consider a collaborative venture in which financial responsibilities would be in your hands and technological quality in mine.

I am not so naive as to expect even your initial consideration without a thorough examination of a detailed proposal on my part and a presentation of the facts. If you feel that this venture might be of interest, I would like to make an appointment to demonstrate my invention, document my qualifications, and present a professional business proposal, which includes data about design and production, distribution, sales and marketing, prospective customers, advertising, and other factors upon which to base questions, discuss alternatives, and reach decisions.

For initial reference, feel free to contact Frederick Bellew, president of Pineland Trust, who has known me for more than 15 years.

Sincerely,

Declining Interest in a Business Opportunity

Dear Brock:

It was a surprise to get your letter, along with the suggestion that my brother and I join you and your associates in forming a new consulting group. Your presentations and charts were impressive, and it is easy to see that the service you propose has enormous potential for future success in the Upper Valley marketing region.

Our bullish impression of your proposition makes it all the more difficult for us to have to reject your offer. As you are probably not aware, my brother is taking early retirement because of his chronic asthma attacks and is moving to the Southwest. Since I have promised to accompany him for the next few months at least and perhaps help establish a small retail business, that eliminates me from any and all other enterprises for some time to come, whether as an active participant or a behind-the-scenes investor.

Thanks so much for thinking of us. Needless to say, we'll look forward to hearing that your new venture is flying high in no time at all.

Sincerely,

PROVIDING INFORMATION TO
STOCKHOLDERS AND INVESTORS

Enclosing Annual Report

Dear Stockholder:

It is with great pleasure that I send you a copy of the Annual Report at this time. Your company has prospered as a result of its steadily increased investment in state-of-the-art technology. And you will note how favorably this is reflected in the year-end figures for 1991 when compared with those of a year earlier. It is our intention to continue our planned program of scientific research and development throughout the 1990s so that your company will remain at the forefront of its field.

Sincerely,

Environmental Policy

Dear Mr. Laffont:

Your concerns about the company's ecological policies were well taken and, in fact, reflect a great deal of the thought that has been given to energy and the environment in our board and committee meetings. Our environmental initiatives have received very favorable comment in the press. I refer most particularly to our formation of citizen advisory panels and the decision to ship our liquid petroleum products only in the new types of vessels that are doubled hulled and invulnerable to any serious degree of spillage, even when grounded or involved in a collision.

The greatest challenge our company faces today is one of credibility in the eyes and minds of a public that questions the sincerity of the environmental commitment of the energy industry, based on past performance. Nevertheless, we take the stand that this lack of credibility and confidence should not make us shrink from confronting controversial issues and taking a stand that is beneficial to our stockholders, to the public, and to the economy. We feel strongly that an open, honest, and communicative approach will, in the long run, strengthen our financial base, as well as serve our expressed goals.

I thank you personally for your expression of concern and assure you that our minds are always open to ways in which we can improve our operations and, thus, the quality of life in every field with which we are concerned.

Sincerely,

Citing a Favorable Quarter Despite Industry Trend

Dear Shareholder:

Getting a letter from me at this time of the year, instead of at the end of the quarter may give you a start and a sudden suspicion that all is not well with your investment in Starwater Savings & Loan. But I assure you that quite the opposite is true. We have had a good quarter thus far, and our record in comparison with that of a year ago is heartening. We see no reason why this favorable trend will not continue.

Why am I writing? Simply to report that all is well at Starwater despite the accounts you have been reading lately in the papers about failures in small S&L businesses across the nation. We have not included any figures with this letter. However, if you want an updating of the last quarterly report, just send us a note. Or, better yet, call the toll-free number on this letterhead.

With excellent prospects for the year.

Sincerely,

Denying Unfavorable Publicity

Dear Investor:

You are among the many who have seen fit to risk some of your money in our small company, with the idea that the investment would be a good one in the long run. And, indeed, it has been during our eight years in business.

Recently, however, we have been the target for rumors and allegations of the kind leveled at the oil industry and firms like ours whose business involves the transportation of petroleum fluids by barges, pipelines, and vehicles. The editorial about oil pollution in the August issue of *Our Land*, which hit the stands this morning, is a striking example.

At this moment, I can only say that the article is very misleading, inaccurate, and laced with serious factual errors. Within the next 24 hours, our director of research will rush to you a detailed "Fact vs. Fiction" report to prove how misinformed the writer was in his evaluation of events and how unprofessional the editors were in publishing a totally biased and fabricated account. What we want to get across immediately, and most forcefully, is that we hope you will continue to have faith in our industry and respect for our company. We assure you that our business will continue to be sound and will grow steadily as it has been doing because we are dedicated to the preservation of the environment and opposed to all actions that might threaten it. We only ask that you reserve judgment until you have the facts in hand.

Very truly yours,

INSURANCE

Letters on the subject of insurance often involve two objectives that are diametrically opposed: the first is to obtain data and/or recommendations; the second, to avoid opening up the door to a flood of correspondence from the recipient of your letter or other insurance agents who might then place you on their mailing lists. Do not let this state of affairs deter you from seeking guidance when you need it for your business operations. Rather, seek help from an agent you already know or one who has been recommended as a reliable source—and who is not too pushy.

Surveying Insurance Benefits

Dear Mr. Demorra:

As part-time counsel for a new construction company being formed as a Chapter S corporation, I have been asked to assemble documents and data relating to various phases of business with which the firm will be involved. One area in which information is desired relates to insurance, including liability, vehicles, medical and health, fire, and theft. Please send me appropriate literature, fact sheets, and premium rates for corporate policies of these types.

At this time, we are discouraging solicitations from agencies until my client has had an opportunity to study the printed information we are assembling.

Sincerely,

Requesting Insurance Information for Company Personnel

Dear Don:

You have been very helpful in establishing and monitoring the group insurance policies we offer to our permanent employees. Several of them have been asking us about individual policies at group rates, which you had promised to offer, once our program had been in effect for a full year. That date is approaching, and we would like to pursue the matter. The most common questions that arise about individual policies are these:

- Would the policy eventually have a cash value?
- Could policies later be used for loans? If so, for what percentage of the face amount and at what interest rate?
- What happens to the status of the policy and the group rate if I elect to leave the company?
- Are any retirement benefits built in?

I'd like to schedule an informal session here so that you could answer such questions face to face.

Sincerely,

Requesting Rate Information—Company Vehicles

Dear Mr. Rawson:

Your name was suggested to me by one of your automobile policyholders in our sales department, and I would appreciate any information and suggestions you might have. We feel that new, increased rates being put into effect by our present agency are out of line, and I would like to compare them with yours. We have six Dodge Caravans, 1990 and 1991, two Jeep Cherokee wagons, 1989, and one Chevrolet Astro cargo van, 1991; our coverage is $250,000 per person and $500,000 per accident for bodily injury, underinsurance, and uninsurance; and the policies have comprehensive and collision coverage, with $250 deductible.

What other data do you need to give us some bottom-line figures?

Sincerely,

Loss Claim

Dear Webster:

In response to your instructions on the phone yesterday afternoon, I herewith submit this letter to initiate a claim under the terms of our $200 deductible Loss and Disappearance insurance policy.

On August 15, we received a shipment of 800 chrome-plated bathroom fixtures, packed in eight large wooden boxes, 100 to the box. These were counted, recorded, and stored in Warehouse "B," to be delivered to one of our customers on or about October 10. A number of other shipments were stored in the same warehouse area at one time or another during this interim period, some of which are still there and others which were removed for shipment.

On October 8, when I instructed my assistant to move the bathroom fixtures to the loading platform for delivery to our customer two days later, he reported that there were only seven boxes, containing a total of 700 products instead of the expected 800. We have taken all possible steps to locate the missing box, including searches throughout all our warehouse areas and communication with every customer to whom we made shipments during this period. This is obviously a "disappearance" that cannot be accounted for and which we feel comes under the terms of our insurance policy.

The value of the missing container and contents is $3,457.89, as clearly specified in the original bill of lading.

We would appreciate your further instructions and a copy of any form that must be completed by us to process this claim.

Sincerely,

Property Damage Claim

Dear Mrs. Bailes:

Regarding your letter to my heavy equipment manager, I am answering it on his behalf in order that we can coordinate whatever action needs to be taken in the claim that has been filed against my firm, Tompkins Land Management, Inc.

Until we have investigated the incident further and talked with the operators of the two bulldozers involved, we cannot release any specific details to you. If the two machines were, mistakenly, over the property line and if indeed they did shatter water conduits and cause extensive flooding, I am certain that our policies will cover such damage. In the meantime, I have placed the matter in the hands of our own agent, Tom Kilington, and have asked him to contact you as soon as he has investigated the facts at this end.

Sincerely,

Placing Independent Agent on Probation

Dear Mr. Parseny:

We have been dealing with you as an independent agent in as professional and impartial a manner as we know how. It is not our desire to try to impose deadlines on agents with whom we coordinate our business, but your case is, unhappily, an exception. At a meeting of the partners this morning, it was unanimously decided that we would give you ten days—or until November 29—to honor your commitment. If you have not by then fulfilled the contract you signed with us, we shall then be forced to take legal action.

Your successive promises have become less and less plausible. We suggest that you apply your time and energy to getting the job done instead of devising empty excuses.

Very truly yours,

OTHER FINANCIAL CORRESPONDENCE

The following models cover a range of typical letters relating to monetary matters common to small businesses. Not Note that each one has the following characteristics:

- Focus on a single basic subject
- Clarification of the matter at hand
- Request for response or action

Transmittal Letter with Sales Contract—Requesting Deposit

Dear Mr. Pollard:

Jake Medding, our sales manager, asked me to send you the enclosed contract for your order and at the same time to clarify our production policy. Because most of our orders—as is true with yours—cannot be filled from stock but must be tailored to individual specifications, we require a 30% deposit in advance. We must also ask you to review the enclosed specification sheet very carefully to make certain that the dimensions, weights, and materials are correct. If you can sign and return the contract and the specifications, along with your check, by February 20, we can guarantee delivery on or before March 5. We also guarantee, of course, that the finished products will meet the exact specifications you have approved.

We look forward to serving you.

Sincerely,

Confirming Financial Terms

Dear Mr. Makeridge:

This letter will confirm our joint agreement and understanding that you will purchase 1,850 16-foot polyester lateen sails at a unit cost of $89, to be paid for within ten days following delivery by us and acceptance by you. For our part, we guarantee that these will be color-fast and will have no more than 5% stretchability, wet or dry, and that we will deliver the entire lot to you on or before May 15, 1990.

If there is any question about these specifications, please contact me at once, since we intend to start production within the next two weeks.

Sincerely,

Confirming a Lease-Back Agreement

Dear Dr. Scudder:

This letter follows through on our discussion during the meeting in your office on June 5. It further confirms our agreement that our firm will purchase the building now used for your office and clinic and lease these premises back to you at the rate of $860 per month for the period from July 1, 1992 through June 30, 1993. We agree, too, that you will then have the option of a lease-back agreement for the next five years at rate increases of no more than five percent (5%) per annum.

As has been specified in the Agreement, during the period of your occupancy, whether for one year or longer, you accept full responsibility for

1. Maintaining the premises in the condition they were in at the time the Agreement went into force.

2. Restoring any portions of the building that might be altered by you for your medical functions.

3. Using the premises as the primary party, with no subleases unless specifically authorized by our firm.

These and other specifications are spelled out in the Agreement, four copies of which are enclosed. Please sign and return three to me and keep the fourth for your own files. At that time, you should also enclose your initial lease-back payment of $860, which will cover your first month of occupancy under the new terms.

We appreciate your cooperation and look forward to a pleasant business relationship.

Very truly yours,

Requesting Job Order Based on Commercial Letter of Credit

Dear Mr. Payton:

The First Commercial Bank has informed us that it is processing a Letter of Credit in the amount of $18,000 to be used by our company for the renovations and extension of space in the south wing of our office. Therefore, we request that you make out a job order and begin the work according to the plans we drew up with you last month.

It is important that we have the space available for use within the next 30 days. So if there is any reason for delay, we must know what to expect as soon as possible.

Sincerely,

Requesting Reimbursement for Faulty Materials

Dear Mr. Partenot:

Three months ago, we received a shipment of lock-and-key assemblies for attaching to our line of Feath-R-Weight™ air-travel hanging bags. We assembled and delivered to our retail customers some 780 of these bags before it was discovered that the lock mechanisms were defective and would jam after being used only two or three times. We recalled all the bags that could be located—about half the lot—and reimbursed the purchasers. Your sales representative, in turn, provided us with replacement lock-and-key assemblies, assured us that he would continue to do so for future returns, and paid us for our expenses in collecting the defective merchandise and replacing it.

As it turns out, however, this reimbursement is just a drop in the bucket compared with the loss in profits that has resulted from the problem. Our accounting department has very carefully evaluated this total loss, using comparative figures to show what our sales *would have been* for this period versus what they actually have been in the end. I feel strongly that, since your company was at fault to begin with, you should share at least 50% of this loss with us. I am willing to rule out losses from merchandise that will still be returned by customers in the coming months, but I see no reason why our company should bear this full load.

Sincerely,

Declining Money-Losing Community Project

Dear Dr. Barthwaite:

I regret to have to inform you that we cannot accept the School Board's proposal that we undertake the decorating and restoration of the junior high auditorium at a fee that is almost 10% lower than what we originally quoted you. We fully understand the Board's frustrations in trying to obtain a larger grant from the state, and our heart is really in the idea of providing badly needed space for developing cultural programs. Yet we see no way we could cut corners and reduce our quote. If you'll recall, when we evaluated the time and work and materials required, we did so with our assertion that there would be no padding and our costs would be pared to the bone. That has been the case. While we would be honored to participate, we have no fat to trim from our quotation.

If a reduction of 10% would put the project in the ball park, we suggest that the

Board consider one or two alternatives: (1) eliminate the music practice room in back or (2) seek voluntary contributions from parents and friends to make up the difference. If either course of action is feasible, we'd be happy to evaluate the project again.

Sincerely yours,

Providing Inventory of Equipment and Furnishings

Dear Mr. Rogler:

Enclosed for your records is an inventory of the press equipment and photocopying machines that were included in the sale of our business to you and your two partners. As you will note, the list also covers the expendable paper, inks, and chemical supplies for use with the equipment.

The valuations, item by item, were supplied by Heller & Heller, an independent accounting firm, which has signed and certified the document and, for tax purposes, attests to the total valuation of $8,990.00

Sincerely,

Enclosure

Reply to Financial Questions from the Press

Dear Mr. Bartell:

Although our phone discussion about our firm, Preferred Business Associates Ltd., covered most of the bases, you will be interested in knowing the central theme of our mission. PBA was established a year ago to work with a variety of clients (mainly small businesses) who need a sounding board regarding their competitive positions in their communities. To that end, we make extensive studies of our clients' operations and then report back to them on such matters as

- Solvency and monetary substantiality
- Credit rating
- Record of fair pricing
- Financial dealings with customers
- Quality of products and/or services
- Avoidance of price fixing

While our firm cannot guarantee any individual client's financial responsibilities, services, or products, we do rate them according to strict, scientific evaluations. Thus, clients can point to us as *objective* analysts of their businesses whenever they need references that have been made in good faith.

I trust that this will provide all the information you need for your editorial.

Sincerely,

Price Increase

Dear Mr. Logan:

When you send out your announcement about our company's financial status at year's end, please make note of one change that will affect our profitability for the coming quarter. There will be a 12% increase in the per foot cost of all plastic piping that we are currently fabricating and molding in our shop at the junction of River Drive and Broad Creek road. However, we are also increasing our discount from 10% to 15% for our regular customers, those purchasing in excess of 2,000 feet of piping per year.

The jump in prices reflects increases demanded by the raw materials producers from which we obtain our own supplies. However, it is our conviction that the better discount, combined with the upswing in building starts, will improve our profit picture during the next 12 months.

Sincerely

To Attorney—Inquiry About Deductible Donations

Dear Mr. Karp:

I am writing to obtain an objective opinion about the validity of certain business deductions we would like to claim. For your purposes, "We" is Books for Business, Inc., an editorial packaging service I founded ten years ago that works largely with book publishers on trade books and with corporate clients on major writings, such as company histories and annual reports. Over the years, we have established a policy of year-end giving, whereby we allocate three percent (3%) of our firm's profits to what we feel is an appropriate cause. We ask editors we have worked with to propose the names of elderly writers who, because of illness or hard times, can no longer earn money in their chosen profession and are now indigent. We then select two, one man and one woman, to whom we make a small grant, usually less than $500.

In the past, we have never deducted this expenditure from our tax return. However, since we intend to increase the allocation and since we anticipate substantial profits this year and next, we want to consider this step. Were we to do so, what would be the best way to allocate funds so they achieved the same purpose but might be donated in a manner that would be acceptable to the IRS?

Sincerely,

Providing Confidential Data to Accountant

Dear Todd:

Enclosed are the data I have accumulated, sorted out, and compiled for our supplemental professional tax return. You will note that the folder marked "Securities" contains (necessarily) some investment information that is marked "Confidential." I ask that you honor this confidentiality in the strictest sense of the word since the data reveal, in effect, what could be considered inside information. I could be held criminally liable should these facts and figures be used to anyone's personal advantage.

Although it is probable that the data are now too outdated for any such exploitation, extreme care is required in their handling and presentation.

Sincerely,

Financial Report

Dear Manda:

You have so much on your hands these days that I hate to ask you to go back to your files again for further material for our company presentation. However, we need copies of the third and fourth quarter financial reports to complete our concluding proposal. We do not need originals—photocopies would do just fine.

Thanks again for your help.

With best regards,

*L*EGAL CORRESPONDENCE

Of all the types of letters there are relating to small business management and operations, those that smack of *legal* subjects are the ones that owners and managers tend to shy away from. When questioned about this distaste for correspondence relating to laws, regulations, injunctions, and other matters of jurisprudence, people who run small businesses often excuse themselves on the basis of being unfamiliar with "legalese." Hence, they tend to delegate the writing of all letters dealing with legal subjects to outside law firms or individual attorneys. As a result, they not only rack up unnecessary bills, but they sometimes lose excellent opportunities to establish worthwhile communication with individuals and groups who could be beneficial in one way or another to their organizations.

Certain categories of documents obviously have to be researched, conceived, and prepared by practicing attorneys or at least by qualified paralegals who work for them. It would be foolish for a layperson to draw up a business contract involving thousands of dollars and risk later monetary loss or lawsuit because of nonprofessional errors and omissions. It would be equally risky to put certain types of commitments in writing without knowing the legal consequences of a failure to live up to specified terms. But such documents generally represent only a small proportion of the common correspondence of a small business, and are easy for an experienced business person to identify.

QUESTIONS TO ASK YOURSELF ABOUT WHERE TO DRAW THE LINE

1. Does the letter involve the commitment of a large sum of money?

2. Is the author, or an associate, going to be committed to an undesirable responsibility or contribution of time?

3. Are laws or regulations being cited that require professional knowledge and understanding?

4. Is the recipient an attorney, judge, or otherwise professionally associated with the law?

5. Is the letter making or responding to a serious complaint that could lead to legal action?

6. Would the signature or letterhead of a practicing attorney carry more weight than that of a nonprofessional?

In most legal matters, *patience* is a valuable asset. Don't plunge into communications that might generate controversy without weighing the possible consequences. If you have ever been unfortunate enough to be the plaintiff or defendant in a lawsuit, you are probably painfully aware of the time that drags on and on from one step in the proceedings to another. The same is true in lesser legal maneuvers at all levels. "Don't invite trouble," advises one corporate counsel with wide experience. "Often, a seemingly touchy condition will deflate itself if you don't keep puffing it up."

HOW TO DO IT

1. Determine carefully what your objective is in writing the letter.

2. Select your addressee carefully if you have a choice of writing to more than one person.

3. Outline the points that must be covered specifically.

4. Concentrate on one subject and cover related topics sparingly.

5. Avoid emotional or aggressive language and tone.

6. Present a spirit of cooperation for mutual benefit.

7. Invite a verbal discussion, face to face or over the phone, if that seems like a realistic and beneficial alternative to further correspondence.

As in the case of all letters, you must leave the recipient with your impression of what action should follow. If you cannot state this clearly, it might be more sensible to scrap the idea of writing this letter. Perhaps it would be more productive to (1) use the telephone and explore actions that might be taken or functions that might be considered, (2) schedule a meeting of the key individuals concerned, or (3) have an intermediary follow through on your behalf.

The model letters selected for this chapter are typical of those whose topics and situations are commonplace in the world of small business. They are not all necessarily "legal" in the technical sense of the word. But they cover subject areas that elate to laws, regulations, and the like. Here you will find letters that can readily, and without jeopardy, be authored by laypersons on such subjects as trade agreements, contracts, equal employment opportunities, mergers, charges of negligence, conflicts of interest, environmental rules and violations, discrimination, liabilities, settling claims out of court, joint ventures, filing legal documents, and requesting relief from jury duty.

Some letters with legal implications will also be found in the chapters on financial matters, sales, collections, and dealing with government regulations.

TRANSMITTAL LETTERS

When legal documents are sent to various addressees they should be accompanied by a brief letter of transmittal, carbons, or photocopies of which can then be sent for the record to all parties concerned. These should be sent by certified mail in most cases, so they can be traced in the event of loss, or by express mail or a private courier, such as Federal Express, if time is of the essence. The following are models of typical cover letters.

Incorporation and Tax Documents

Dear Mr. Hannamon:

Enclosed, via certified mail, are the documents you requested regarding our firm's incorporation three years ago and the tax relief statements and approvals granted by the county. As you will note, we were granted these benefits on the basis of the fact that we employ only the elderly or the disadvantaged and thus qualify for tax relief. If you will phone me when you have finished reviewing them, I'll arrange to have them picked up by hand.

Sincerely,

Testimony

TO: Hawley & Hawley, Attorneys
FROM: Abbey & Company
RE: Testimony

Enclosed, as you require, is the testimony of our personnel manager regarding the charge of discrimination brought against us by your client. This has been duly signed and notarized.

Real Estate Transaction

Dear Ms. Hickman:

Under separate cover, via Federal Express, we have sent to you all the documents we had on hand relating to the transfer of our Bond Street property to your Houston affiliate. There are 8 papers in all, as well as 12 items of related legal correspondence. After you have had a chance to compare them with your files, please return them by certified mail or other assured carrier.

Sincerely,

cc: Bobson and Hall
Mr. Anson Garner

Legal Action

Dear Judge Dorfmann:

Following through on my phone conversation with your court clerk, I enclose herewith the papers relating to the fraud committed by the salesperson we recently fired. It is my understanding that these photocopies will suffice for your records. Should you require the originals, however, we will send them by certified mail, or however you may specify.

Sincerely,

cc: Arlen, Arlen, and Baker, Attorneys

Contracts

Dear Tom:

I understand from Joe Smalley that you need copies of all our legal contracts for the past year in order to review our tax records before filing a return. Since all these accumulated documents—mostly originals—weigh about 6 pounds, we have sent them to you by way of United Parcel Service (UPS). We are told they will reach you within a week.

Sincerely,

cc: Joe Smalley

Drivers' Licenses

TO: Chief Clerk, Municipal Traffic Court
FROM: Star Trucking Company
RE: Parking Tickets

Enclosed are the drivers' licenses and related papers of the two truck drivers from our firm whom you have placed on probation. These are being sent by certified mail to prevent loss. After the 30-day probation period is over, please let me know and we will have the drivers in question pick them up personally at your office.

cc: Messrs. Warner and Childs

Miscellaneous Legal Documents

Dear Messrs. Powell and Peete:

As you requested, I am herewith transferring the following *original* documents from our files to yours, since they deal with legal matters and are more appropriate in a law office than a car-rental agency:

- Property lease
- Insurance papers covering negligence
- Contracts with automotive suppliers
- Letter of Agreement with Standard Gasoline

We have kept photocopies on file here.

Sincerely,

Inventory

Dear Mr. Roddey:

This will complement the recent contract we signed, making it possible for my firm to assume the office space you have vacated for a period of two years.

As you requested, I enclose a complete inventory of the furniture and furnishings we are taking over, along with the space. This inventory represents our inspection of all the items in question and describes the condition in which we found them. If any such description is at variance with your own listings or understandings, please let me know so that we can resolve the differences prior to the February 1 start of the sublease.

Sincerely,

AGREEMENTS AND CONTRACTS

The average owners of small businesses are qualified to prepare and expedite most agreements and contracts without having to hire a lawyer. The degree to which these are valid and binding depends to a great extent on the simplicity or complexity of the arrangements covered. In between the two extremes is the contract which you write yourself but then give to an attorney for review. The first model that follows falls into this category. Basically, it covers the essentials. However, a discerning lawyer might find certain loopholes that would be detrimental to the writer—such as an unexpected occurrence that could negate part of the payment specified.

The final example, Assigning Power of Attorney, is adequate for the situation and circumstances that are described in the letter. However, it would be wise to place this document in the hands of an attorney should any of the following be true:

- Much larger sums of money are involved.
- More people are possible participants.
- The business owner has a chronic health condition that could cause death or leave him or her physically or mentally incapacitated

Letter of Agreement

Dear Mr. Holenbrook:

This will serve as a *Letter of Agreement* between the undersigned and Mallon Plate & Glass regarding the planning, preparation, and shooting of photographs for the company's Annual Report. It is agreed herewith that we, Anne Landon, Ltd., will assume the following responsibilities:

1. To confer with all department heads, technicians, and others designated by you to determine which glass-making operations and technology should be visualized.

2. To outline all the subject areas that seem appropriate, following this research, and present a written proposal to you that describes the theme, viewpoints, and visual treatment.

3. To schedule the individual photographic shootings for the convenience of the departments in question, to cause the least amount of disruption of normal job functions.

4. To obtain legal releases from all personnel identifiable in these photographs.

5. To provide complete data for each photographic subject for the use of copywriters preparing the text for the Annual Report.

6. To process and supply all photographs—no fewer than 200 in all—for review and selection by the Public Relations Department of Mallon.

7. To complete the above on or before February 2, 1991, in accordance with the production plans discussed earlier by Mallon and Anne Landon, Ltd.

8. To submit an assignment sheet and expense report that includes costs related specifically to the research, planning, and completion of photographs, as specified.

It is further agreed herein that Mallon Plate & Glass will have the following responsibilities and commitments:

1. To provide the necessary background information about the firm and its operations for the edification of the photographers assigned.

2. To approve and schedule interviews with department heads and others for the photographer(s) assigned.

3. To assume full responsibility for safety procedures on the job, supply photographers with instructions and any safety equipment needed during filming operations on company premises.

4. To reimburse all photographers approved for the assignment at the rate of $350 per diem, the accumulated sums to be paid to Anne Landon, Ltd., at the conclusion of the job.

5. To pay all expenses incurred, and satisfactorily substantiated by the photography crew while on location.

It is mutually agreed and understood that, should the project be terminated for any valid reason by either party before completion, compensation will be prorated according to the proportion of the assignment completed.

Signed and acknowledged this date: _____

_____   _____
For Mallon Plate & Glass   For Anne Landon, Ltd.

Acknowledging Contract and Commitments

Dear Travis:

This will acknowledge the receipt of your contract and order for 7,800 rolls of our Mastercraft *Z-35A* Panoramic Film. As specified, the film will be moistureproofed and will have a heat tolerance of no less than 165°F. We expect to have no problem meeting your January 20 deadline and, in fact, should have the complete order in your hands by the 15th.

Just a note about the *Z-35A* formulation. Perhaps you noticed in the November issue of *Photo Marketing* that our manufacturing affiliate, Pro-Lab Films, received an accolade from the American Press Association. The citation referred to *Z-35A* as "fireproof" when ten rolls survived a fire during a plane crash and was later used for filming, with no loss of clarity. So don't worry about its heat tolerance!

With best wishes,

Acknowledging Verbal Agreement

Dear Mr. Molson:

This will confirm our telephone conversation of last Tuesday, in which you requested that Alder & Alder assign an attorney proficient in environmental law and maritime codes to negotiate your contract with the Coastal Commission. It is our understanding that the contract will be drawn up solely for the design, construction, and installation of tide retainers along the South Narrows Inlet. As you explained, it is vital for your firm and the government supervisors to be in perfect agreement on all specifications and materials from the outset, to avoid the kinds of problems that in the past have plagued contractors in coastal areas that are environmentally fragile and sensitive to man-made incursions.

Our candidate for this assignment is Arthur Albritton, an attorney who has been with our firm for 12 years, has always specialized in environmental law, and has never negotiated an offshore or onshore contract that had to be revised after the initial planning stage was underway.

I have taken the liberty of asking Arthur to send you his professional resume, to assure you that his qualifications are without question. At the same time, he will provide a checklist of the ten most sensitive strictures and conditions that must be resolved in order to prepare a foolproof contract that will stand up in court and against the most aggressive conservationists, should any part of the project come under public scrutiny.

Thank you for selecting Alder & Alder for this noteworthy and much-needed project. You have my personal pledge that you and your associates will be pleased with the results.

Sincerely,

Requesting Termination of Agreement to Reflect Change in Situation

Dear Mr. Delahanty:

As you know from your records, our two firms have done business for a number of years under the terms of a loose written agreement, signed at the time of origin by our legal counsel and by the former owner of your fleet. Since this document is no longer binding, we feel that this is a proper time for us to conclude the agreement and go our separate ways. We have been planning to purchase several vans of our own, of a type that would be specially air-conditioned, moisture proofed, and cushioned to prevent damage to the art that we transport and store. I'm sure you can appreciate the fact that, with the skyrocketing cost of works of art and authentic antiques, conventional vans and trucks just are not designed or equipped to minimize damage and wear and tear. This letter will serve, therefore, as our legal termination of the agreement.

Sincerely yours,

Terminating Contract for Cause

Dear Wilson:

Physical pain can be alleviated by a strong drug.

Emotional pain can be destroyed by suicide.

Psychological pain can be smothered by a blackout.

But the pain of being sold down the river by a longtime friend is something that can never be erased. Especially if it has now been emblazoned in print for all the world to see and the victim put to mockery.

When you sold me the rights to Dr. Schweiker's brilliant book on Spacemarks of Science, I immediately labeled it top priority and predicted it would be acclaimed as a breakthrough in scientific publishing. The book's publication and our support of it through extensive advertising and promotion were fully justified by the reception it had in all quarters.

Then came the pain, like that of a dull knife that has been plunged into the breast and twisted so that no organ of the body has been left untouched. I learned just this morning that—in total violation of our contract—you had sold the serial rights for the book to a British publisher. You did not even have the decency to tell me to my face what you were doing, or intended to do.

This act is so clearly a violation of our contract that I am terminating all the agreements contained in its 26 clauses. I have ordered that all copies of the book be impounded in our warehouse, that bookstores return shipments not yet opened, and that plans for a second printing be scrapped. If you try to sue me to reverse these decisions, you do so at great personal risk. I have asked our general counsel to review the contract with meticulous care, and she has just reported that your violation is specific, premeditated, and without the slightest iota of justification.

The book will be forgotten long, long before the pain will ever subside.

Sincerely,

Explaining Contract Terms

Dear Harlow:

It seems unbelievable that, after all these years, you have never done business with Festival Music, Ltd. But there always has to be a first time. To answer your question about royalties for writers of music and lyrics, our contracts are drawn up quite differently from those of other music publishers. In specifying author's rights, we generally offer a much higher royalty than the conventional publisher. Why? Because we leave it up to the authors and/or their agents to undertake the initial stages of production. Since we do not have to maintain a production studio on our premises, this preliminary step cuts our overhead immensely and thus makes it possible to increase the royalty scale. Expressed from another viewpoint, our policy puts a greater demand on authors and agents at the start, asking them to get the ball rolling. But then they share greater profits when everything is in motion.

Sincerely,

Avoiding Liability—Contract Terms

Dear Annette Jarrett:

Welcome to better health and fitness! We hope that you will be fully satisfied with everything the Club has to offer and that it will provide many rewarding hours of enjoyment and accomplishment.

In welcoming new members, I always make it a point to ask that they reread our contract carefully and be sure they fully understand the various clauses in it. *We* have certain responsibilities. *You* have certain responsibilities. And *we both* share certain other responsibilities. One liability we cannot undertake regards each member's physical condition. Only you and your doctor can determine how much exercise is healthy for you and how far you can push yourself safely. So please review the very first clause in the membership contract and make sure you can comply. That way, we'll all breathe more easily and have more fun.

With every good wish,

To Supplier—Potential Breach of Contract

Dear Mr. Bryden:

It came as a shock to be told by your Madison production manager that you are not going to ship me the 38 ribbed steel "I" beams specified in our contract for delivery no later than August 28. He did not respond in what I felt was a responsible manner when I informed him quite forcefully that this was a breach of contract. As you well know, we rely on that shipment to meet our deadline with AT&T, for which we also have a contract with very specific commitments. I can sympathize with the fact that you had a three-week strike on your hands two months ago. But your Madison office assured me that it would not affect our order.

I urge you to take whatever action is necessary to meet our deadline. It may be costly to get into overtime and other costs. But we take the stand that if we have to face a loss because of our construction delay, we will expect like compensation from you, even if we have to sue for breach of contract in order to collect. Meeting the terms of our order would be much simpler, and less costly, for all concerned.

Sincerely,

Requesting Reconsideration of Denial of Lease

Dear Mrs. Theraux:

Last month when we applied for a lease in one of your West Park office buildings, we were flatly turned down. It was acknowledged that our financial report was accurate and fully acceptable, that our management has a reputation for honesty, and that our hiring policies are fully in accord with EEOC and state regulations. The fly in the ointment was the fact that we are in the business of designing and manufacturing signs and are not strictly engaged in the kind of "office" operations for which West Park was developed and constructed.

This response is sheer nonsense. While our headquarters office would indeed contain drafting and layout rooms where our clients could visualize the designs and units we recommend for their use, we would not be a "manufacturing plant" in any sense. A visitor to the area, for example, would see nothing to suggest that we were any different from the other lease holders in the building. The amount of traffic to and from our offices would in no way resemble that of "a department store," as one of your clerks commented. In fact, there would probably be a lot less traffic than there is at the insurance agencies now ensconsed in Building C or the accounting firm located in Building F.

I sincerely hope that, with these facts in mind, you will overrule the hasty and ill-advised rejection of our request for a five-year lease at West Park.

Very truly yours,

Assigning Power of Attorney

POWER OF ATTORNEY

I, Arlen Turner, the sole owner and manager of Turner Home Designs (THD), expect to leave the country on business abroad and will be unavailable to transact any architectural matters during a period of approximately six weeks from this date. With this in mind, I transfer power of attorney to my brother, Samuel A. Turner, during this interim. He is hereby assigned the following powers in my name:

1. To negotiate and sign contracts regarding several architectural proposals that have been drawn up by me

2. To write checks on the THD account at Centennial National Bank to pay bills that become due during my absence

3. To endorse and deposit checks payable to the firm

4. To take any other reasonable action that might be required to protect my professional interests

Copies of this Power of Attorney are herewith provided to my bank, agent, clients, suppliers, and other organizations that might be concerned in one or more of these matters, and they are requested to honor its contents and intent. All such actions taken by my brother, as attorney thus empowered, shall, in the event of my death or disability, be binding upon me and my heirs, legatees, and legal counsels.

The following is a specimen of the signature of my empowered attorney, Samuel A. Turner:_____ .

In witness whereof, I have signed this Power of Attorney this _____day of _____, 19____.

Arlen Turner

I, Notary Public in the county of _____and the state of _____, hereby certify that Arlen Turner, known to me as the person who signed the foregoing instrument, personally appeared before me this day and acknowledged that he signed the instrument as a free and voluntary act, for the purposes set forth therein.

Given under my hand and seal this_____ day of _____, 19 ____.

_____
Notary Public

LEGAL ACTIONS

When you anticipate the necessity for some kind of legal action, consider a carefully worded letter as a first step before you call in a lawyer. You may achieve the desired results and save yourself substantial legal fees. If not, the most you have wasted is postage, paper, and a little of your time. The first two model letters are pertinent examples of this approach.

Threatening Lawsuit—Uncooperative Neighbor

Dear Mr. Paradoo:

When we opened our restaurant here two years ago, it was with the understanding that your firm was going to clean up your lumberyard and get rid of the piles of scrap wood and metal littering the area that adjoins our property. When it was obvious that no such cleanup was about to take place, we made the not unreasonable request that you erect a high, attractive fence that would totally shield this junkyard from view, both from our restaurant building and from the street front approaching our door. You seem totally indifferent to our pleas. It is not our intention to become entangled in a lawsuit. But we have no other recourse. If your junkyard is not entirely cleaned up or the fence erected within 30 days from this date, we will take the matter to court. We intend not simply to sue for the cleanup or the fence, but to place our case in the hands of the zoning board and request that your license to do business be rescinded. Be assured that our attorney has researched the matter very carefully and is fully convinced that such action could be expected.

Yours truly,

Response to Threat of Legal Action

Dear Mrs. Brownstone:

The manager of our Eaglebrook store phoned me to say that you have threatened legal action unless we replace the television set you purchased last year. If you will read your warranty, you will note that it is good for only six months, whereas you have had the set for almost ten months. The time frame on the warranties of the products we sell are set by the manufacturer and not by us. We wish they were longer, but there is not much we can do about that.

Please remember that we repaired and adjusted your set at no cost to you four months ago when it was brought to the Eaglebrook store. At that time, it was still under the manufacturer's warranty. We are sorry that you are displeased with us, but believe me we do everything we possibly can to provide fine products and reliable service.

Sincerely,

Accident on Premises—Letter to Victim's Family

Dear Ms. Franck:

It was a pleasure to see your mother again, as one of our former employees, and I was happy to talk to her about her pension and the reinvestment program for retirees. But I was distressed to hear the next day that she had been slightly injured upon leaving the office when the elevator stopped abruptly and she fell to the floor. The operations of the building, including the elevators, are in the hands of Five Star Properties, Inc., from whom we lease our offices. Since this firm is responsible for maintenance and safety on the premises, I immediately called the building manager to report the incident. And I have asked my assistant, Jim Anglade, to look into the matter and determine what form of compensation would be available to pay for any medical or other costs incurred as a result of the injury.

Please pass along my sympathies to your mother and assure her that we are ready to assist in any way we can.

Cordially,

SOLICITING LEGAL ADVICE

How do you obtain reliable counsel without paying any initial fees? There are numerous resources available to the managers of small businesses, several of which are explored in the model letters that follow.

Out-of-Court Settlement

Dear Dennis:

No lawsuit has been initiated. No legal action has been taken. But I feel it in my bones that our firm, Hegler and Holden, is about to be taken to court. Before anything happens, I'd like to take the bull by the horns and propose an out-of-court settlement to the "injured party."

Fundamentally, what happened was this. One of my young engineers inspected a residence for a retired couple who were considering its purchase and wanted to make sure everything was in applie-pie order. That's the nature of our business, and we are quite good at investigating the nooks and crannies and detecting potential trouble spots. In this case, my engineer gave the place a clean bill of health. But he goofed badly in one respect: he failed to detect the deterioration that had taken place inside the attic air handler of the heat pump/air-conditioning system. Result: Four months after purchasing the house, my retired clients had to plunk down $4,400 to replace the equipment in full. After they registered a protest, I visited the premises myself and made the kind of inspection that should have been done in the first place. I came up with some lame excuses ("these things can't be anticipated", "There's a chance an electrical surge or lightning damaged the works," etc.). But I knew that we were remiss.

By way of compensation, I intend to write a letter to my clients and, though disclaiming negligence, offer to reimburse them for half of the cost.

Do you feel that this will suffice? Or is there a danger that my offer in itself will be an admission of guilt and lead to legal action?

With best regards,

Company Substance Abuse Programs

Dear Judge Poberton:

Your name was suggested to me by the Municipal Bar Association as one who could advise me in my position here as chairman of the company substance abuse committee. I understand from the MBA that you had at one time specialized in legal matters relating to crimes committed by people under the influence of alcohol or other drugs. As medical director of the company and an internist by profession, I am experienced in dealing with the problems of employees who are drug users or alcoholics. We have a recovery program that we feel is effective and are constantly improving our procedures to increase the record of successful recoveries.

We have not been so successful in another facet of the program, however. And we need to find an accomplished attorney who can act as a consultant when the substance abuse problems of employees lead to legal difficulties as well. In that department, we are admittedly novices who are ill-equipped to assist employees in trouble. For example, we have two men in our program who been convicted of driving while intoxicated and whose jobs are threatened if they do not fulfill certain requirements. We need an expert to counsel them on their rights and restrictions. Others have been threatened with lawsuits because of actions taken while "under the influence."

I would appreciate any recommendations you might have.

Sincerely,

Charges of Age Discrimination

Dear Counselor Clarke:

Our firm is located in Mountain Valley, which, as you know, is a community heavily populated by people who are over the age of 60. Because of the rise in the cost of living, many seniors who otherwise might be in retirement are going back to work. Others seek part-time employment to keep themselves solvent. As a result, we have found that the number of older job applicants coming to our personnel office has more than doubled in the past three years. This results in what has become a problem: We have to keep turning down many older people. Age is not the reason, but rather the fact that these applicants simply do not have the right qualifications.

We have been threatened with legal action by several rejected applicants. To make matters worse, a recent column in the *Courier* published excerpts from the Age

Discrimination in Employment Act and implied that a number of local firms, including ours, were guilty of age discrimination. We have reviewed the wording of this act carefully and are convinced that we are legally, as well as morally, in full compliance with the law. Yet I am still uneasy that we might become the target of lawsuits or other legal action by older job seekers who are rejected. Would you be available to assist us, perhaps on a per diem basis, and counsel us about the steps we should take to avoid such disputes, as well as adverse publicity?

Very truly yours,

Joint Venture

Dear Secretary Whiting:

To introduce myself, I am the founder and publisher of a firm engaged in the research, design, printing, and mailing of professional journals that are produced on contract with private companies, associations, and other organizations whose business depends heavily upon marketing. Because our long-range objective is to expand our format in some instances into hardcover and paperback books, we are about to propose a joint venture with an established book publisher in the state. In so doing, however, we will be stepping into sensitive areas whereby we will be using editorial formats for material that is substantially advertising in concept and purpose. If we do not employ considerable tact and objectivity, this combination of strange bedfellows could expose us to claims of conflict of interest or perhaps mislabeling.

To prevent such occurrences, we intend to establish rigorous policies and codes for our editorial staffs, as well as our salespersons, to follow. We would appreciate it, therefore, if you could send us copies of your fact sheets covering pertinent, related subjects. I have seen state-produced reports, for example, on such topics as "misrep-resentation," "fact versus fiction," "advertorials," "the invalidity of surveys," and the misuse of quotes. We would also appreciate copies of forms needed by two firms intending to merge legally or undertake a joint venture.

Sincerely,

Company Logo and Imprint

Dear Nell:

You have seen Sanford Security vehicles around town for more than ten years and are familiar with the "SS" imprint and the uniformed cartoon owl we have used as the logo in our advertising and mailings. But now we want to make it all official, largely because we expect our business to double within the next two years, but also because a couple of other security systems have used birds as emblems, in one case we feel to infringe on ours and ride on our coattails.

To do this, I understand we need to file a written application for any symbols and lettering we intend to use, along with exact replicas of the art. I'd appreciate it if you could send me whatever information the Chamber has on file about such matters. Also, am I correct in thinking that we have to submit these for publication in the *Official Gazette* that covers such matters?

With best regards,

Labor Regulations

Dear Judge Parsons:

Since our firm is located in a commercial area which has had problems with drinking water because of recent contamination of the local source of supply, we have been forced to use bottled water for our employees. When we listed this cost in our state tax return, it was rejected as not being deductible. The state auditor referred to our use of bottled water as an "optional" choice.

We feel that we can reverse this decision in our favor. But what we need is a copy of a regulation or ruling that employers must supply all personnel with fresh, potable drinking water and avoid any source that is tainted or questionable. Can you provide us with such a ruling? If not, what can we do to convince the state auditor that we have no choice in this matter?

Sincerely,

Paralegal Services

Dear Mr. Roraback:

Three years ago, a group of business managers and I formed the Cold Harbor Commercial Association whose purpose is to acquire better information about policies and procedures that we should know about in our own small businesses. We have long been in need of legal assistance when drawing up work-related documents or seeking sources of data. Quite frankly, we have never had enough money in our CHCA budget to afford anything more than do-it-yourself efforts or the occasional hiring of a lawyer in time of crisis.

One of our members suggested that we hire a paralegal part time for this kind of assignment. As I understand it, a paralegal could not replace an attorney, but could be counted on to undertake legal research, make contacts with various government offices, and prepare certain kinds of documents and forms. We would appreciate it if you could send us whatever literature you might have on hand describing the qualifications of a paralegal. We'd also be interested in knowing where to turn to locate a likely candidate for the job.

Sincerely,

Company Liabilities

Dear Judge Cook:

You may recall that we met at the Bar Association last October at your anniversary party, at which time you mentioned that you were going to devote yourself to part-time volunteer work in the village in several fields of public service of interest to you.

I don't know whether this fits your category of either "voluntary" or "public service," but we are anxious to obtain some advice that would be helpful to our neighborhood. As you know, in our commercial area where Rogers Street and Warehouse Road intersect, there is a grassy park that was once one of our equipment storage sites and which we donated to the community as a Little League ball park.

Recently, the township sent us a notice that the park has been considered a "liability" because no individual, group, or organization bears direct responsibility in the event that someone were injured on the property. But there is considerable confusion about what jurisdiction the township has over this park or our administration of the property. We would welcome your opinion about (1) such jurisdiction and (2) what steps we should be taking to avoid what could be costly liabilities in the event young ball players were hurt while engaged in their sport.

Respectfully,

GOVERNMENT AGENCIES

When writing to government agencies, the most common mistake made by the letter writer is not in the writing but in the selection of the addressee. This causes many of the complaints you hear about the frustrations of dealing with the government and the lack of appropriate response. Before even touching pen to paper, do your homework and make certain you are addressing the right person (or title) in the proper government office.

To Environmental Commission—in Response to Charge of Pollution Violations

Dear Dr. Kagelman:

The MEC has charged Container Renewal, Inc., with a serious violation, namely, polluting the waters of the Derby River with toxic chemical wastes. Quite frankly, your inspector assumed a good many "facts" that were not true and gave every evidence that he had not done his homework before making the rounds. For one thing, he alleged that "at least five drums" of ammoniated chemicals had trickled into the Derby River from our container cleaning workshop. The fact is that the only facility we have anywhere near the Derby is our marketing office. The workshop he referred to is more than 20 miles from the river, on a plateau totally devoid of streams of any kind. He charged further that we were using an illegal substance, chlorine dioxide, as a cleaning agent. The fact is we don't use CD at all because it is absolutely useless in the kinds of container renewal we are contracted to do.

In light of the above, may I suggest that you (1) assign your inspector to functions he is more qualified to perform and (2) you drop the allegations against our company.

Sincerely,

To Town Sanitation Review Board—Denial of Illegal Procedures

Dear Cedric:

This letter is written on behalf of KleenKare, the trash removal service that has a contract with our firm to help us keep our area environmentally free of pollutants. I have before me a copy of the minutes from last week's meeting of the town sanitation review board and would like to take issue with several misstatements in the report before anyone in the Council reaches the conclusion that some form of punitive or corrective action should be taken. I have listed below the inaccurate assertions from the minutes, followed by the facts as they stand:

Minutes: KleenKare uses soluble chemicals to break up solids and make sludge removal easier. *Fact*: The firm uses no chemicals of any kind in the removal process.

Minutes: KleenKare operates tank trucks that were originally designed for transporting gasoline and are not suitable for heavier fluids. *Fact*: The trucks were designed by the manufacturer, Mack, specifically for sludge removal.

Minutes: The supervisors of the trash removal operations are not properly versed in environmental matters. *Fact*: All personnel, including the drivers, have attended authorized training seminars and are certified by state inspectors for this field of work.

If there is any doubt on the part of the Town Council or members of the sanitation review board that the company is fully qualified to continue its operations, please let me know at once so I can respond to any questions they still might have.

Sincerely,

Requesting Waiver of Jury Duty

Dear Counselor Kerryman:

This is to request that you waive the requirement for jury duty for a period of six months for one of my associates, Michael Burkehead. His jury duty and consequent absence at this time would place an inequitable burden on our firm, which was formed only five months ago to assist in the improvement of county drinking water systems, an action that has long been overdue. Dr. Burkehead is in charge of our water research program, the demands of which have kept him occupied for an average of almost 50 hours a week. We anticipate that this initial effort will diminish by the end of six months, at which time he would be happy to serve on any jury called.

Sincerely,

COMPANY POLICIES

Among the most sensitive issues relating to company policies and functions is the matter of sexual harassment, the topic of four of the following letters.

Crime Prevention

Dear George and Travis:

As longtime partners in the firm, all three of us have been increasingly dismayed at the inroads of crime in our commercial neighborhood and its direct effect on such matters as losses through theft, threats to our employees, the cost of alarm and security systems, and consequent increases in annual insurance premiums. I propose that, in addition to running the business, we consider ourselves a tripartite crime prevention committee to counter these drains on our profits. While we cannot take legal steps, per se, we can take positive action by orienting all personnel so that they take steps like these:

1. Report the presence of suspicious persons on our premises.

2. Double-check inventories regularly to spot any illegal depletion of equipment and supplies.

3. Make sure doors and windows are properly locked after hours.

4. Have emergency police and security phone numbers handy for instant use when necessary.

Any suggestions you have would be welcome.

Cordially,

To Employees—Filing of Legal Documents

TO: File Clerks
FROM: The Business Manager
RE: Filing of Legal Documents

All legal documents that are signed originals or which for any reason may be considered one-of-a-kind, should be filed in the fireproof library vault, rather than in the general files or on the shelves. This vault, as we all know, is kept open only when in active use by an authorized employee when in the same room and must be closed and locked at other times. Recent examples of the documents in this category are

- The corporate property lease
- The Letter of Agreement with the design contractor
- Certificate of authorization from the State Manufacturing Safety Commission
- Power of Attorney affidavits

If you know of any papers that should be in the vault and are not, please consult with me about them.

Sexual Harassment—Nonbusiness Hours

Dear Ms. Renner:

Because of the legal, moral, and occupational problems that can arise from sexual harassment—or charges thereof—our firm is instituting the following policy:

When the press of business requires members of your secretarial pool to report for work before the normal business hours or to remain after closing time, you are to institute a "buddy" system. There will thus be at least two secretaries within comfortable sight or voice distance from each other in any particular location of our building during these times.

Sincerely,

cc: Personnel Office

Sexual Harassment—Information Meeting

TO: All Office Personnel
FROM: The Management
RE: Sexual Harassment

You are requested to attend a meeting of about one hour's duration on Friday morning at 10:00 in the company cafeteria. At that time, a representative from our attorney's firm will discuss sexual harassment—what it constitutes legally and ethically. You are not only free to ask any questions you have on this controversial subject, but are encouraged to do so.

Your management wants to make certain that every individual in our company, regardless of sex, age, or position, is fully aware of this legal and moral issue and that the chances of anyone being in jeopardy from harassment will be all but nonexistent.

Sexual Harassment—Legal Interpretations

Dear Mrs. Rohrback:

As the paralegal assigned to our company by your law firm, you could be of considerable help to us in a subject area that seems to be generating more and more attention in the press: *sexual harassment*. It would be helpful to us if you could make a copy of an appropriate legal paper describing the actions and attitudes that are relevant, which we could post on our employee bulletin boards. If the language involves too much "legalese," perhaps you could paraphrase the stipulations and terms and type a description that would be clear to laypersons.

You might also include your name, address, and telephone number, should anyone want to contact you with questions or even discuss an alleged violation.

Sexual Harassment—Making Complaints

TO: All Employees
FROM: The Management
RE: Sexual Harassment

By now, thanks to the press and recent cases that have been discussed in newspapers and magazines and over the air, all of us are aware of the widespread existence of sexual harassment. If any individual feels that he or she has been subjected to such harassment—or any other kind—a complaint should be made to our outside attorney, Ms. Powers, by phone or mail, at the address below. *All such contacts will be held in strict confidence.*

CORPORATE MATTERS

Recommending Change in Corporate Status

Dear Don, Jake, and Thelma:

Because we are in the communications business and often shepherding into print a great many statements that can be considered provocative, if not controversial, we are sitting ducks in a manner of speaking. I refer to the fact that we can be sued in certain instances if what we print is damaging to any individual or organization. Sure, we check out our facts with great care, and we require editorial researchers and the writers we hire to document their quotes, reports, and data in a precise, reliable manner. But if something backfires, the buck doesn't stop until it reaches our desks. Then—boom!

What I am leading up to is that I propose that we get together and change our partnership into a *corporation*. That would protect us, as individuals, from having our private lives shattered should we be gunned down by the legal sharpshooters.

I can already hear the objections. Sure, we formed a partnership to begin with because it is simpler in structure than a corporation, is more informal, and could be formed without a lawyer and a lot of legal red tape. And we all liked the idea that each partner could work on a parallel basis and make decisions as an individual, without being stifled by the whole, enveloping infrastructure.

Maybe I'm getting timid in my advancing years, but I just don't like the idea that life could become a nightmare for each of us if we stick our necks out too far without any protection.

With best regards,

Transferring "S" Corporation from One State to Another

Dear Sir:

We are a small business in Kansas City, officially registered as a chapter "S" corporation under the laws of Kansas. Now we are about to relocate, and though the move is only a distance of one mile, we will come under the laws of your state, Missouri, rather than Kansas.

As I understand it, this kind of transfer is not difficult or complicated, but one that can be transacted by supplying copies of our present charter and supporting papers to you, completing a form, and paying a fee. Is this true, or do you advise our turning the matter over to an attorney in the State of Missouri?

To acquaint you in more detail with our business, I enclose a copy of a descriptive leaflet we send to prospective customers, as well as suppliers.

Sincerely,

Enclosure

To Stockholder—Response to Inquiry About Company Stock and Issue

Dear Mrs. Drury:

Thank you for your thoughtful inquiry about the proxy letter for Amalgamated Metals. You can rest assured that your comments about the stock issue have been noted and will be reviewed by our management, as well as the AM board. In our analysis of new issues, we make every effort to present the information as objectively as possible. We examine the total assets, liabilities, portfolio, objectives, history, stability, and other factors that determine the value of an issue. Our responsibility is to reports that are as accurate as possible and to avoid any semblance of recommending or discouraging purchases. We always welcome and encourage letters like yours because it is vital to know about the opinions of stockholders. So we appreciate your comments and thank you for writing.

Sincerely,

$\mathcal{G}$OVERNMENT

Frustration is the prevailing sentiment in many cases for people who, for business or professional reasons, have to communicate with government administrators and bureaus. In the first place, it usually requires a major effort just deciding which individual should be addressed. And it is difficult, if not impossible, to try to match a title with a personality and determine how that recipient might react.

There is an old saying in Washington that, if you want to accomplish anything in the government, you have to "speak governmentese." The situation is not quite that bad. However, it is always helpful and beneficial to think of the governmental recipients of letters as people whose situations and objectives may be quite different from those of customers, clients, and professionals to whom most business letters are addressed.

The model letters in this chapter will help you evaluate government agencies at all levels and develop the right approach, one that will stimulate a *useful* reply. The letters have been especially designed to include the kinds of words, phrases, and approaches that will prompt reasonable action.

POINTS TO REMEMBER

- Do your homework so you know which government agency the letter should reach to stimulate a proper response.

- Ascertain the title of the person whom you feel is most likely to respond positively to your letter.

- Provide enough pertinent data and statistics so the recipient can zero in on a response without having to check too many references.

- Avoid references to side issues that have no direct bearing on the subject at hand.
- Schedule the mailing so that the letter does not arrive at a time when the recipient is likely to be busier than usual.
- Allow more time for transit, since government mail tends to go through more channels than regular business mail.

State facts and avoid hearsay or assumptions.

- Use technical or specialized words only when you fully understand their meaning.
- Address the agency by its full name at the beginning. Later, it is permissible to use the acronym (the word formed from the organization's initials), if it is in common use.

One of the common problems in writing letters to government officials and agencies is that—unlike sales and marketing communication—they are not written regularly. You may have to communicate with a particular area of government only once in a decade. Thus, it is difficult to compose a text from scratch, without the help of model letters. Here, for example, are some of the occasional subjects for which you can receive guidance in this book:

- Recommendations to a highway department
- Complaint to a public service agency about energy policies
- Inquiry to the Office of Veterans Affairs
- Request for long-range forecasts from the Weather Bureau
- Proposal to Parks Department about softball fields

The agencies with which small businesses are likely to have the most communication are the ones relating to employee benefits and rights, such as Social Security branch offices, the Equal Employment Opportunity Commission, the Internal Revenue Service, or the Board of Health.

When writing to the government (as is also true in legal correspondence), it often expedites a proper response if you use the preposition *re*, "in reference to." Common usage calls for this to be capitalized and included in the letter right after the salutation, in this manner:

Dear Mr. Johnson:

Re: Medicare Benefits for Employees

Other subjects that can be readily summarized in this manner are the following:

- Re: Age discrimination policies
- Re: Location of Equal Employment Opportunity offices in St. Louis
- Re: New property tax assessments

- Re: Public Health Department pamphlets on air and water pollution

Generally speaking, letters to the government representatives are more formal in tone than other small-business letters and are seldom likely to contain personal comments. Thus, they rarely contain apologies, comments of appreciation for the recipient's time and counsel, or references to mutual acquaintances or associates. Messages should be as brief as possible, without disregarding necessary data, and to the point. If you have several unrelated points to discuss with the same agency or individual, it is often better to compose separate letters and mail them at suitable intervals. It is not unusual for government addressees to forward requests to other units for response or for additional information and comments. Thus it confuses the issue and results in delays if a letter has to be routed in turn to more than one person.

HOW TO DO IT

1. In the first sentence, introduce a key word or phrase that can serve as an identifying "label."
2. Be specific about names, titles, job specifications, and locations.
3. State the problem or situation.
4. Request that the letter be forwarded to the right party or information provided to you, if the addressee is not the one to whom the letter should have been addressed.
5. State clearly what you expect in the response.

TAXES

Letters dealing with taxes (like those sent to other government officials) should be addressed to the right person. Information must be precise, and the tone of the letter should be as professional as possible. On critical issues, such as tax delinquencies or filing failures, do not make any statements that could later be used against you or your company's interests. If you have complaints, use restraint. End on an up beat, that you are certain everything will be resolved to the mutual satisfaction of all concerned.

To IRS—Tax Status

Dear Mr. Delafield:

Thank you for reporting that our Form 2553, Election by a Small Business Corporation, has been received in your office. We have not yet received the the notification of our status as an S corporation. So, since more than the 45 days you specified have gone by, we will consider ourselves a corporation and will file the Form 1120, U.S. Corporation Income Tax Return, when it is due in April.

In the meantime, should our status be confirmed or changed in any way, please notify us immediately.

Sincerely,

To Property Tax Commission—Land Variance

Dear Commissioner Jeffords:

Your letter to the president of Highland Acreage Farms, Inc., has been turned over to me for two reasons: (1) I am responsible for handling corporate tax matters and making certain we comply with the state and county in all respects, and (2) I am the only officer in the company who was with HAF when we negotiated with Halbrook County for the variance. I recall the discussions very clearly. We were granted the land variance through mutual consent with the Tax Commission because we agreed to share what had been our sole water rights with the county for the government land reclamation project that was then being approved.

You will find the record intact: we still have the variance and the tax relief and the county still has the share of water rights. If you cannot find the legal instrument for this in your files, try the records of the Land Reform Office.

Sincerely yours,

To Municipal Tax Assessor—Response to Questionnaire

Dear Ms. Dunegan:

We received your letter and the tax questionnaire that you send each year to local businesses that might be subject to the rooms and meals assessment. We have not completed this form since our business does not fall in the category described in the foreword. While it is true that my company, Ridgefield Leases, Inc., does from time to time rent small properties on a short-term basis, these are not for vacations or purposes that could be, in any sense, related to the region's tourism. Rather, they are for basic residential use, and in some cases for adaptation as offices or display rooms for merchandise. In no instance could they be interpreted as "rooms" in the sense for which the tax was instituted, nor are they ever used for meal service.

Thank you for your inquiry.

Sincerely,

To City Tax Administrator—Supplying Documentation

Dear Mr. Twigg:

As requested, we submit herewith complete documentation of the deduction we claimed on Form 27-A2. As you will note, the claim resulted from damage incurred on the top floor of our headquarters building when a 75-foot angle-arm crane buckled and caused a load of steel beams to crash through the roof. You indicated that our claim was "duplication," but such is not the case. We reported only the damage to our property and not to the crane, which was owned by the Neil Construction Company and was not under contract by us. It is possible that Neil duplicated one of our loss figures on its tax return. But we most certainly did not.

Thank you for your courtesy.

Sincerely yours,

Enclosure

To Local Politician—Business Tax Assessment

Dear Laura:

You have always expressed an interest in our firm's progress since we founded the business two years ago. So I know you will be equally interested in our reaction to, and opinion about, a proposed state amendment that will assess retailers. The avowed purpose of the amendment is to collect funds to improve waste management and collection in commercial properties, such as shopping malls.

Although we do not fall into the "retail" category and would not be assessed, we oppose the amendment on the grounds that it would be of no benefit to businesses located in areas outside the "commercial" districts. We are thus going to vote against the measure at the polls and urge our friends to do likewise.

Enclosed is a copy of the amendment, which I am sure you are not familiar with as yet.

I hope all goes well with you.

Sincerely,

TRANSPORTATION

Sad, but true, most of the letters written by small-business spokespersons to government trans-portation officials are critical in nature. As the following samples indicate, they relate to such topics as inadequate mass transportation, unsafe highways, traffic congestion, and the lack of parking facilities. It is your right to complain, with the hope that some of the problems can be alleviated.

However, whenever it is possible, bolster your letter with suggestions that are both constructive and realistic. After all, the recipients of your letters are citizens, too, and possibly just as frustrated!

To State Senator—Proposal for Cutting Transportation Costs

Dear Senator Stallway:

As several of your staunchest supporters, my partners and I at Whitney Wheels have long appreciated your work as chairman of the State Transportation Committee and your efforts to solve the transportation problems, particularly in Sutton County. We were delighted to hear your recent comments, therefore, about the unfairness of the existing limousine service tax, which has been on the books for six years. During that time, our firm alone has paid out more than $86,000—money that has to come out of the pockets of our drivers in reduced paychecks and ourselves in hard-earned company profits.

By contrast, how much do the taxi companies pay? Zero!

How much do the bus companies pay? Zero!

How much do the shuttle services pay? Zero!

We hope you will make this—as you have hinted—a major campaign issue. And, while you're about it, please see what you can do about the Sutton County Airport gate fee. That adversely affects private limousine companies, and no one else. It is nothing but legalized pickpocketing!

Sincerely,

To Selectman—Recommendation for Better Public Transportation

Dear Selectman Curtiss:

Your speech about the healthy growth in our community impressed me in all respects save one. While small businesses like ours have multiplied and the region has grown in economic strength and population, there is one element that has been dismally lacking in growth. In fact, you could say it's in danger of remaining dwarfed if it doesn't get proper attention and financial nourishment. I'm speaking of the badly outmoded mass transportation system. From the heights of City Hall, you may not see the debilitating effect it has on the economy as much as I do, looking at it from the ground level of a company headquarters. But bus delays and breakdowns are very costly. I asked our auditor to assess the damage. Using a two-week record of employee late arrivals and lost time caused by poor bus service, he estimated that our company alone is losing more than 1,000 person-hours a year. Using a payroll average, he transposed that statistic into dollars and cents and reported a company loss of more than $12,000.

I suggest that you form a panel immediately to study the problems and make recommendations. I'd be happy to serve on it.

Sincerely,

To Senator—Mass Transportation Safety

Dear Senator White:

Safety at sea has been such an enormous issue in recent American history that Congress traditionally goes to great lengths to make sure that ships built in U.S. yards are the most seaworthy in the world and the least prone to fire, capsizing, split hulls, and other disasters. This is well and good, and all of us in shipbuilding are truly proud of the results of our labors and their performances on the high seas.

It is ironic, therefore, that one of the most hazardous and life-threatening trips anyone can take is from our own shipyard to our places of residence, from 5 to 25 miles away in the heart of this sprawling urban metropolis. This year, my division alone, with a complement of some 150 people, has amassed a pathetic record while using mass transportation: 3 deaths, 11 broken legs, about 16 other assorted fractures, and 4 head injuries. Not being a statistician, I cannot tell you what this means to the company in terms of lost time or to the individuals in terms of unrecompensed medical costs. But the data must be horrendous.

As I sit at my desk composing this letter, I can see at least four posters in the outside shop with block letters that say SAFETY and with messages urging care on the production line. But step beyond the steel fence surrounding the yard and SAFETY is a factor as remote as the Neanderthal Age.

The focus of all of the above is simply this question: Cannot Congress take effective steps to eliminate at least some of the perils we face when we risk travel on mass transit in any major city in the USA?

Sincerely,

To Municipal Highway Department—Traffic Congestion

Dear Mr. Schneerson:

Re: Alleviating an Acute Commuter Traffic Jam

The enclosed municipal map pinpoints the Grafton Street area where our insurance company offices are located, and I have marked the particular intersections where traffic problems have been escalating during the past couple of years. A survey of our employees shows that, on the average, they are taking 8.9 minutes longer to get to work in the morning than they did two years ago and more than 10 minutes to leave at the end of the day. If you multiply those figures by 130 (our employee total), the amount of lost time is prodigious. And I am speaking only for our own firm, let alone a dozen others in the area whose highway commuters experience the same delays.

One way to ease the situation would be to make Grafton a one-way street for ten blocks (as marked on the map with a yellow highlighter) going from east to west between the hours of 7:30 A.M. and 9:30 A.M. And between the hours of 4:00 and 5:30 going from west to east. It would alleviate the log jam also to put up a sign at the Hart Street Bridge intersection advising city drivers to avoid the Grafton Street area during those periods if they can take alternate routes.

I would like to meet with you as soon as possible to hear your opinion of this plan (or any other) and discuss what can be done. It is obvious that we can no longer tolerate the situation or let it get any further out of control.

Sincerely,

To Town Council—Parking Problems

Dear Members of the Town Council:

I have been appointed by a group of 36 merchants in our block at the northeast section of Main Street to call to your attention a situation which must be dealt with if we are to survive in business. In a word familiar to all of you, it is *parking.* The subject has been discussed endlessly and what few "corrective" measures were instituted in the past have been about as visible as a puff of dust on a windy day.

The purpose of this letter is to urge the Town Council to take the following steps:

1. Place parking at, or near, the top of the village priority list
2. Establish an active parking committee
3. Hire an outside professional consultant with documented success in alleviating small-town parking problems.

We stand ready to cooperate in every way possible in whatever studies or actions are necessary to launch an effective program. We feel certain that most other business and professional people in town would be equally supportive of this badly needed venture.

May three or four of us meet with representatives of the Council, at your convenience, to discuss what can be done?

Sincerely,

To Mayor—Lack of Parking Facilities

Dear Mayor Leach:

Parking! I'm sure at this stage you could scream every time you hear the word. But I'm not writing the usual complaint letter. I simply have a plan of action I think could lessen hassles for customers and improve business for merchants in a village whose center was unfortunately designed with streets too narrow and buildings too many. The biggest problems arise during weekends and holidays because of the heavy influx of shoppers who come here from the city. Since the high school parking lot is not used on weekends, why not promote that as a parking area and run a shuttle bus the half mile to the center of town? I, along with other merchants I've talked to, would be willing to deduct the round-trip fare from goods purchased. And there would be a lot fewer parking tickets to build up the resentments of the local populace!

Sincerely yours,

To Labor Commissioner—Request for Assistance in Resolving Ongoing Labor Problem

Dear Commissioner Albright:

Re: Failure of Arbitration Board to Take Action

To introduce myself, I am the owner of a small business engaged in providing individuals and businesses with limousines for a variety of purposes, including transportation to and from the Municipal Airport.

As you know, our area has been severely affected by a strike that involves trucking firms, but which has nothing whatsoever to do with limousines or passenger-vehicle service. Yet my business has been all but halted by the action of pickets who block our access to highways, threaten limousine drivers, and frighten away potential passengers.

We have asked local officials in the Labor Department and on the Arbitration Board, as well as the police and airport security officers, to take steps to alleviate this senseless and implausible situation. If we do not get some form of relief, my firm will be out of business before the month ends.

We implore you to assume your responsibilites and take some kind of prompt action on behalf of those of us who are being unjustly victimized.

Sincerely,

REGULATORY ISSUES

The recipients of letters about regulatory issues are on the receiving end of so much mail that their reactions are blunted and their responses often indifferent. It helps if you can write a letter that...

like the first model here, uses humor

like the second model, suggests an unwelcome sacrifice for the governing and governed alike

and like the third model, calls on the recipient's sense of fair play to right a wrong.

To Congressman—Food Labeling

Dear Congressman Brown:

Re: A Plea to Help Stifle Bureaucratic Babysitters

In all my 45 years in the American food business, in a career that has spanned just about every aspect of obtaining, processing, packaging, marketing, and distributing edible products, I have never seen so much hullabaloo and brouhaha as are reflected in today's headlines. The government has jumped in, up to its big nose, and is attempting not only to regulate what humans can and cannot eat but to censor the very way in which food products are described. When it comes to labeling, there isn't a word in the English language that is acceptable. How fresh is "fresh" ? How dry is "dry" ? How light is "light" ? How thin is "thin" ? How sweet is "sweet" ?

Why I ever got into the seafood processing business I'll never know. The most natural of our products are damned for every possible reason. Even if one were to come, pure and adulturated, out of a test tube, it would be censured for being exposed to light rays or faulted for being off color. There doesn't seem to be an element in all of creation that does not contaminate our products, from mercury and sodium to iron, magnesium, oxide, and just plain sea salt. All we have to do is to start marketing a product successfully and have it accepted popularly to bring down the wrath of the FDA. Or Congress. Or both.

Trying to stem the tide of villification is like placing a cobblestone at the entrance to the Bay of Fundy. But I hope you'll consider my small voice a plea, not a whimper, and ask those labeling experts in Washington to take up crossword puzzles and stop hounding the food industry.

Respectfully,

To Mayor—Excessive Government Regulation

Dear Mayor Bostwick:

When I retired from a corporate giant, tired of the internal bickerings and road blocks to innovative thinking, I established my own business, The Glass Factory, here in Green Falls with the idea that now I could be innovative and get things done without having to go through endless committees and boards. My experience during two years in business has shown, ironically, that I escaped one form of bureaucracy only to land in the clutches of another that is equally cumbersome and frustrating.

I no longer have to hurdle committees to pursue my objectives. Instead, I have to fight City Hall. For one thing, every time I design a window that is unconventional or want to install a new kind of glass never used in the village before, I have to get approval from the town Safety Review Board. The designers and installers of lumber products don't have to do this. The suppliers of aluminum and steel products don't have to do this. The producers of bricks and ceramics don't have to do this. Why *glass?* Is there something ominous or life-threatening about glass that does not apply to other building and decorative products? I am truly perplexed.

Everyone at City Hall must have extensive childhood histories of having cut their fingers on broken glass!

Is there any chance your administration can review the legislative situation and take glass off the hit list? If not, you may give birth to an endangered species and eventually find yourselves living in windowless houses.

Sincerely,

To State Legislator—Requesting Government Intervention

Dear Representative Trenton:

When your Environmental Committee members meet next week at the State Capitol, we hope you will voice an official condemnation of Royal Chemical Producers, Inc., for the part it has played in perpetrating a fraud against our pest-control industry. To be specific, my firm and several other companies recently protested to the RCP management that three of the chemicals they supply us with were deliberately mislabled to hide the fact that they contained formulations injurious to the environment. Their action was in direct violation of the law, as well as injurious to our reputation as pest controllers.

I have registered several additional protests, including a demand for reimbursement for illegal chemicals unknowingly purchased by my firm and used in recent applications completed for our customers. These protests and demands have fallen on deaf ears. It is my belief that RCP will take no compensatory action until it is hauled into court and forced to do so. However, the mere payment of fines, a slap on the wrist, and a phony consent to "cease and desist" mean nothing to a company like RCP. The only language its owners understand is the kind that you and your committee could publish in an official document threatening to put the company out of business if it does not comply with the law and conduct its business in an ethical manner.

The enclosed copies of our joint protest and my individual correspondence will provide the basic information you need. We will supply anything else you might want at any time.

Sincerely,

RECOMMENDATIONS

Recommendations and suggestions take their place with a few other subjects as ones that are likely to be low on a manager's letter-writing priorities. In many cases, though, opportunities are lost that might have proved beneficial to small businesses. Here are some sample letters that suggest this kind of correspondence that can often achieve favorable results.

To Community Services Commission—Mutual Cooperation

Dear Mr. Chairman:

As one chairman to another, I am writing to determine where we might be able to take mutual advantage of opportunities we both can share. As a Commission, you have expressed continued interest in improving community services throughout the state by coordinating plans and activities. As an association of people in retailing, we and our members have also dedicated ourselves to similar improvements. As has been said repeatedly in our newsletters and reports, "What is good for the community is good for business."

We, therefore, propose that we "lend" one of our members to the Public Service Commission for a period of four weeks in order to study potential areas of mutual participation. The person we have in mind is Ms. Julia Gooding, who served as an aide to the governor before going into business for herself and who is capable of looking at all sides of the picture.

Yours in service,

To Police Department—Weekend Office Patrols

Dear Chief MacDonald:

Re: Request for Increased Police and Security Patrols

The recent newspaper accounts of drug dealing in the Overbridge Farms mall and office development may be news to readers of the *Times*, but they are old hat to us. If you will check your police blotter, you will find that we have telephoned and registered no fewer than eight complaints to the desk sergeant in the last three months alone. I also reported the problem in writing to the mayor's office twice last year. But thus far, the response from your department and City Hall have been negligible.

Because of vandalism, break-ins, and other property damage caused directly and indirectly by drug operations in the Overbridge Farms vicinity, our attorneys have counseled us to institute a lawsuit against the city for negligence. In fact, a legal instrument has already been drafted to that effect. Before taking this action, we would like to make one last request for your cooperation. We feel that the situation can be brought under control through regular police patrols at night and on weekends when the drug dealers are reported to be most active.

We are willing to assign two of our own officers to assist in this program, but we cannot do it alone. Won't you please promise us some action and institute patrols before the situation worsens.

Sincerely,

To City Purchasing Office—Cost-Cutting Proposal

Dear Sylvia:

Re: Proposal for a Plan to Slash Municipal Costs

It was with considerable interest that I read the newspaper account in yesterday's *Eagle* about the city's budgeting crunch and the tax increase proposal. We all hate to see that phrase, "tax increase," and it occurs to me that perhaps there is something positive we can do about it, if we all work together. Your own department is a case in point. I'd be willing to bet I could save the city 40% or more on the purchase of office supplies alone, just by pinpointing overstocks that are available, gauging the best times of the year to order, and coaching purchasers in ways to obtain better deals from their suppliers. You know as well as I do how that works in private industry, and there is no reason why a city government should be any different.

Translate that into all other departments, and some enormous savings could be effected. I'm sure, for example, that the purchasing agent at Sullivan Motors could give the city some hefty suggestions for buying automotive parts at discount. And the buyer at Wayland Clothes could show city purchasers of fire and police uniforms how to up the quality and quantity—and still cut the budget.

I propose that we organize a study group to look into this proposition. If industry can help the city slash its budget at no sacrifice in goods and at the same time avoid tax increases, then we'd all be better off. And a little richer.

With best regards,

To Governor—Code of Ethics for State Employees

Dear Governor:

Re: Urgent Need for an Improved Code of Ethics

Having just moved to your state from the Southeast, I have been quite distressed to find some very slipshod practices here in the ranks of government employees at all levels. With all due respect, may I suggest that you adopt the following code of ethics, which emphasizes

Integrity. State workers should follow personal codes of conduct supporting the moral values necessary for good government.

Honesty. Workers should avoid even the appearance of wrongdoing and should confront and challenge unethical behavior.

Respect for others. Workers should serve with care, compassion, and concern for the well-being of the compatriots.

Fairness. Workers should make decisions in a fair, impartial, and objective manner.

Accountability. To the end, workers should protect the public trust by upholding the state and U.S. constitutions and laws.

These precepts worked well back where I came from. But I don't want to look back. I want to be here where I am, and I want the same code of ethics to be evident. It pays off in every way.

Respectfully,

To State Public Information Office—Publicizing Services

Dear Ms. Booker:

During the seven years since I joined Empire Employment, the number of disadvantaged people for whom we have secured remunerative positions has increased by at least 50%. We are making a special effort to improve the statistics and reach a goal of 100%. We have found—much to the surprise of a great many employers—that their most loyal and reliable workers are often found in the ranks of the deaf, the vision impaired, the handicapped, and others who a decade ago might have found no work at all.

We would appreciate it if you would mention in your monthly newsletter, or publicize in any other way appropriate, the fact that Empire Employment welcomes applications from disadvantaged people. We don't intend to make a specialty of this, but we are far more experienced than most agencies when it comes to matching good jobs with disadvantaged candidates.

Cordially,

To Parks Department—Proposal for Softball Teams

Dear Sheridan:

Now that you have joined the Parks Department and are enjoying a little more fresh air away from City Hall, I have a proposal to make that should be of interest to you. Last year, we formed a company softball team at Highland Foods and have been scheduling informal games with two neighboring firms, after business hours and on occasional weekends. Several other company managers have asked about doing the same thing, and I can see where we could have an entire league going in no time at all.

What we need at this point, however, is coordination with the Parks Department, so we can line up playing times and reserve diamonds regularly on an annual basis. If a program of this scale would be disadvantageous to noncorporate softball players in any way, we need to be alerted to the situation and do something about it. I think, for example, that we could raise enough funds to underwrite the cost of two or three more diamonds. But these are things we need to know, and I propose that two or three of us get together with you for lunch some day soon and talk things over.

I hope all goes well with you.

Sincerely,

To Motor Vehicle Department—Recommending Change in Procedures

Dear Commissioner Parmer:

Last week, one of our staff members wasted the better part of two days touring license commission offices at the municipal building, the county center, and the state office building. Through what seems like a "simple oversight," she had neglected to reactivate her license on time, and there was no information readily available on the procedure to follow in such cases. Hence, she bounced from here to there, and no one seemed able to provide the right guidance.

The problem was that your office had mistakenly mailed the renewal form to her old address, although she has been registered at her current address for more than two years. We feel strongly, therefore, that she should not be penalized with a delinquency charge to be reinstated.

If I may offer a suggestion, I think that your renewal letters and forms should be mailed to the applicants' firms, rather than home addresses. That way, there should be a minimal chance of error.

Sincerely,

INQUIRIES AND REQUESTS FOR INFORMATION

For additional letter-writing ideas, see Chapter 1, Providing and Requesting Information.

To Small Business Administration—Consulting and Advisory Services

Dear Mr. Chandell:

Re: Business Assistance Available to Entrepreneurs

As I understand it from my past experience in establishing my own business, the Small Business Administration makes available to perspective entrepreneurs a number of consulting and advisory services at little or no cost. I would appreciate information about such services or suggestions about other sources of pertinent data.

To be more specific, several engineers who have worked for me in the past on a part-time basis have expressed a desire to start their own businesses. They would then, in effect, become suppliers and help my own business to grow. Though I have made suggestions based on my personal experience in this regard, I am not familiar with developments that may have occurred in the SBA within the past five years.

Would your available consulting and advisory services help people with these objectives? I'd appreciate it if you could send me whatever literature the SBA may have in print about the incorporation, development, and staffing of small businesses of this nature.

Sincerely,

To Equal Employment Opportunity Commission— Potential Sexual Harrassment Charges

Dear Ms. Redding:

RE: Possible Charges of Sexual Harrassment

Our company, Baylor Brass Plate, has been in business for more than 60 years, founded by the grandfather of the present owner. Even before the formation of the EEOC, the firm was noted for its fair hiring policies and lack of discrimination in the workplace. We have had no serious complaints and no injunctions by the EEOC or any other regulatory body dealing with discrimination. Now, however, we are concerned that several female employees who bear unfounded grudges against the company are conspiring to claim sexual harrassment and to cite supposed slurs made by male employees on the assembly line.

Anticipating trouble, we would like to obtain from you a copy of the question-naires or other papers you require, both from the Charging Party and the Employer. If possible, we would also like to see examples of actual cases in which sexual harrassment charges were made and actions taken.

Sincerely,

To Mayor—Minutes and Report on Zoning and Taxes

Dear Mayor Belknap:

As a new member of the Chamber of Commerce and the business community in Summit, I strongly support your stand on the zoning issue and tax relief for small businesses. One of my first acts since moving here from Georgetown was to register to vote so that I could express my opinions at the polls. After I become better acquainted with our new hometown and have had a chance to get our packaging design and service company rolling as it should, I plan to take an active part in politics and government—as I did in Georgetown.

In the meantime, would you please be good enough to have your secretary mail me a copy of the minutes and your report from the October 18 open meeting on zoning and business taxes. I'd appreciate having them for reference.

Sincerely,

To State Representative—Supporting Position and Requesting Assistance

Dear Representative Comely:

By now, you are probably inundated with mail from the owners of businesses in towns larger than 30,000. I can't blame them completely for feeling that they are being discriminated against by the "hicks" who elect to do business in rural areas rather than the big cities. But it only makes sense from a business viewpoint. As one who is about to move the family business from a city location to a farm belt community, I know full well that our income and profits will drop markedly. So why shouldn't our real estate taxes do likewise?

I'll do you a favor and voice support for you next November, as well as cast my vote on your behalf. May I ask a favor in return? I have been trying without success to get a copy of the tax proposal from the State Tax Division. I guess its staff is too busy. Could you send me a copy?

With best wishes for '92,

To IRS—Tax Information

Dear Director:

Please send me the necessary forms and instructions for filing corporate federal taxes for 1990. We are a Chapter S corporation conducting a service-oriented business in seven states. Our three offices comprise a total of 167 salaried employees and 24 people who function on a part-time, hourly basis.

Sincerely,

To Social Security Administration—Educational Program

Dear Ms. Prince:

If you will recall, we had some correspondence last year about our corporate employee committee and plans to provide information and assistance to older employees who were nearing retirement age. At that time, you sent us some leaflets to distribute, as needed.

Now our plans have been activated, and we intend to hold a series of monthly meetings for employees. Each session would be no longer than one hour, would be held in the company cafeteria, and would take place during regular business hours, preferably in midmorning or midafternoon.

My question: Would it be possible for you to send a representative to assist us, and particularly to respond to questions that we may not be qualified to answer? We would schedule the sessions on whatever weekday and time of the month were most convenient for your representative.

Sincerely,

To State Public Health Official—Air Quality Data

Dear Dr. Beerbahm:

My three partners and I, all with medical degrees, plan to open and operate a community health clinic near the town of Burnwood. We have selected a site two miles north of the center of town, adjacent to the Salinac River and within half a mile of the intersection of Route 87 and River Road. Before buying the property and contracting for the building, we would like to get a reading on the air quality in this location during all four seasons of the year. Since the site is in a valley, we also need to know whether surface air is trapped for periods of any duration or whether it flows readily, and in which prevailing direction. Many of our patients will be suffering from lung and throat ailments, either chronically or occasionally, and the question of air pollution is a vital one for us.

We would appreciate any data you can send us.

Sincerely,

To Office of Veterans Affairs—Postmilitary Employment Policies

Dear Major Chutnick:

Re: Military-Style Physical Fitness Enterprise

I am about to incorporate a rugged physical fitness training and testing program tentatively named Vets in Action, based on the type of jungle and mountain obstacle courses you and I were so familiar with in Company "C." However, I would like to clarify several points with the VA and am asking you whether any of the following would be subject to rejection by either the military or civilian employment bodies:

1. To staff the company about 75% with men and women who had qualified for these programs in the field and attained a rank of not less than corporal
2. To mention their specific military experience in promotional brochures or advertising
3. To use the name "Vets" or "Veterans" in the company title
4. To specify my own former rank and achievements in the military service

I'd be interested, too, in your reaction to the venture I am undertaking. I think it will succeed, but there is always a high risk in any small-business enterprise and this one is probably no exception.

With kind regards,

To Weather Service—Predictions

Dear Director Hartell:

As co-owner and captain of a small fleet of offshore fishing vessels, I am writing to inquire about the possibility of obtaining better long-range weather forecasts and marine oceanographic readings within the next few years. Thus far, the predictions have been dead wrong or contained serious miscalculations for a high percentage of readings that extend more than two days ahead of time.

Our problem is that we not only have to lock in our fleet schedules a week or more in advance, but we have to select the fishing grounds and contract for crews. We lose money—lots of it—when we pick less productive fishing banks, overbook crews, or time departures poorly.

The recent article in *Fleet Management* entitled "Better Forecasting" gave us some hope that the situation will improve. How much improvement can we expect?

Sincerely yours,

To Better Business Bureau—Imposter Using Company Name

Dear Mr. Farthingame:

For almost ten years, we have been doing business as HighStar Audio, Inc., and have become known in Charlotte not only for our highly competitive prices, but for our prompt, courteous service and our know-how and experience when it comes to repairing or reconditioning electronic products of many kinds.

Recently, we have become aware of a startling situation that actually threatens both our business and our reputation. We have complained to the police department, but have been told that no action can be taken until we provide positive "evidence" of criminal intent and wrongdoing. So we are hoping you can give us the necessary advice, based perhaps on similar scams that have been dealt with by the BBB in the past. A telephone salesman, armed apparently with our own customer list, has offered "reconditioned" compact disk (CD) players at ridiculously low prices. He claims to be from the "High Star Company," says he is "in the vicinity," and suggests stopping by to show the line he has just picked up at the "reconditioning plant." He demonstrates the equipment and about half the time makes the sale because the price is one few people can resist. Also, he assures the buyer that "High Star stands behind every purchase, unconditionally" and mentions how the name stands for reliability and superb service. But the set he actually gives the purchaser is pure junk—not the demonstration model—and so people get stuck.

Why, you may ask, don't buyers ever call our store for confirmation before laying down their money? Because this imposter always calls and appears on the scene after hours, on Sundays, or whenever he knows our shop is closed.

What action do you suggest we take, both to avoid any further misrepresentation and, ultimately, to catch the culprit in the act?

Sincerely,

RESPONSES TO INQUIRIES AND CRITICISM

When your company is charged with any kind of offense or impropriety which prompts your response by letter, use the following as guidelines:

1. Reply directly to the person responsible for the charge, unless someone else has been specified.

2. Make certain that you understand the nature and implications of the allegations.

3. Discuss your options, if necessary, with an expert more familiar with the situation than you are before writing your letter.

4. Be specific in your rebuttal and address your comments only to the issue(s) cited.

5. If you acknowledge being at fault, describe any countermeasures being taken.

6. Avoid mentioning any nonpertinent matters.

7. Close with a positive statement.

To Municipal Manager—Affirmative Action Program

Dear Squire Dardon:

Re: Company Affirmative Action Program

In response to the inquiries you sent to determine the nature and extent of affirmative action programs of companies in River Bend, I am answering on behalf of the the Bowden-Beck Luggage Company, which has been a family-owned operation here for almost a quarter of a century.

B/B subscribes to the belief that the most advantageous way to attract top employees is to judge individuals on their performance on the job, without regard to race, religion, sex, color, or ethnic background. In this spirit, we instituted an ongoing affirmative action program more than ten years ago and have always considered it a vital force in building employee morale and developing our business. We are continuing to do so and are active in encouraging employment by minorities, veterans, and disadvantaged people.

Sincerely,

To State Department of Labor—Employment of Minorities

Dear Mr. Hernandez:

My wife and I are happy to submit the information you requested about the proportion of our employees who belong to minority groups or are disadvantaged. As you can see from the figures, Ho-Ho Car Wash, Inc., makes a practice of offering steady jobs to people in these categories, as long as they are qualified, reliable, and honest.

We appreciate your concern about the hiring of minority groups and are happy to see that the state is keeping an eye on labor practices and policies in our region. If we can be helpful in promoting better opportunities and improving the relationships of people of different races and faiths, believe me we would want the chance any time.

Very truly yours,

To Public Safety Office—Response to Criticism

Dear Mr. Goldspan:

Your letter to our chairman was neither appropriate, timely, nor factual.

You have no basis on which to make a claim that fleets of small delivery trucks like ours are operated by "kids who are immature, inexperienced, ill trained, and often guilty of substance abuse." The fact is the average age of our drivers is well over 40. They are hired through reputable employment agencies, must pass rigid written and physical tests, and are put through a course of instruction at our own driving school before being permitted to represent us on the road.

As for common courtesy, they could surpass your manners any day!

Sincerely,

To State Licensing Board—Responding to Charge of Racial Discrimination

Dear Chairman Beecher:

Re: Response to Unjust Charges of Discrimination

You have every right to question innkeepers about their conduct in dealing with travelers who stop for meals or rooms, and in fact it is one of your prime responsibilities to do so. I would not like to see licenses granted to hostelries and restaurants that discriminated against the public because of color, race, religion, age, sex, or ethnic background.

Nevertheless, the state has been dead wrong in its allegations that any employee of the Durango House unlawfully discriminated against the six tourists from Juarez who, on February 18 of this year, applied at the desk for lodging. They were turned down, and rightly so, for the following valid reasons:

1. Despite their claims, they had never phoned or written for a reservation on that date or any other.

2. It was obvious from the discussion my manager had with them that they had mistaken our inn for another with a similar-sounding name, the Dorado, 12 miles away.

3. Since we have only 11 rooms and they were all occupied except one small single, we could not have provided suitable (or even legal) accommodations.

4. My manager was gracious and obliging and provided the group with the names and phone numbers of five other hostelries within ten miles of ours. He offered to make calls himself, but was turned down.

The problem was compounded by two situations. In the first place, only one of the six could speak English very poorly and none of my staff could speak Spanish. In the second place, it was obvious that the three males in the group had been imbibing to the point where they were not acting either courteously or rationally. I rule out any reference to drinking, however, since neither I nor my staff make it a practice to conduct tests for alcohol consumption.

In view of the above, I request that you drop any and all allegations against us for discrimination.

Sincerely,

To Equal Employment Opportunity Commission— Responding to Complaint

Dear Mr. McGuffey:

This letter follows up the discussion you had on the phone yesterday with Ms. Haldeman, my administrative assistant, about the complaint of one of our employees, Charles Tooley.

As I understand it, Mr. Iguano, who is Hispanic, alleged that the company violated his Equal Employment Opportunity rights because he was suspended for one week for participating in an altercation at the plant warehouse whereas two others who were involved and were not Hispanic received no punishment but verbal admonitions.

The fact is that Mr. Iguano was the main offender, according to four reliable witnesses at the scene, and had to be forcibly restrained after punching one of his associates without just cause. The other two men cooperated and were guilty only of some rough language.

After a complete investigation, our EEO committee is convinced that the punishment was fair and without any kind of racial overtones. Our policy here on EEO matters is rigid, and we feel that we consistently make every effort to comply with both the technicalities and the spirit of the law.

I trust that this letter will render unnecessary any further action on the part of the EEOC review board.

Sincerely,

COMPLAINTS

The model letters that follow are typical complaints relating to small businesses. For additional letter-writing ideas, see Chapter 2, Making and Answering Complaints and Effecting Adjustments.

Consumer Affairs Complaint—Denial of Wrongdoing

Dear Councilman Marietta:

Unfortunately, I was out of town attending a funeral when my wife, who serves as my business manager, opened the notice from the Director of Consumer Affairs, which implied that Dollar Photo Supply, Inc., was guilty of price collusion and might be subject to punitive action. I returned home to find her greatly agitated and without a kind word to say about the Consumer Affairs Office or its threats.

My own initial reaction was one of anger and bitterness. However, after I calmed down and perused the report, I could see that there was some reason for the implication. It is quite true that the price structure we publicized for our 35mm cameras was influenced by competitive pricing. In no way, though, did we conspire with competitors to agree on prices that would be favorable to our mutual interests and put the consumer at a disadvantage. I guess you could say that, in the end, our decisions were influenced by the marketplace and to that degree were "collusive."

Please accept this letter as our official apology for any infringement made and our assurance that we will maintain both the spirit and the letter of all laws and regulations relating to the best interests of the consumer.

Respectfully,

To Post Office—Delays in Service

Dear Mr. Krantz:

When the U.S. Postal Service sent us a copy of your new booklet, "Addressing for Success," we distributed it to all of our office secretaries and agents and have made every effort to comply with its suggestions. We use the right envelope sizes and the correct address abbreviations and line sequences for your automated equipment and optical character readers (OCRs). And we purposely send our policyholders stamped return envelopes that meticulously follow the address formulas cited in your booklet.

Yet still we have problems almost daily because of delays in both incoming and outgoing mail. You can well understand that delays can be very critical when they involve payments of premiums in order to avoid policy cancellations. To give you some examples, last week we received five letters that, according to the postmarks, had taken four days to go less than 100 miles. And one of our agents in a branch office some 10 miles from here stated that it regularly takes four to five days for some of our first-class mailings to reach her.

What can we do to correct this continuing problem?

Sincerely,

To Post Office—Lack of Response to Complaint

Dear Mr. Ogden:

My distribution manager and I have tried on numerous occasions to reach postal officials by phone, but have had a total lack of success. Since you are much better geared to communication by mail than by wire, perhaps this letter will achieve the hoped-for results.

We have experienced very serious delays in mailing small packages from our plant at this address to locations in northern Wyoming and Montana, as well as elsewhere in the West. Since the food products we ship are perishable, we have been receiving increasing calls from customers complaining that some items are not as fresh as they hoped for. As you can imagine, this discourages repeat orders and damages our reputation.

We'd appreciate it if a representative from the USPS could meet with us to determine how we can improve our mailing procedures and minimize delays.

Sincerely,

To Post Office—Lost Shipments

Dear Mr. Vordock:

Your name was given to me by the postmaster's office as the person whom I should contact to help resolve a problem relating to our mail delivery. With my wife, I operate a small specialty mail-order business. We sell sports shirts and caps to customers, imprinted with their names or whatever short message they instruct us to apply. We offer these in our ads and a small catalog on a money-back guarantee, warranting that we will refund the cost plus postage for any items that are returned. During the six years we have been in business there had been no problems with returned merchandise—until three months ago. Starting in March, we began receiving letters from people saying they had returned items, but received no refunds.

How can we find out what has been happening to return mail of this kind? The complaints have come from various parts of the country, not just one or two locations. And the return labels we supply have not been changed in any way.

Sincerely,

To Public Works Department—Trash Removal

Dear Commissioner Longfellow:

Re: Public Works Department Spillage and Pollution

Two years ago, the city filed a formal complaint and promptly extracted a fine from our company when one of our leased trucks was in an accident and spilled 10 gallons of salad oil at an intersection. As the records clearly showed, the trucking firm, not Italia Oils, was at fault, yet it was we who removed the spillage as quickly as was possible under some difficult circumstances.

Last year, in a "turnabout is fair play" motion, we complained to the Public Works Department that two of your tank trucks were leaking raw sewage along the public road adjacent to our food storage warehouse. As we pointed out then, the spillage was never cleaned up properly and for weeks on end attracted flies and rodents to an area where we are superstrict about health precautions. Three weeks ago, exactly the same spillage took place, and it is evident that PWD has not repaired the hose connections or gaskets where the leaks have occurred. Despite five phone calls to PWD and two written complaints, we have yet to see a single piece of equipment or a single person doing anything about the spillage.

If you have any doubts, I invite you to drive over here and *smell* for yourself. You will be nauseated.

And nauseated is a good adjective for our present opinion of PWD and its operations.

Sincerely,

To County Office—Failure to Remove Garbage Efficiently

Dear Mr. Tuthill:

It has been many months since I last saw a sanitation inspector on or near any of the five premises where we have supermarkets in Powell County. And the results show it. The streets in these vicinities are constantly littered with trash, including raw garbage, mainly because the operators of the municipal haulage facilities are not properly supervised and the firms are never cited for violations. We have had many complaints from customers who don't like the idea of buying food in an area that resembles a city dump. As we lose more and more customers, we naturally become more desperate to take some kind of measures to save our business.

The purpose of this letter is to ask that you dispatch more inspectors and generate corrective action. If you cannot do so, we may have to take the matter to court.

Sincerely,

To Traffic Court—Parking Tickets

Dear Judge Simmons:

Re: Relief from Business Parking Problems

I am a small businessman and have been serving the township of Brownsville for eight years supplying a healthful, much-needed product at competitive prices. But my margin of profit has been drying up steadily for a number of reasons, not the least of which is the substantial sum I have to set aside to pay for parking tickets and summonses for our fleet of ten trucks which deliver bottled water to offices and other commercial and residential customers. Because of the parking and traffic problems in town, it is almost impossible for our drivers to park and make deliveries most of the time without incurring some form of vehicular violation.

Is there no solution to this problem? Or should we simply fold up the business and go away?

Sincerely,

To Public Service Department—Energy Policies

Dear Foster:

I am astonished to find an old hand like you, who grew up in the oil fields of Oklahoma, letting the public Service Department get away with an energy policy that is so biased and unrealistic. One of my clients is Radial Tubing, which manufactures conduits and tubing used mainly in refrigeration equipment. After a lengthy study, I advised the production manager how to cut fuel by reducing production during electricity peak-load hours and increasing his runs during the off-peak hours when demand for electricity is lowest. The idea obviously was to take advantage of the lower rates passed along by the electric cooperative.

Don't tell me you are ignorant of what happened next. The PSD refused to allow the change unless Radial Tubing pays its employees overtime for working during "nonconventional" hours! This is sheer nonsense, and I hope you can do something about it before we all blow our stacks!

With disbelief,

To County Attorney—Filing a Damage Claim

Dear Solicitor Marin:

Re: Damage Claim Against Randolph County

As I mentioned to your assistant on the phone yesterday, our firm is instituting a suit against Randolph County to claim redress for damages suffered to one of our discount outlets last fall. Our building at the corner of Hillcrest Road and Harding Road was so badly discolored by mud and grit splattered carelessly by the county sewer excavators that it had to be completely steam-cleaned and repainted at a cost of more than $3,000. Since our initial damage claim was rejected by the county, we are taking the matter to court.

We'd appreciate it if you could send us a copy of the Claims Assistance statute enacted in 1985, along with the necessary forms for instituting an action of this nature. It is our opinion that the county will honor our claim when it is realized that we intend to go to court.

Sincerely,

To Fire Commissioner—Potential Hazard

Dear Commissioner Lagmount:

Re: The Critical Deficiencies of Firefighting Resources

When the Apex Company moved into the buildings we occupy in the Medland section, there were only three industrial plants in the area. Today there are more than 20. Last year, we wrote an official complaint to the developer for what was then purely a commercial reason: we were having difficulty maintaining the water pressure needed in our cold metal processing. We received a few promises and the addition of a secondary water line and holding tank. But that improvement was minimal and reflects, I suppose, the developer's reluctance to put any capital into features that do not tend to beautify the environment and thus attract new office leasers.

Now I intend to take a firmer stance, but this time based on what I feel is a real threat to life and limb. Were we to have a major fire in Medland, I doubt that it could be extinguished through the use of existing water conduits. What I am asking, really, is that you authorize a realistic study of the water supply and other firefighting resources in Medland as they now exist and report on their quantity, quality, and effectiveness under duress. Should there be any cost involved, beyond your normal budget, Apex is willing to underwrite it.

Sincerely,

CHAPTER 11

ℳEDIA, PUBLIC RELATIONS, AND BUSINESS AND PROFESSIONAL ASSOCIATIONS

Experienced letter writers often admit that some of the most challenging letters they have to write are those that are addressed to people who themselves are in the business of writing and presenting ideas and thus are likely to be highly critical of anything that is amateurish. This group includes people who work for the media and public relations agencies. The next most challenging assignment, they say, is writing letters aimed at staff members of business and professional associations. Why? Primarily because those recipients have to send out so many letters in their daily work that they are likely to cast a critical eye on their own incoming mail.

If you have a hang-up about writing letters to these discriminating audiences, you can relax. You may be better off with less experience because you can be yourself and express your own ideas in an honest and straightforward fashion. The pros recognize and respect letters that come from the heart rather than the copywriter's formula bank. The model letters in this book have been deliberately composed with fresh points of view and flexible styling so you can adapt them easily and personalize them for your own use.

WRITE TO A PERSON, NOT TO AN ADDRESS

Before you write the first word in your letter, close your eyes and imagine your letter being read. Do you see a flesh-and-blood person in that image? Or do you visualize an office, a bank, a repair shop, a retail store, or some other structural entity?

Once you envision a real person opening the envelope, you are on the right track. But you still have to overcome a second hurdle, which is to have a reasonably realistic understanding of the recipient's interests. Many letters fail to make their mark because they stress situations and ideas relating to the writer, rather than the reader. How often have you read letters, for example, from friends or associates and ended with the distinct thought that the writers were looking for sympathy or understanding for themselves and were not really too concerned with how you were making out these days? Don't fall into that trap. When composing your thoughts, think in terms of *you*, the person who is the recipient. Even when the subject of a letter is routine and conventional, there are ways to bring the reader into the picture.

ANALYZING YOUR AUDIENCE

Here are some keys to the types of people you will be writing to in the four specific fields with which this chapter is concerned:

1. The Media. These people are in the business of working with ideas and issues and communicating them to people through magazines, newspapers, broadcasts, and other media. They may be writers, editors, publishers, administrators, or marketers, but they are dedicated to better communication, and they respond favorably to letters that clarify ideas and issues and give them something substantial to think about.

2. Public Relations. Like those in the media, these people are concerned with ideas and issues. The main difference is that, whether because of personal convictions or loyalty to clients, they are likely to have preconceived opinions about the issues. They respond well to suggestions for improving relationships between organizations and the public.

3. Business Associations. The kinds of staff members you are likely to write to in business associations are much like people in public relations, but more specialized. They are committed to the goal of helping business in general and their own field in particular to flourish and be economically healthy. They respond well to requests for information and to ideas that will be mutually beneficial to the recipient, as well as the letter writer.

4. Professional Association. Picture the staff member you are writing to as a person who is more "vertical" in both interests and experience. He or she will be perhaps less knowledgeable about general business, but substantially informed about the work and goals of the profession that the association represents. These people react positively to requests for data and publications that can spread their message, as well as ideas for improving any relationships affecting the association.

HOW TO DO IT

1. Imagine yourself having a face-to-face meeting with the recipient (rather than writing a letter), during which you will briefly discuss a topic of mutual concern or interest.

2. Begin with a personal or favorable comment.

3. Swing the dialog naturally around to the subject.

4. Be specific about what is needed or what you hope to accomplish.

5. Focus on one subject.

6. Use language and style that the recipient is familiar with and finds compatible.

7. Provide a brief description of anything pertinent the recipient needs to know and may not be familiar with beforehand.

8. Make it clear what reaction and/or action you expect.

9. Close on a positive, upbeat note.

Sometimes, in dealing with these four kinds of audiences, the subject at hand may not be simple or brief enough to cover in a single page. If what you have to present is so long and complicated that it requires more than a page or a page and a half of typescript, your letter might be more effective if it makes the necessary point(s) and then refers the recipient to an attachment or enclosure.

Some examples of situations in which enclosures might be useful:

• Sending information to newspaper editors in the hope that they will publish a story about your business

• Submitting material about your business to a public relations account executive who represents your industry or causes in which you are involved

• Listing the kinds of information you would like to receive on a regular basis from a business association

• Providing a professional association with technical data on your company or the text of a position paper you have written concerning your profession.

COMMUNICATING WITH THE MEDIA

When writing to newspapers, broadcasting stations, magazines, and other media, follow these guidelines as closely as possible:

1. Select the editor, publisher, commentator, columnist, or other staff member most likely to be interested in, and responsive to, your letter.

2. Make sure you understand the nature of the medium you are addressing and the demographics of its audience.

3. Stick with your primary theme or topic and resist the urge to digress.

4. Use your own personal language and style and don't attempt to be a literary show-off to impress your reader just because he or she is probably an experienced wordsmith.

5. Provide an enclosure if it will help to describe or visualize the subject at hand.

6. Make it clear why you are writing and what action or response you hope will result.

7. Close with the assurance that you are readily available for further information or an interview should the reader desire a follow-up.

To Newspaper—Community Problem

Dear Phil Davison:

If I were to dine at your home and spill drinks and crumbs all over the carpet, you'd be reluctant ever to see me as a guest again.

If the kids next door were invited to a neighbor's pool and dropped candy wrappers and soda cans in the water, they'd quickly be blacklisted.

If I hired an electrician and he flicked cigar ashes on the floor, that would be the last time he'd be a candidate for a job in my house.

We have certain choices when it comes to the quality of the environment in which we reside. Unfortunately, those choices don't seem to exist in the workplace. If you'd like a graphic example, please come visit me in my place of business at 29 Vine Street any day of the week. What used to be a green triangle of lawn opposite our front door is a quagmire of weeds and sludge. What once passed as a hedgerow along the block, looks as though it had been raked by machine-gun fire. What were erected some years back as neatly painted trash receptacles are brimming over with refuse whose age can easily be determined by the foul patterns of mold and slime. The once clear air, buoyed by the fragrance of blossoms and pine, is sickening and laden with soot.

Needless to say, in such an environment is it any wonder that customers and service people feel no guilt about dropping crushed cigarette packs on the sidewalk, tossing scraps of paper and containers in the gutter, or letting their pets use the shrubbery as convenient latrines?

As a result of these surroundings, my business has nowhere to go but downhill. The irony is that I can hardly promote interior (or exterior) decorating from the heart of a slum. I have appealed to the Town Fathers, whose ears appear to be clogged; to the Chamber of Commerce, which suggests that I move my business; and to a noted judge, whose response was that prosecuting litterbugs is not very high on any lawyer's list.

So where do I turn next?

Dejectedly,

To Newspaper—Announcing New Product

Dear Amy:

Be my guest.

I am delighted to be able to send you samples of a brand-new product that will prevent a lot of pain and trouble for users in the sunbelt regions of the world. SunTurn™, perfected by our Skin Enhancement division after three years of research, contains oils that (as the name implies) turn away the harmful rays of the sun. At the same time, our product, which is available as a lotion or as a cream, will permit a smooth and glorious tan for those who insist on sitting in the sun.

SunTurn™ will hit the market on Memorial Day weekend. Please try it. And if you like the way it lives up to its promise, we'd appreciate a mention in your column.

With best wishes,

To a Magazine—Responding to Inquiry

Dear Mr. Jardine:

I am flattered that you have selected our firm, Carpet Collection, for inclusion in your article on employment goals and policies. In answer to your questions:

1. We comply with Equal Employment Opportunity laws and regulations not simply because we have to but because it makes good business sense to us to do so. Since our customers represent the same broad range of people in regard to such criteria as race, faith, age, sex, and ethnic background, it is important that our employees are on a parallel basis.

2. We encourage applications from disadvantaged people and have five in our employ in this classification—two who are deaf, one with a vision impairment, and two who have lost limbs in accidents. We also have a learning-disabled part-time helper who has an uncanny eye for colors and the slightest variations in tone. We find that these employees more than make up in dedication and determination whatever they may lack in physical or learning capabilities.

3. Our policy regarding age and retirement is to let older men and women continue on the job as long as they are able. Since our company is barely a year old, we have not yet had any experience in retaining "old-timers." But we do have three employees who are over 65 and one who is 77, and they are just as efficient in their jobs as their younger counterparts.

4. We are "multilingual" only in the sense that we have several employees who can speak Spanish, French, and German, respectively. If we had numerous customers who could speak little English—which we don't—we would adjust our language capabilities accordingly.

If you want more information, let me know. In any case, feel free to publish these facts or edit them at your discretion.

Sincerely,

To Newsletter—Announcing Awards

Dear Ms. Setzer:

As an enthusiastic reader of the *SBB Newsletter*, familiar with the topics you cover regularly, I think it would be quite appropriate for you to recognize the accomplishments of three of our salespersons in your forthcoming issue. The facts are as follows:

Galloway Reference Books Ltd. has just awarded Gold Success Seals to three of its most active salespersons, Ms. Hilary McCown, Ms. Vera Randall, and Mr. Everett Maxwell. Ms. McCown and Ms. Randall had sales of more than $400,000 for the six-month period from January through June, and Mr. Maxwell's sales exceeded $350,000. In keeping with its policy of offering sales positions to disadvantaged persons, GRB is especially pleased to announce that of these recipients, Ms. Randall is deaf and Mr. Maxwell is visually impaired.

If you would like further information, please call me.

Sincerely,

To Newspaper—Statement of Company Policy

Dear Mrs. Holden:

As chairman of the Deep River Group, I was greatly dismayed to receive a phone call this morning from your business editor asking why we were trying to "suppress" information about the automobile accident in which one of our officers was seriously injured following a "party" at our office.

I assure you, first, that there was no party, social event, or other function on our premises. The injured man had, in fact, just finished making a presentation to the Board of Directors and was on his way home. When our public relations manager was phoned by your newspaper and asked for details, he responded that he had no information at all about the accident and that it was our company's policy not to divulge any data about employees until (1) the facts were in hand and (2) it was determined that the inquiry was valid and did not jeopardize a person's right to privacy.

If you will call me, I will provide the necessary information to the extent that it does not invade the injured man's privacy or compromise his integrity.

Sincerely,

To Newspaper—Responding to Inaccurate Editorial

Dear Mr. Haskell:

Your editorial, "The Cancer Mill," was not only grossly inaccurate and misleading, but was an atrocious example of how the press can distort facts and alarm the public. It is one thing to alert people to life-threatening substances and habits, but quite another thing to point an accusing finger directly at a supposed villain in order to satisfy some egotistical editorial urge to make the *Carrier* look like an investigative champion of heroic causes.

Let me set the record straight. Wilson Chemical, Inc., does not "add a potent dye to its antifungal spray to make it look as natural and fresh as a sprig of mint." Our products contain no pigments whatsoever. The "death by cancer of two Wilson employees on the production line" had nothing whatsoever to do with company functions. One died of lung cancer from smoking. The other had complications from an earlier illness and a cancerous condition that had been diagnosed before she ever joined the company. Last, we have never in our 14-year history "marketed products judged to be risky by the Texas Agricultural Testing Board." The Board was a body established temporarily to undertake experimental research in the field of plant foods and was never involved with the examination of pesticides.

Wilson Chemical is a recognized leader in its field and develops and produces its products in a responsible manner, adhering strongly to all safety standards and practices. We—including the company's 345 employees—deeply resent being erroneously labeled by the *Carrier* as threats to society.

Sincerely,

To Newspaper—Responding to Published Misinformation

Dear Dean Stribling:

It is my understanding that you are the faculty adviser at the university and, as such, would be concerned about the accuracy of remarks made on the editorial page of your undergraduate newspaper, the *Big Blue Press.*

As you are probably aware, last Friday's edition ran an editorial headlined "Local Store Barons Assume All Parents Are Rich". Along with my fellow merchants, I take strong issue with the statement that our prices reflect "what the market will bear" rather than the fair value of the merchandise offered. During the past few days, several of us have carefully studied our prices in Durham versus those in the shopping center of St. Edmonds, which is frequented by very few college students. We were interested to see that our prices—for merchandise ranging from clothing and small appliances to electronic items and sports goods—were actually *lower*. And we know that, without question, we hold more sales, offer more "twofers," and extend more personal credit (often at our own risk).

In closing, I'd like to emphasize that there is no "widespread collusion" in our price structures. Were we to indulge in this infamous practice, we would soon lose our licenses, thanks to the watchful eyes of the state business regulators. I hope you will ask your editors to be more professional in the future if they intend to publish a newspaper worthy of the name.

Sincerely,

To Newspaper—Responding to Unfavorable Article

Dear Elmer Reynolds, Editor:

Your pun-pal columnist Dottie Woodward has too many tongues in her cheek to be let loose on subjects any more serious than selecting goldfish bowls. While her recent column, "Parking on a Dollar, Not a Dime," was geared for a lot of belly laughs, it was hardly an appropriate place to refer to my well-researched traffic proposal as "Fatty, the Fast Fooder's Folly."

The data on which I based my proposal were taken from studies made by mass transportation engineers from RPI who had been selected by the Cook Regional Vehicular Commission to study traffic congestion and flow in key locations, including ours.

Just because I run a restaurant service and am more concerned than many in town may be by the parking problems of customers and suppliers, I do not need to be labeled a "rush-hour gourmet whose thoughts are as hasty as the fast foods he serves." Perhaps dotty Dottie could spend her time more commendably sweeping your floor than insulting the intelligence of your readers.

Yours truly,

To Television Station—Controversial Issue

Dear Mr. Samson:

The viewers of your "Topics Today" show deserve better than to be conned by you into believing that the solution to the drug problems in our community can be achieved by forcing businesses to ante up a share of their profits to support an "anti drug committee." Our company has always supported worthy causes, but we are not in any position to pour money into harebrained schemes such as the one you propose. In the matter of drugs, we are opposed to the proposal of your recent "Topics Today" guest, who suggests a "citizen's committee" to oversee the county substance abuse program. That program will fail, we are convinced, if it is administered by lay persons rather than health and medical professionals with proven track records in treating drug addicts and alcoholics.

If you come up with a sensible program, we'll gladly reconsider a donation.

Sincerely yours,

To Television Station—Disagreeing with Editorial Statement

Dear Harvey and the Staff of "Harvey Speaks Out":

Your biased, untimely, and ludicrous on-air attack on "nepotism" in our community made it sound as though it were incestuous for relatives to work in the same company. What is wrong with a husband and wife going to work under the same roof when they also share a roof at home? What is so offensive about a brother and sister driving buses for the same public transportation line? Why should not a father and son be part of a team working in a corporate accounting department?

I am astonished that you did not mention Nelson & Sons on your ill-advised program, as the ultimate in companies favoring that despicable art of nepotism. We are a family company. We encourage husbands and wives to work for us, not to mention mothers and daughters, uncles and aunts, and in a couple of cases even ex-spouses. Wow!

"Nepotism" used to be an ugly word, used to charge organizations with family-tie favoritism to the disadvantage of employees not related by blood or marriage to others on the payroll. But that concept has long since gone down the drain, along with one-week vacations and six-day work weeks.

If you decide to do a follow-up show on nepotism, why don't you interview some of us "nepotics" from Nelson & Sons.

By the way, all of us relatives engage in collusion and conspiracy to beat out the non-relatives by producing a product in which you'll find a great deal of nepotism mentioned: We make Bibles!

Sincerely,

To a Doctor—Suggesting Response to Newspaper Inquiry

Dear Dr. Sterling:

You are undoubtedly besieged by requests from the media to let their people visit Jim B. in the hospital. And I can understand why they want a firsthand account from a popular personality who was involved in a serious accident. But I am greatly concerned about his physical condition, despite his seemingly hale and hearty appearance and his eagerness to give interviews. As I understand it from his physician and surgeon, any exertion, however small, puts him at risk and lessens his chances of early recovery.

Please hold off on visits for at least a week.

Sincerely,

To a Competitor—Questioning Stand on an Issue

Dear Edson:

Receiving my copy of the Charlotte *Post* in the mail this morning, I read with some misgivings about your speech to the Rotary on Friday. While it is too late to undo what has been done, I hasten to caution you about the sensitive nature of the remarks you made about our recycled paper shopping bags versus those made from plastic. You may already have gotten some repercussions. Recent laboratory tests have proven that, when discarded, the plastic material does not disintegrate nearly as fast as was originally claimed—and certainly not as fast as paper. The bald fact of the matter is that a lot more research and development will be needed before manufacturers can make that type of plastic environmentally acceptable. In the meantime, recycled paper—which we use on this stationery as well as in our shopping bags—has passed all environmental tests with flying colors.

Sincerely,

Canceling Magazine Subscription for Inept Reporting

Dear Mr. Shutt:

When I subscribed to *Outdoor World* more than ten years ago, it was because I was delighted with your quarterly's handling of sensitive ecological subjects and the obvious professional knowledge of nature displayed by your authors. During the last three years, however, the awareness and sensitivity have steadily eroded, and your publication has become "popularized," I suppose to broaden your advertising potential and income.

I continued to subscribe and pretend you were what you used to be. But the whole editorial content continued sliding. The last straw was the article in your April/May/June issue, "Save the Birches." Whoever wrote it couldn't discern a birch from a beech, let alone save it. And the procedures he outlined were in direct contradiction to those that experienced tree experts recommend.

So, please cancel my subscription as of this date.

Sincerely,

LISTINGS IN DIRECTORIES

Describing the Company—Regional Directory

Dear Mr. Latano:

The following is a brief description of our company, which we give you permission to publish in your directory:

Designs for Action is a package-design firm whose expertise lies in the layout, rendering, and production of small containers for use by speciality shops and other retail and wholesale outlets whose requirements are print runs of 100,000 or less. Recent clients have included producers of jams and other preserves, hand-crafted toys, fruit-scented skin lotions, and tie-dyed sports shirts with local emblems. For information contact Art Leavitt at 660-1111.

We would appreciate seeing a copy of the typesetter's proof at your convenience, just to check for accuracy. Thanks for your interest in *Designs for Action*.

Sincerely,

Describing the Company—Chamber of Commerce Directory

Dear Ms. Charlene:

Thank you for your inquiry about Borchard & Peate Fine Woodworking Ltd. If you are going to include us in the Chamber of Commerce annual business directory, you can explain that our firm hires 12 people, 8 of them experienced woodworkers or experts in woodcrafts. We have been in business on the Peninsula for 15 years, originally simply as two friends and artisans who were available to repair antiques and refinish fine furniture. Today B&F undertakes what we advertise as "quality work at reasonable prices." That includes custom-built furniture, cabinetry, kitchens, cabinet refacing, antique restoration and repair, and built-ins. During the past two years, we have also engaged in the restoration of wooden boats, which have lately increased greatly in price and demand, and the rebuilding of shelves, cabinets, bunks, and other wooden elements of smallboat interiors.

Sincerely,

Describing the Industry—Student Handbook

Dear Dean Simmons:

As you requested, I offer the following synopsis as a suitable description of our field of activities relating to the development and application of ultrasound in an increasing number of high-tech corporations.

The ultrasonics industry was developed when it was discovered that certain sound waves could be used for a variety of purposes, including the nondestructive testing of materials, cleaning small parts of jewelry, serving as a safe replacement for X-rays, and even enabling the surgical removal of tissue within the body without having to cut through the skin and outer flesh. Ultrasonics is the study and application of the energy of sound waves vibrating at frequencies greater than 20,000 cycles per second, which is beyond the range of the human ear. With only a primary course in ultrasound, totaling not more than 15 hours, a business school graduate would be qualified to serve in any business-oriented or non-scientific department of a company in the ultrasonics industry.

I hope this fills the bill, but if you need anything further, please let me know.

Cordially,

Describing the Locale—Real Estate Directory

Dear Mr. Riggs:

Orangeburg was conceived in the 1920s as an "American Riviera," lying as it does along a wide, sandy beach with numerous inlets and waterways and a sunny and warm climate during most of the year. The first homes were designed in the Mediterranean style, with later emphasis on the Spanish and some elements of Dutch Colonial. One important advantage stems from the original planners' use of broad avenues with central park strips in both the residential and commercial sections of this town of 45,000 people. This overall layout not only increases the feeling of spaciousness but minimizes parking problems, even during the busiest seasons of the year. Today, every new building plan requires approval from the Board of Architects, which has banned billboards and neon signs. Orangeburg Township includes a lake, a combined zoological/horticultural garden, three major parks, and a cultural center. A small industrial complex, confined to the northwestern part of the town, houses three office buildings, two small technology plants, and a railroad/truck terminal.

Sincerely,

Profile of Sales and Marketing Staff—Association Yearbook

Dear Mrs. Carmichael:

As you requested, I have written the following profile of our sales staff for inclusion in your *Yearbook* for 1991, "in 100 words or fewer":

Marlborough Motors was founded by the father of the present owner, Keith Marlborough, in 1976, with a sales manager and three salesmen. Today, it has two sales managers and eight salespersons, all of them specialists in the sales and servicing of passenger cars, vans, pickup trucks, and other vehicles. The youngest of these staff members has been in automotive sales since 1986, while the most experienced is a veteran of more than 30 years in the business. Mr. Marlborough was himself a salesman and manager for 18 years before taking over the business from his father.

Please feel free to edit this text in any way you deem appropriate.

Sincerely,

PUBLIC RELATIONS

One of the joys of corresponding with people in public relations is that you are more likely to get a response, even if the topic of your letter is of little interest to the recipient. One of the unwritten rules for public relations practitioners is that they be communicative, whether by phone, letter, or other means. As one p.r. executive confessed, "We can't afford not to respond, because who knows where we might find future clients!"

This kind of outlook does not mean, however, that you can be overly casual in making your point. Though they may be creative, affable, and open, public relations people are first and foremost business specialists. They are concerned with facts as well as in some instances fantasies, and the bottom line as well as economic generalities. The more specific and expressive you can be in your correspondence, the more likely you are to get productive results. If you have hang-ups about writing letters, this is one field of business in which you can usually obtain good responses with a phone call.

Transmittal Letter with Sample Press Release

Dear Sarah:

Since we have no public relations manager or anyone on our staff experienced in this field, we hope that from time to time you can help us with p.r. and publicity. As a starter, we'd like to send a press release to broadcasting stations and newspapers throughout Beaufort County and possibly the northeastern portion of Harmon County.

Our purpose is to announce the fact that all of the cartons, packages, and wrappings, we use for the household products we process are (1) biodegradable and (2) formed from recycled papers or plastics.

To give you an idea of what we have in mind, I enclose a release that was sent to me recently by one of our suppliers in Michigan who knows our objective. You could almost type this as is, substituting our name and address for Smith's.

Sincerely,

Enclosure

THE A. B. C. SMITH COMPANY
10 Orchard Row
Pinehaven Springs, MI 49500

For Immediate Release   *Contact: Sandy Richards*

CONSUMERS HAIL USE OF RECYCLED, DISPOSABLE PACKAGING

According to the chairman of the County Ecology Commission, retailers and consumers in the area have been profuse in welcoming a recent decision of the A. B. C. Smith Company in regard to its packaging policies. Starting this week, the company will package its food and household products only in materials that have been recycled and are fully biodegradable. The decision relates to large shipping cartons and containers, as well as to packages, wrappings, and labels for products consumers themselves buy and take home.

"Our aim," says Roger Smith, president of the company, "is to play a greater role in reducing pollution, avoiding waste, and conserving forests and other sources of raw materials used in packaging." He strongly urges that consumers pay as much attention to the way a product is packaged as to the price and contents. The company has initiated a special indoctrination program for its route salespersons. Once knowledgeable about the environmental benefits of recycled, biodegradable packages, they can then more easily convince buyers at retail stores that they, too, should consider this factor in the brands of products they select for their shelves.

The time will come, forecasts Smith, when people will be as much influenced by a "recycled" label on a package as they are about assurances that a food product lacks cholesterol or a household product contains no hazardous chemicals.

Response to Inquiry about Public Relations Event

Dear Ms. Tallibay:

Your inquiry was well timed because normally, at this early spring season, we have hosted our "Indoctrination Cruise" off Block Island to acquaint the press with our marine operations and plans for the spring, summer, and fall seasons. Unfortunately, inflation has finally caught up with Castaway Cruises, and we find that we just don't have enough surplus in the budget to continue this very popular press event. However, we would like to invite you to a special showing and reception at Mystic Seaport on June 10 from 5:00–7:30 P.M. At that time, we will show some exciting footage taken by skippers during last year's single-handed, globe-circling sailing race. We will be serving drinks and light refreshments. So we hope you can join us.

With our best wishes,

Apology for Tactless Statement by Company Spokesperson

Dear Major Bambard:

As a former submariner, I hasten to inform you that the tasteless remarks about the military base made by one of my colleagues in his speech before the Lion's Club do not in any way reflect my attitude or the outlook of my compatriots. His comments were, in fact, totally opposite to my own views on the subject. While I acknowledge that we are fortunate enough to live in a free country where a speaker has every right to his own opinion, we have already made it clear to our fellow executive that we question his judgment in expressing his sentiments as he did.

Please accept our apologies for the incident and any embarrassment it may have caused to you and other local residents who are in the military service.

Sincerely,

Denying Conflict-Of-Interest Charge

Dear Mr. Blanchett:

It was with shock and disbelief that I read the report of the Media Review Board accusing me of representing, at the same time, two different clients who are competitive and have harshly divergent interests. Your members have acted rashly and without provocation. Most assuredly, they have not gone to the trouble of obtaining facts before taking such a groundless and preposterous stand.

If it were not for the fact that the Committee's inference jeopardizes my professional standing, I would not even bother to respond to the accusation. You say that I am guilty of a conflict of interest by taking an assignment with two organizations that are in direct competition with each other and whose policies are poles apart. The fact is that I am affiliated solely with your agency in the promotion of print media, as I have been for many years in the past. My "relationship" with your competitor has nothing whatsoever to do with the promotion of broadcasting or any related business, function, outlook, or policies. I am serving as an adviser to an employee group that is engaged in fighting drugs in our community. The fact that some of its members are in the world of broadcasting is beside the point.

For this commitment, I receive no remuneration other than my personal satisfaction with helping people in trouble. And I certainly need no smug reprimands to force me to quit.

Sincerely,

Description of Presentation to Chamber of Commerce

Dear Charlotte:

The five subject areas I will cover during the two hours you have allotted me will be the basic functions of a press lettershop service such as mine. They include

- *Printing:* how to produce a personalized mailer by laser printing when supplied with the necessary units to appear in the finished piece, such as letterhead, logotype, slogan, symbols or thumbnail graphics, and personal signature

- *Folding:* why this simple procedure is often mishandled, but when done properly can result in lower costs, easier opening, a more favorable impression, and less work

- *Inserting:* A labor-intensive, often overly expensive process when done manually, which can be achieved cheaply and almost instantly with state-of-the-art equipment

- *Sealing:* A time-consuming, often messy job that ruins the appearance of a mailing, but can be automated and completed at little cost

- *Metering:* the proper way to plan for and use postage meters and electronic weighing to effect postage savings that can lop off as much as one-third of the cost of mailing, along with a look at current postal rates and options

- *Mailing list management:* how to determine which lists are most productive and which prospective recipients are most likely to generate orders or anticipated action

I will close with a brief question-and-answer session, timing my presentation so we will have about 10 minutes for this. If you have any suggestions about my participation, as planned, let's discuss them.

Cordially,

Industry Outlook—Chamber of Commerce Speech

TO: Phil Sanger
FROM: Debbie Plante
RE: Chamber of Commerce Speech

Reviewing the subject and content of recent speeches delivered before Chamber members, it is quite evident that the audience is not really interested in statistics and survey data, regardless of how well these might document the speaker's comments. Therefore, I think you should avoid giving out any economic and financial figures or citing any statistics, most especially since the only ones we could supply you with would tend to be negative and discouraging. Here are some positives to express:

- Tourism has declined in many regions because of terrorist activities and threats. However, the area served by the Chamber is likely to benefit by that decline by attracting visitors to a place where no such perils have surfaced.

- During the past three months more than half our advertising budget has focused on the benefits of travel and vacations in the region served by this Chamber.

- Two of the towns in the area were recently listed in *Travel & Health* magazine as being among the 50 locales in the United States with the cleanest air and purest water.

- An article in the May issue of *Beach and Surf* described the region's public beaches as "so clean you could walk a hundred yards without seeing a candy wrapper or cigarette butt in the sand."

- The federal government has, during the past five years alone, designated more than ten residences and churches in the area as national historic sites.

To sum it all up, you might add that our agency is willing to help the Chamber fulfill requests for information about the area when it has its hands full during the height of the tourist season. That pinpoints our belief that there really will be a big—and welcome—crunch.

MEETINGS AND SEMINARS

Persuasiveness is often a valuable gift when you are writing letters in this subject area. You often have to use great tact and some creative flattery to get readers to respond affirmatively to invitations to participate. And if you yourself are in the position of being invited to make a speech or attend a function outside your field of interest, you sometimes have to be quite ingenious in the way you turn down the offer, yet hurt no one's feelings. Here are some characteristic examples.

Invitation to Participate in a Seminar

Dear Dr. Thorndike:

It has been almost a decade since the Engineering Society hosted the heavy metals research seminar that stimulated such widespread acclaim and resulted in some innovative revisions in the ASME Code Book. Looking through the Achievement Reports of the ten-day seminar, I noted with interest that you were the committee chairman for the iron and steel studies.

With this in mind, I have been asked by ASME to invite you to participate once more in a seminar that we feel will be even more meaningful and productive than the last one. The proceedings will take place at the beginning of next year, probably from February 15 to 24. Once again, the site will be Tucson, Arizona, where an entirely new research and testing center was constructed two years ago. We can guarantee that the surroundings will be appealing, the facilities superlative, and the programs exciting.

I sincerely hope that this is an event you just cannot turn down and will await your response with anticipation. In the meantime, I enclose a brochure describing the laboratories and residential accommodations that will be available for all who participate.

Cordially,

Invitation to Sales and Marketing Seminar

Dear Tyler:

Once again, the sales and marketing group invites you to attend our annual seminar, which this year will be held on June 17 and 18 at the Biltmore Club. I know you'll want to be on hand because the program will include group discussions with Dr. Horatio Barger, president of your alma mater, and Vaughn Marsella, newly elected chairman of Southwestern Gas & Electric and author of the forthcoming book, the *Energy Conservation Crisis*.

Anticipating your acceptance, I have assigned you a room in the Palmetto Wing, which you found so convenient and comfortable last year.

Sincerely,

Invitation to a Reluctant Attendee

Dear Chester:

You are going to call me names and insist that I am badgering you into an enterprise that you want no part of and whose objectives are foreign to your interests.

But, believe me, I have given the matter considerable thought and am looking at the picture objectively and realistically.

We are holding a joint meeting of the Property Owners' Association and the Tenants' Board on Tuesday evening, October 16 at 7:30, to try to resolve the question of taxes on public lands used by all of us for recreational purposes. You are the only person in either group who was in residence when the POA was founded in 1978 and, as such, your recollections of the original covenants are valuable and could make a difference in the proceedings.

I know that you have steadfastly resisted involvement in the Association's activities. But this is a case in which you could do a service to yourself as well as to your fellow property owners. I assure you that we will preempt no more than 20 minutes of your time, and probably less.

For this, we will offer you a drink and a sandwich—and, of course, our thanks for your participation.

Hopefully,

Follow-up Letter to a Reluctant Attendee

Dear Chester:

Although I had hoped that my letter would induce you to attend our Property Owners' Association meeting, your silence is mute evidence that you do not wish to be involved or bothered with such matters.

Perhaps the following data will motivate you to change your mind. Yesterday, the county notified the POA that the taxes on the property in question will be $8,600 next year—if we cannot resolve the dispute right away. Apportioning that amount among the 89 individuals who own property here means that each and every one of us will have to shell out almost $100 apiece—you and your wife included. And that is just for one year.

Isn't it worth 15 minutes of your time to keep that money in your pocket?

Sincerely,

Recruiting Speakers for a Seminar

Dear Dr. Antonini:

You may recall that we first met at the American Dental area seminar in Houston last June, and again at the reception for the new dental clinic in Austin in September. At that time, you mentioned that you maintained a list of dentists and other specialists who were available for speaking engagements before lay audiences when the programs warranted their appearance.

My dental supply firm is planning to sponsor a series of orientation talks and presentations on periodontal mouth care and gum health to be given in public high schools in our region to audiences of young people between the ages of 14 and 18. While we do have a few speaker candidates in mind, what we need most are dentists who are not only professionally knowledgeable but who can relate to young students. Is it possible that your list contains some qualified candidates who would be willing to speak on this subject and to this audience?

Sincerely,

Thank You Note Confirming Plans

Dear Senator Dunwoodie:

The members of the small-business commission join me in thanking you for your positive response to our invitation. I enclose a newspaper clipping from Sunday's *Tribune* that aptly describes two of our recent projects.

As planned, I shall be at the Airways Commuter Terminal of the airport at 11:45 on the fifth to meet your plane and drive you to the Chamber of Commerce building. Our luncheon meeting will be at 12:30, and I'll have you back at the airport for your return flight at 4:30.

Appreciatively,

Request to Speak at Seminar

Dear Mr. Selectman Trottan:

Judge Farbison has informed me that the County Development Board is hosting a series of seminars on the economic development of our region. As I understand it, one panel of speakers will be assigned to talking about products and services that have enhanced our way of life in Parsons County.

I would very much like to be considered as one who can talk about factors that have greatly reduced air pollution and improved the quality of the air we breathe—both in our homes and at work. How should I enter my name as a candidate for participation?

Sincerely yours,

Canceling Program on Short Notice

Although the writer's secretary has phoned those who planned to attend, he writes this letter to assuage any bad feelings.

Dear Arnold:

We scheduled the symposium as a vital step to take.

We disrupted the plans of two dozen people who had to rearrange their own daily affairs in order to accommodate two extra days at the end of June.

We touted the conference as the most important event on our spring business calendar.

And now I have called everything off!

The fact is that I have no choice. Our legal consultant has just advised me that a competitor has challenged our right to the patent we were to discuss at the symposium. Although we'll win in the end, apparently any such group discussion would be considered to be "collusion" until such time as our rights are legally confirmed.

We hope to reactivate our plans in the fall.

Regretfully,

Request for More Professional Orientation Seminars

Dear Sol:

While looking through the *Association Newsletter* for the fourth quarter, I was encouraged to see how many orientation seminars are being planned next year on topics relating to waste disposal and the environment. But, upon further reading, I was discouraged to note how many of these are scheduled in the Northeast, on the West Coast, and in the Midwest, with almost none in our region here in the Southeast, where our firm is certainly the most active.

So I propose that we take the bull by the horns and create our own seminar, inviting other environmental firms to participate to spread the costs and improve the quality of the lectures. Atlanta would be a good location for the program. I'd be happy to make an informal survey to see how many firms would be interested and whom we could enlist to lead the proposed seminars.

Does this sound possible, and practical?

Sincerely,

Invitation to Participate in Trade Show

TO: Roland Timbermann
FROM: Al Weir
RE: Caring: The Ultimate Homecare Exposition

Most commercial shows and exhibits are DUDS—*D*ull, *U*norganized, *D*reary, and *S*illy. But this latest exposition is being put together by a group of experts who know their stuff, and most particularly their audience. I've done my homework and learned that they have organized 18 shows in the past three years and haven't had a flop yet.

The theme of the show is such that what we have to offer is of direct interest to the people who'll be attending, not only for their offices but their homes as well. The focus will be on such matters as carpet renovating, upholstery cleaning, tile stripping, floor waxing, and soil proofing. What more could we ask for? It's all tailor made for our kind of business. Let's take advantage of a sure thing? I can show you my plan of action anytime.

Purchase of Booth for Town's Spring Fair

Dear Maria Mannix:

We understand that you are the person to contact to arrange for space at the annual town fair. Our company, the LeatherWorks, would like a booth described as "Size D," which is listed as having dimensions of 15 feet in front and 12 feet in depth. If possible, we'd appreciate a location in the tent marked "Apparel" rather than "Crafts." Most of our leather products are belts and accessories, and we have found from past experience that our sales are better when we are in an area where prospective customers are looking for clothing instead of art or decorative objects.

We wish you much success in organizing this popular community event.

Sincerely,

PROPOSALS FOR LOCAL BUSINESS COOPERATION

Data Processing to Reduce Costs

Dear Jake:

At Chamber of Commerce meetings and industry sessions, you and I have often exchanged mutual gripes about the rising costs of doing business compared with the way things used to be. I would bet my last dollar that computerized data processing is one of your biggest profit drains, just as mine is. But I think we can beat the odds if you and I and perhaps three or four others in various parts distribution fields could share one system large enough to handle all our combined orders.

I have described this problem to the technician who has been servicing our equipment, and he suggested that we meet with him to discuss our current needs, future goals, and budget limitations. Since he represents four major manufacturers of equipment and holds a recent electronics degree, he seems like a reliable adviser to whom we can turn.

A letter similar to this one has gone off to 12 other parts distribution firms like ours, and I expect to receive a positive response from perhaps half of them. If you are at all interested in exploring the idea with us, please get in touch. Monday the 11th at 10:30 has been set as a tentative date for and initial discussion.

Cordially,

Action on Local Traffic Issue

Dear Mac:

Increasingly over the past couple of years, I have had the distinct impression that business would be better, parking would be easier, pedestrians would be safer, and life would be more pleasant if Market Road could be changed into a one-way street. Not content with the fact that several of my neighbors in business have felt the same way, I did some informal research on my own. My first step was to talk with merchants in White Plains on three streets that had been made one-way last year. They were unanimous in their approval, and several said quite bluntly they wished the city had made the change long ago. My second step was to visit the County Engineer's Office and browse through a tremendous file of data on city street designs, including a massive file on one-way traffic. And my third step was to ask my son-in-law, who is an executive with the Gallup Organization, to interview a sampling of local people—motorists and pedestrians alike—to get candid opinions about one-way and two-way streets in our town. The comments were interesting and supportive of the idea.

All of this has convinced me that we—those of us with business interests on Market Road—should band together to petition City Hall to approve the change. To that end, we are holding an informal meeting in the council room of the Lion's Club on Saturday, September 14, at 10:00 A.M. I hope you will join us.

Sincerely,

Increasing Local Security

Dear Mr. Thorling:

Twelve years ago, when the developers of Park West began constructing the office buildings familiar to us today as our places of business, the area was almost rural and inhabited during the day only by business and professional people with valid reasons for being on site. Since then, with the unexpected growth and urban sprawl of the city and the construction of overly commercial strips practically in our backyard, we have witnessed the increasing incursion of outsiders—not all of whom have been welcome. Many, of course, are promoters, sales representatives, and others seeking to peddle wares and services. Unfortunately, we are also under assault by people whose motives are suspect, as evidenced by the steady increase in break-ins, thefts, vandalism, and in some cases, physical abuse.

Having consulted at length with city police officials and the Park West security office, a group of us have formed PWW (Park West Watchers) as a step toward foiling further criminal encroachments. Like you, we are tenants or owners or managers of offices in the Park West complex. As we have been told by the experts, a multitude of alert eyes and ears is the best deterrent to crime, particularly when the effort is well coordinated and reinforced with an effective system of immediate accurate communication. The purpose of this letter, therefore, is to urge you to join us as a member of PWW. Participation consists simply of learning some reporting basics: what to be on the lookout for, what to report, when to report, and where to report.

There are no membership dues, no bylaws, no formal meetings. Simply give us your name and address, by phone or mail, and we will send you further details. We do urge you to join us. The effectiveness of our anticrime venture is directly influenced by the percentage of people who join in this effort.

Sincerely,

COMMUNITY INVOLVEMENT

Letters that relate to civic affairs are of special importance because they reach out into the community and act as "calling cards" for the writers and their organizations. They are, in effect, public relations media since they reflect a great deal about management, policies, and outlooks. If the writers of the letters and/or their organizations are going to be involved, it must be clear to what extent they expect to do so. If they are regretting requests for participation or contributions, they must do so graciously, forthrightly, and without closing too many doors.

This category of "community involvement" covers a wide range of subjects, events, people, and places. These range from fund raising and volunteer recruitment to hospital aid programs, Chamber of Commerce participation, environmental enhancement, municipal beautification, public meetings, adult education courses, help for the handicapped and the homeless, preserving historical sites, establishing behavior codes, fighting crime, improving library resources, fighting pollution, combating drugs, planning fairs and festivals, and keeping the streets clean.

Walking the tightrope of community involvement can be tricky, especially for those who really want to help improve their communities, but are hard pressed to find enough time to build their own businesses. Well-worded and well-timed letters, however, can go a long way toward keeping a busy executive's professional affairs in balance.

QUESTIONS TO ASK YOURSELF
ABOUT BECOMING INVOLVED

1. What percentage of my time can I devote to community affairs and volunteer work?

2. How can I be a good communicator and a catalyst to enlist the help of others to make my contributions and time more valuable?

3. In order of priority, which worthy causes are most important to me personally? To my business? To the community in which we work?

4. Which of my skills and what career experiences can offer the greatest contributions?

5. What kinds of letters and other communications can I generate and produce to motivate the most effective action?

6. Which people are the most important for me to reach?

Community service letters fall into several categories, including those that request funds, plea for assistance, reject a plea for assistance, offer a productive action plan, recruit helpers and participants, review proposals, organize arrangements, praise programs, and criticize programs. It goes without saying that the composition, tone, and context of the letters you write will determine the reception they get at the other end of the line and will largely determine whether your intentions are realized.

HOW TO DO IT

1. Do enough homework so you address your letter to the most appropriate person.

2. Introduce yourself and describe your position if the addressee is not likely to know you.

3. Explain the letter's purpose concisely and as briefly as possible.

4. Indicate what benefits will ensue to the community.

5. Refer to an enclosure if such is necessary to present the subject more clearly.

6. Make it clear just what is expected of the recipient.

7. Enclose a self-addressed, stamped envelope if that will elicit a quicker, or more promising, response.

Like the tip of the iceberg, the *writing* of a letter relating to community service is only a small proportion of the project at hand. The larger, unseen dimension is the *research* that should be undertaken before you write a first draft, or even an outline. Unless you are already very familiar with the project, the circumstances, and the current situation, you need to spend time with your homework. Here is where—if you are a busy owner or manager of a business—you can enlist the aid of a business associate, family member, or perhaps an already active participant in the project to provide the data you need.

What if you have to send the same letter to more than one addressee, as in the case with fund raising or recruiting volunteers? The most effective procedure is to use actual names, such as "Dear Mary" or "Dear Dr. Johnson" rather than "Dear Friend" or "Dear Member." If you can personalize the letter in any way, perhaps by adding a postscript, by all means do so. The extra effort is worthwhile if the project is important to you and the community. Perhaps you would do well to concentrate your efforts. If any statistics are available, for example, you might be more successful focusing on the 10% of the addressees who have responded well in the past. However, when mailing multiple letters with the hope that recipients will donate money, volunteer their time, or otherwise contribute their efforts or something of value, don't be discouraged if fewer than one out of ten responds. If only 5% of your letters achieve a positive response, your success ratio is about average.

DONATIONS AND FUND RAISING

Ingenuity. Innovation. Imagination. Originality.

These are some of the key aptitudes that help writers of fund-raising letters jump from the mediocre to the sublime. Unfortunately, we cannot all be clever with words, phrases, and themes. The best approach when appealing for money or participation on behalf of worthy causes is to write in a way that is natural for you and that expresses your honest opinions. If you try too hard to be clever, you may alienate the reader. If you use humor, you risk offending people who find this no time for a joke.

Writing a letter or note to decline a request for a donation usually requires tact. Make it clear that you respect the volunteer efforts of the person to whom you are responding, but don't go into long explanations about your reasons for not giving at this time. Even more important, unless you seriously intend to give the matter further thought, don't give the impression that you might be a donor in the future.

Community Youth Organization

Dear Mr. Meeker:

"A penny for your thoughts."

That old saying seems ridiculous these days when a penny is worth so little that few people even stoop to pick one up from the sidewalk. Yet consider what just 22 of these pennies can do, even with inflation:

- They can provide a full meal for an infant.
- They can buy enough gas to transport a vanload of children 5 miles to a park.
- They can supply a paperback learning book for a fifth-grader.
- They can fill a glass with vitamin-rich juice for an undernourished orphan.
- They can do a great many other things too.

But, most important, like grains of sand forming a barrier dune, these insignificant little coins can provide mountains of assistance when multitudes of people give a little and then a little more.

Our firm was asked to come up with an idea for helping the more unfortunate young people in our community. This is it. We call our program PENNIES WITH A PURPOSE.

How many pennies can we count on from you? Or dimes? Or quarters? Or dollars?

A convenient, self-addressed envelope is enclosed for your contribution. We thank you.

Sincerely,

Books for Libraries

Dear Commissioner Quinn:

As an executive in a firm that produces papers for the book industry, I spend a great deal of time with publishers and librarians as we explore ways of improving our products for their special use. In the course of visiting libraries around the state, I have noticed that, while many library users are interested in literature on professions and careers, little space seems to be devoted to exhibiting and suggesting new books on the subject. Therefore, my colleagues and I have formed a committee to foster "Career Shelves" in conspicuous locations at public libraries. Toward that end, we have made a corporate donation and are soliciting funds from other firms for the same purpose.

If you favor the idea, we'd greatly appreciate a statement from you that we could use in promoting "Career Shelves." It would be strictly noncommercial.

Sincerely,

Historical Society

Dear Mr. McClelland:

With McClelland and Quinland about to commemorate its 25th anniversary next year, this seems like an opportune time for me to write you about a project close to the heart of history buffs throughout the state. We have four state-supported historical societies in Maynard County that also rely on financial aid and donations from private individuals and groups. One of their ongoing projects is the addition of archives and exhibits of companies with significant histories. We would therefore like to consider your company as a prime candidate for inclusion. If you are planning a company history, an exhibit, or the compilation of photographic memorabilia for your anniversary, we invite you to send us duplicate material you feel is pertinent. And, once your anniversary is concluded, you might consider donating materials from your own exhibits.

Several firms, including ours, not only like the idea but have decided to make financial donations to the Historical Society as one activity to be associated with their own anniversaries. We urge your consideration of this option as well.

Happy Anniversary!

Sincerely,

Contribution to the Community Hospital

Dear Doc:

The enclosed check for $1,000 is our annual company contribution to the Rolling Hills Hospital fund. If it's not too much paperwork, we'd like to earmark it for improvements in the children's ward in the East Wing.

I'm sorry our donation is not as high as last year, but we have to base it on our end-of-the-year balance sheet, and 1991 was not the best year for us. We are hoping to improve our financial status—and our giving—next year.

With our best wishes

Contributing Used Furniture for Church Rummage Sale

Dear Reverend Edgerly:

Business has been so good at our Starlight Motel, I am happy to report, that we are completely renovating our lounge and part of the breakfast room. We are also modernizing the kitchen. As a result, we will shortly have more than 70 pieces of wooden and metal furniture and quite a few cooking utensils to dispose of. As it turns out, the business manager has learned that we can sell very few of these items, and even if we did the cost of hauling would exceed the value received in a secondhand market. So I've decided to donate the lot. My plan is to recruit volunteers for the forthcoming church Rummage Sale to transport the items from the motel to the rectory hall. There, they could be sorted, cleaned, and made presentable for the sale. I estimate that at least 75% of the items would be salable. A few remainders might then go to the church Bargain Box. And the remainder would have to be carted to the dump. But, judging from what I have seen in the motel lobby, breakfast room, and kitchen, the Rummage Sale should turn a neat profit from them.

What do you think?

In good faith,

Offering Art for a Benefit Auction

Dear Salty:

You have a big job on your hands with this year's Fan Fair. But we can make one aspect of it a little bit easier for you. As you may know, I run a company that creates props for "Grand Ole Opry" and many other radio, TV, and theatrical productions. We have some talented and ingenious artists and illustrators here, and several have offered to contribute original works of art and sculpture to you for public auction to help fund the Country Music Association.

Now we can't in all honesty claim that much of this art equals in artistry the musical skills of members of the Country Music Foundation. However, many pieces are ingenious, most are colorful, and they are all signed by their creators. All in all, they should not only bring in a tidy sum for the Association but would make for an amusing and popular event for the Fair.

Come on over and I'll show you some!

Enthusiastically,

Contributing Sports Equipment to Senior Citizens Committee

Dear Mr. Newhouse:

Your letter to our sales manager, Gordon Duffy, has been passed along to me since both my father and uncle have been active in senior citizens clubs, and we are all interested in supporting your programs in every way we can. I suggest that you, and anyone else you care to bring with you, come to my office next Thursday, the 17th. We can have lunch in our little cafeteria, and I'll then take you over to our warehouse and you can select from our regular stock the items that would be most useful to your members.

Please bear in mind, too, that we make the company playing fields and two tennis courts available to the public whenever they have not been reserved by our regular employees. I'll take you on a tour and give you the necessary information about sign-up procedures.

With every good wish,

Declining Request for Donation—Already Committed

Dear Mrs. Sebastian:

Your plea for financial aid for the "Help the Homeless" United Way program is well taken, and I appreciate your concern about a problem that has been increasing in our city, as it has elsewhere. We have closed the books on our company donations for this year, having already exceeded our budget. So there's no way we can extend our financial aid at this time. For that, I am truly sorry.

Yet there is a way in which we might give you an assist, one that involves little expenditure, but that could provide very positive and substantial assistance for home-less people. In the course of fabricating mobile homes, we frequently have older models that have been turned in by repeat customers for credit on the purchase of new models. A number of these are parked for indefinite periods of time in a lot behind our shop and are eventually repaired, remodeled, and sold as "rebuilts" at discount prices. If the city can provide parking space in a public area that has proper waste and water facilities and can be regularly patrolled, we could supply at least eight mobile homes, each one for a period of, say, six months. We would rotate these vehicles, making regular replacements as we continued our normal remodeling program.

The units we'd offer would be clean, safe, and supplied with all necessary household appliances, bunks, plumbing, waste disposers, and furnishings. They would be just as serviceable, in other words, as they had been when their previous owners turned them in. They could easily be converted, therefore, into homes for the homeless.

If you would like to pursue this proposal, please let me know.

Sincerely,

Declining Request for Donation—For Cause

Dear Mr. Trendall:

Your request to our business manager for a donation for your "Purify Our Streams" campaign has been assigned to me, since I am in the best position of any of our officers here to explain why we cannot comply with your request. As a trout fisherman myself, I have long been familiar with the work your society has been doing to outlaw pollutants and clean up our region's streams, lakes, and other freshwater bodies. Along with many other sports fishermen, I commend you for your efforts and your accomplishments. In the past, I have made personal donations to your causes and will continue to do so.

However, we as a company cannot give public support to your current program. As you must surely know, members of your society were instrumental in establishing a "road block" to the plans we had instituted to construct a small reservoir to provide water for our North Field vineyards in time of drought. While the Society had its reasons, some of them realistic, it was felt by our company agronomists, in toto, that your position was extreme and that the proposed reservoir would in no way violate environmental regulations or the spirit of the law. Having just gone through a period of drought with less than adequate emergency water supplies, we have felt the pinch severely. Were we to make a donation to the "Purify Our Streams" campaign, we would surely have a mutiny on our hands right here at company headquarters.

Sorry, but I wish you well.

Sincerely,

Declining an Invitation to Join a Fund-raising Drive

Dear Dr. Nobosky:

Knowing how unstintingly you have given your time to medical research and health programs for the aged, we deeply regret that we cannot participate in your proposed fund-raising drive. We are a small company, with fewer than 30 employees, and hence have to allocate our public service commitments more sparingly than larger corporations. Since we have only recently agreed to assign six of our managers and supervisors to helping the United Fund this year, we simply cannot stretch our joint community involvement any further.

We do extend every good wish to you in your work and trust that you will find many willing volunteers.

Cordially,

To Better Business Bureau—Verifying an Unfamiliar Charity

Dear Mr. Cronin:

As owner of the Crown County Bottling Company, I encourage my employees to contribute funds or time to worthy causes. To that end, I annually ask the editor of our quarterly magazine, *CCBC News*, to print a short, informative article for employees, which is really a listing and description of various charities and institutions that regularly request donations from consumers. We don't try to influence anyone's philanthropic habits, but simply to give readers enough information so they can make their own judgments.

Recently, we have received inquiries from several people who have been asked to give money or sign up as volunteers for an organization that is unfamiliar to us. This is the *North Country Recycling Association*. We can find no address, phone number, or ready reference. The organization is apparently quite new. Can you give us a reading on its makeup, goals, membership, and needs? We welcome any data you have.

Sincerely,

INVITATIONS

The following model letters have been selected to provide a range of typical invitations of the kind that are pertinent to small businesses.

To Participate in Local Historical Event

Dear Michael:

Normally, my partners would look askance at my writing a letter with a *cooperative* tone to one of our most aggressive retail competitors (i.e., you). In this case, though, I don't think they can charge collusion or collaboration with the enemy. Very few people realize it, but there is a local "Fourth of July" that is vital to our very being, even though it may pale as insignificant in other locales. That was the date when, in 1823, a group of settlers, facing starvation, elected to explore further along the Continental Divide rather than retreat with the main party back to St. Louis. Had they also turned back, the whole central region of Montana would have remained total wilderness for half a century longer than it actually did.

I suggest that we combine forces, perhaps with the help of our sales departments, to publicize this local Fourth of July, for the benefit of our citizens and our community.

Can I talk you into it?

Hopefully,

To Tour Recycling Plant

An Open Invitation to the People of Greenville:

In keeping with the community's program to "Save the Forests and Plant a Tree," we are holding an open house for all interested residents at our XYZ Plant on the corner of White Birch Lane and Spruce Avenue. This is our recycling plant, where you can see at firsthand exactly how newspapers, crushed cardboard boxes, and other used paper products can be reclaimed, sanitized, and formed into new products. A lighted, moving display will also demonstrate how many trees can be saved by the recycling of just one day's input and output at this modern recycling center.

For further information, phone our receptionist at 123-4567.

Sincerely,

Accepting Invitation to Participate in Adult Education Program

Dear Dr. Couriere:

Having attended several adult education courses at Thomas Jefferson High during my 12 years of residence in Jefferson County, I compliment you on your ability to offer programs that are both instructive and diverting at the same time. Your idea of starting a new curriculum next fall for working women certainly strikes my fancy, and I am eager to participate. I would like to give further thought to the concept and scope of the fashion-and-beauty course the Adult Education Board proposes and draft an outline for consideration. It seems to me that your audience would be more interested in personal applications than in historical aspects. History might enliven the course. But, believe me, I could provide enough practical discussion material for 20 sessions, let alone 10.

Cordially,

Accepting Request to Participate in Training Program

Dear Dr. Gradley:

We greatly appreciated your interest in the facilities we have established here to train our engineers in practical applications of energy conservation methods. While it would be difficult for us to turn the seminar rooms and training grounds over to the university on any regular basis, we could certainly make them available to your science department from time to time when they are not booked by our field managers. Generally speaking, this means you would have to set up your university program on very short notice—perhaps only one week ahead of time.

I have a suggestion, though, that might be workable in a different way. Since the number of engineers attending any particular session seldom utilizes more than 50 or 60% of the seating capacity, we would be happy to have your students sit in, a few at a time. Thus, they might see and hear firsthand what petroleum engineers are actually doing to conserve oil and gas and other forms of energy.

There would be no charge to the university in either case. I suggest that your science or engineering professor stop by my office one day, and we can get into more specific detail about the possibilities.

Sincerely,

Soliciting Merchant's Cooperation— Display Health Related Literature

Dear Mr. and Mrs. Bolter:

This letter is being sent to you and about 20 other store owners in town in an effort to ask for your cooperation in an endeavor that is beneficial to all of us in this community. It is vital to educate the public about ways to combat major illnesses like heart disease, cancer, diabetes, AIDS, and Alzheimer's. For that reason, those of use who serve as volunteers had hoped that the business community would respond quickly and favorably. But the response has been sluggish, if not negative.

Like you, I am the owner and manager of my own business and have frequently displayed health-related literature and posters where they can be easily seen and read by customers. While these have in a few cases prompted other organizations to ask for display space, I have by no means been inundated by requests. Occasionally, I make room for a poster about the school play, a church supper, or the Scouts' flea market, but that is no big deal.

So, if you will let us change your mind, we'd very much appreciate enough room in your window for a poster and enough counter space for a packet or two of booklets. If things get out of hand, you can always refer aggressive solicitors to me and get them off your back.

Cordially,

Soliciting Cooperation—Historic Preservation Effort

Dear Ms. Donovan

By way of introduction, I am the owner of a local enterprise engaged in producing fibers, cloths, and yarns, 50 % of which are handmade reproductions of historic and antique materials. Many of these are purchased by historical societies that are preserving old homes and national monuments. We have been a strong supporter of this kind of preservation in our area and have just been alarmed to learn that the old structure at 116 Liberty Road, two blocks down the street from us, is to be torn down for the construction of a mall. You may not be aware of it, but this was known as the Commercial Lane Building, erected in 1772, and was first used as a trading center for locally manufactured goods.

This building most certainly should be preserved and restored to its original condition. I urge you and the other members of the Tourist Board to support us in a drive we are undertaking to prevent its demolishment. Instead of being a piece of land on which to build a store, it could well be part of a central historic theme for the mall and an important tourist attraction.

Sincerely,

Accepting Invitation to Speak at a Public Meeting

Dear Councilman Haight:

It is with great pleasure that I accept your request to join the other two speakers and talk for half an hour during the tree-planting ceremonies at Central High on Arbor Day. Of the topics you suggested for consideration, I feel best suited, from the standpoint of education and present commercial experience alike, to give your audience a practical overview of tree care in our region. My talk, therefore, will cover descriptions of types of trees that are appropriate for shade and beauty with a minimum of care and vulnerability to disease in the county. I will also talk about feeding, fertilizing, spraying, pruning, and the place of tree surgery in preserving older trees that grace one's property. In other words, my discussion will be quite practical, and I'd be happy to respond to questions.

Thanks for the opportunity to be of service.

Sincerely,

Canceling an Invitation to Speak

Dear Colonel Hudspeth:

Knowing how full your schedule is and how sought after you are as a public speaker, I cringe at the very thought of having to inform you that the Founder's Day program has been scrapped. We were all looking forward to having you as our guest and hearing your report on military developments in the Middle East. The decision to cancel the plans was entirely out of our hands, a judgment made by the college Security Board. The Board has become increasingly concerned about problems with student activists and tensions that could result in physical violence on campus during a major event like this.

You may not be entirely dismayed at the turn of events, however. Senator Lippert, who was also to have appeared on the program with you, has suggested that you be his guest at the State House that day and present your viewpoints to the Committee on International Cooperation. You might find this exchange stimulating and informative.

Sincerely,

Declining Request to Speak at a Public Meeting

Dear Jeffrey:

You were thoughtful to ask me to speak at the Labor Day commemoration of the Civic Action Group, and I appreciate the fact that you think my oratorial capabilities are on a par with those of the distinguished guest speakers you mentioned. However,

I have already made family commitments for that day—indeed, the entire weekend—which preclude my ability to be present at that time and place.

I wish you well and hope the program lives up to your fullest expectations. Please give my regards to your colleagues in the Group.

Sincerely,

Accepting Invitation to Serve on Environmental Planning Committee

Dear Mr. Contiglio:

In response to an invitation from the Mayor's office, I am pleased to reply that at least two officers in our firm will serve on the new committee he has formed to improve the environment and reduce pollution, in all forms. We feel, as he does, that if we can improve the looks of our town, we'll attract more customers from outside the limits. And we'll also encourage more businesses to relocate here, which will be good for business all around.

We'll let you know within a week which of us will join the committee. Over and above that, you can expect all of us in the firm to support this program.

Sincerely,

Accepting Invitation to Participate in a YMCA Musical Event

Dear Luther Midding:

Regarding your solicitation of candidates with musical talents to join your program for the summer music festival, how could we refuse!

I never go into one of my restaurants without hearing musical reverberations all over the place, sometimes to the point where I think I'll have to plug my ears. What I hear is largely canned. But it was a revelation for me to find out that many of our employees themselves have, in addition to ironclad ears, music-related skills and can sing and play all kinds of instruments. So I am posting notices asking all who are interested to phone your office for information or audition time.

As an added contribution, I'd like to set up a booth at the festival to serve complimentary soft drinks and cookies to the guests and participants.

With best wishes,

Declining Request to Serve on Board

Dear Dr. Saarinen:

You were very thoughtful to write me and ask whether I would serve on the board of the Retirement Research Coalition next year. I have great respect for the work of the RRC and have been told that it has conducted excellent research on aging since its founding six years ago. Unfortunately, I shall be unable to accept your flattering offer. I am already serving as a volunteer for two philanthropies and, what with the increasing responsibilities of running my own business, I find that I have to spread my services a little too thin already. It would not be fair to the Coalition for me to accept duties and face challenges I could not promise to fulfill.

Sincerely,

VOLUNTEERING

If you are active in volunteer programs, whether for business or personal reasons, the following model letters will provide ideas and guidance. Some suggest ways for you to recruit volunteers, while others depict methods of assisting or launching new programs of benefit to the community.

Recruiting Volunteers—Village Fire Department

Dear Kingman:

Five years ago, I became a volunteer firefighter the wrong way. I was a salesman peddling tires and I thought maybe if I could get involved with the action, I could sell the fire department a lot of tires. Well, you wouldn't believe how seldom the fire engines need to change tires or how much paperwork there is in peddling tires (or anything else) to town governments. But in the course of all this, I discovered that I could perform a real, solid community service as a part-time, no-pay fighter of fires. Now, with a lot of blazes under my belt (and no tire sales to the department), I am convinced that this is one of the finest, and most needed, of all personal contributions to a community.

Come on down to the Central Avenue fire house this Saturday at 11:00 A.M. and see for yourself. While sipping coffee and munching a doughnut, you can watch an exciting film about firefighting and then chat with some volunteers, like me, who have found this activity very fulfilling.

Sincerely,

PS: You'll also get a chief's badge to give to King, Jr.

Establishing Sports Program

Dear Commissioner Belfast:

During the last three years, the employees of Palmetto Foods have organized softball and volleyball teams on their own and in an informal manner. This sports activity became so popular, however, that our company management has now decided to endorse and support amateur teams by providing playing fields, uniforms at cost, and equipment through a realistic budget that will grow according to the number of participants.

As the newly appointed sports director for Palmetto, I have put out feelers to see what other companies in our area would like to pit their company teams against ours. I thought it might be productive, too, to mention this to you in the event you know of organizations that would like to participate. We'd be happy to share the use of our three playing fields on company-owned property and perhaps offer a few trophies.

Sincerely,

How May We Help?

Dear Dr. Sterne:

My wife and I decided we would start a fire in the fireplace last evening because it was damp and cold outside. As I tore off part of the morning paper to light kindling, I happened to glance at a story that caught my eye. It was the account of your recent work on behalf of children with impaired vision. It suddenly seemed very symbolic that you had brought light to young people just as I was trying to bring light into a dreary night. How would mankind exist without such glowing moments—the little, inconsequential ones as well as those with impact and meaning?

My partners here at our small-business firm and I have for some time wondered just how we could make a contribution to a worthy cause. And suddenly now it comes to me. We'd like to help you to continue to bring light into young lives through personal participation as volunteers. How may we help?

Sincerely,

Soliciting Advice for Helping with Cultural Programs

Dear Judge Cranstone:

The idea for the Hilltown Cultural Center was a grand and glorious inspiration, which at its inception made so many of us feel that our inhabitants are moving away from the harsh and material things of life and back into a world with vitality and meaning. So it is agonizing to see the dream slipping and life settling back into the same old doldrums. The contrast is brought home daily, and acutely, whenever people confer with me about music or come into my back barn shop to look at the selection of instruments we offer. As one recent graduate of the Eastman School of Music said to me the other day, "We can play music anywhere: in a forest primeval, on a lonely beach, in our private bedroom. But what we really need is a symphony hall that has ears—thousands of ears—which make the musicians' playing not an exercise, but an event."

Hope for construction of the Cultural Center is fading, according to everything I hear or read in the paper. The problem seems to be that there are not enough people who respect their ears and want to put them to better use than listening to gossip or the blaring of electronic sound boxes. How can we generate a better respect? How can little people like me, who cannot donate substantial sums or influence the shakers and doers, keep the dream from fading?

I'd like to *do* something. To volunteer to help our community. But what?

I welcome your advice.

Sincerely yours,

Offering Firm's Services or Facilities

Dear Ms. Pointer:

Your recent plea to merchants to help the United Youth Fellowship locate missing children in our area has given us pause for thought. As the owner of a firm that manufactures paper labels and marking tags, I have what I think might be an effective plan. I call it "Stamps for Humanity." The idea is to print gummed stamps the size of large postage stamps, imprinted with pictures of missing children. Informative lettering up to about a dozen words would be feasible. These identification stamps could be sold to merchants, and others who use the mails frequently, to help defray the cost of your UYF program. The purchasers would then affix the stamps to envelopes being mailed throughout our region and, indeed, to many other parts of the country.

Our firm, Mini Label & Tag, Inc., would be honored to produce the stamps at cost, in whatever quantity and with whatever pictures you decide to order. I'd be happy to discuss details with you at your convenience.

Sincerely,

Proposing a Volunteer Survey

Dear Mr. Dorfinger:

You and your associates at Kiwanis devote a substantial amount of your time studying problem areas that are in need of assistance from active volunteers, as well as financial support from many quarters. When it comes to the participation of volunteers, we have seen from our own experience in consumer research that only the surface has been tapped. There are many, many people who would volunteer their time and talents if they were more aware of the need, and if they were given positive assurance that their capabilities are substantial and their help would be valuable.

With this in mind, we propose being a volunteer ourselves long enough to undertake a limited survey, just within the 4 square miles that comprise the town of Suffolk. The objective would be to find out how many people who are not volunteers would be interested in some form of meaningful public service. We would expect to obtain answers to the following questions:

1. How many people, out of the population of 21,000, would have to be interviewed to provide an answer?
2. How long would it take?
3. When would be the best time to schedule these interviews?
4. How much would a complete study cost?

Armed with these answers, we would further volunteer our services to conduct a complete study, *at cost.* Kiwanis could play its role by soliciting financial assistance from member organizations, pointing out that the end results would be a much larger volunteer army to help improve the community in a multitude of ways. It is always possible that the state or county would underwrite part of a survey of this kind, since it is obviously for the general good.

Sincerely,

"Lending" Company Volunteers

Dear Elbert:

After reading about the budget cutbacks and dilemmas facing the Cherokee County Planning Commission, I felt guilty that I had not accepted a request last year to serve on the appropriations council. Now I'd like to make amends—not by a late acceptance, but by offering some valuable expertise in a way that will not tap your budget by so much as a penny. The problems you face in financial analysis are much the same as the ones we deal with on a day-to-day basis in our accounting department. It would be realistic for one of our analysts here to study your monetary problems and make recommendations to the planning commission.

My partners and I would be happy to "lend" a couple of our whiz kids to you from time to time to help you find the solutions you need. If that seems agreeable to the Commission, let me know, and we'll get the plan in motion whenever you are ready.

Cordially,

Participation in Medical Volunteer Program

Dear Dr. Parsons:

As you may know, several of our managers have worked with your hospital committee to provide medical information to employees, along with schedules of blood pressure, sugar, heart, and other tests that are available from time to time.

We are pleased, therefore, that the Medical Association has accepted our invitation to use our small auditorium for its public seminars on diabetes, emphysema, and kidney disease.

We have already lined up employee volunteers who will assist in handling the arrival and seating of those who want to attend one or more of the sessions.

Our advertising department has prepared an informative leaflet to mail and hand out to the public. A copy is attached.

We are delighted to participate in this community service.

Cordially,

Offering Help to Better Business Bureau

Dear Spencer:

Although we are a small operation in what you might call a "cottage industry," we do rub elbows with a good many other businesses in the area and are concerned about some of the questionable marketing plans being practiced hereabouts. We cannot send the BBB much of a donation each year, but we certainly can contribute in other ways. I, for one, would be happy to serve on your review board for two or three hours each week. Because we are marketers ourselves and I have been in the selling field during most of my business career, I can generally smell a scam or swindle a mile off. I suggest that you regularly let me look at current complaints from consumers and provide whatever correspondence or documentation you have. I can then do my homework on any schemes that seem fishy and report back to you.

When can I start? Right away.

With best wishes,

Offering Help for Regional Historical Seminar

Dear Dr. Lowry:

Recently, the Reverend Dimock asked me if I would like to attend the seminar of the Kendall County Historical Society, since I have long been a history buff. After I had asked him where it was to be held, and he replied that he did not know, I asked around and realized you had *no* meeting room lined up. Dr. Dimock was greatly concerned, knowing how expensive it is to hire a hall in the metropolitan area, and asked me if I had any suggestions about solving the problem. He came to the right person. It so happens that our company has a cafeteria for employees that can seat about 80 people comfortably. It is adjoined by a large hall with a cork wall that is suitable for posters and displays. Since we have a well-equipped kitchen and serving tables, you could easily provide refreshments for participants, should you so desire.

Please accept our invitation to use these facilities for Historical Society seminars. We'd be honored.

Sincerely,

Improving Employee Response

Dear Reverend Hardy:

Last month, your office mailed a request to the owners of local businesses requesting that they undertake to collect and donate canned goods to help feed homeless people in your parish.

This letter has two purposes. The first is to report that our employees responded in a positive way to announcements we placed on our bulletin boards, and we were able to deliver more than 200 canned and packaged items to your Bargain Box storage area.

The second purpose is to suggest that you also place announcements in local papers well in advance of collection dates when planning any future food contributions. The only such notice we saw was printed barely two days before the event, and it was probably too late for many people to participate.

Respectfully,

Description of Community Programs

Dear Mr. Stanley:

Our firm does volunteer work for the Chamber of Commerce, so it was fitting we should have received your inquiry about community programs in Northampton that you might want to know about when your firm relocates here. Since you are in the business of supplying animal feeds and nutritional supplements, you will be likely to want to participate in the seasonal Grange fairs that are held in the early spring, midsummer, and late fall. These are basically commercial, underwritten by individuals and groups who take booths, and used to present new products and services to visiting farmers and agriculturists.

Our big event is the annual Labor Day Fair, which runs for ten days in late August and September, ending on Labor Day. While this also does involve commercial booths, the Fair is a major family event, with all kinds of recreational activities for people of every age. Under separate cover, we are mailing you a descriptive folder and application form.

Sincerely,

To City Clerk—Thank You for Assistance

Dear Winthrop:

Recruiting volunteers is always tough, even for a worthy cause like stocking a small-business reference room in our public library. But the job has its rewards, and one of them is certainly working with dedicated coordinators like you who don't mind contributing their time and effort to projects for the public good. We would never in this world have gotten the project in motion and progressed so far had you not stepped forward and offered to give us a big assist.

The Small-Business Library Committee thanks you heartily.

And to that I add my own

Thanks for a job well done,

CONGRATULATIONS

Among the letters that are the most satisfying to write are those that offer congratulations to friends and business associates for their accomplishments. Such letters, even though brief like some of the ones selected here, can go a long way toward building employee morale or improving your company's public relations.

Recognizing an Accomplishment

Dear Doris Ivey:

The write-up in the *Packet* about your work with young handicapped children was very moving and will go a long way toward interesting other volunteers in the work of the local Guild. To the many praises mentioned, however, I'd like to recognize an accomplishment that went unrecorded: your program to distribute large-print books to elderly shut-ins who are visually impaired.

I have taken the liberty of sending last month's Guild *Newsletter* to the newspaper editors so they can add a postscript to yesterday's article. And, as one who has two elderly parents whose vistas have been gloriously widened through large-print books, I commend you for your commitment.

With deep appreciation,

Appreciation of Special Effort

Dear Mrs. Reardon:

In my capacity as medical director of the Commonwealth Health Center, I commend you and the members of your program who participated in our *Cancer Alert!* project. Your people seemed to be tireless when it came to arriving early, staying late, and working hard all day long. As a result, we were able to distribute more than 450 posters, 3,200 personal wallet cards, 1,700 brochures, and 780 mailing requests. In addition, your financial delegation handed out about 500 pledge cards and received 232 monetary commitments during the day.

All in all, *Cancer Alert!* was a big success. More important, we are sure that it will play a part in cancer prevention and early detection of the disease.

Thanks, thanks to all of you.

Sincerely,

Commending a Client or Prospective Client on Winning an Award

Dear Thelma:

The Municipal Citation for community service could not have been more aptly awarded. All of us here have been well aware of the long hours you have devoted to helping young people in trouble get a second chance. I know you'll receive many other notes of appreciation, as well as many silent prayers for what you have accomplished. But I just wanted you to know that you have been—and are—a continuing inspiration to all of us in Harborville.

With warm regards,

PS: Thought you might want the enclosed clipping for your files.

Appreciation for Stand on a Public Issue

Dear Harcourt:

"If they're over 65, get 'em out of the work force!"

I couldn't believe my ears when I heard Assemblyman Donart voice this crass and heartless statement at the Rotary's reception for recent college graduates who are making their mark in the business world. Sure, we want to encourage the young and express our enthusiasm for their vigor and gumption in getting ahead in our highly competitive world. But we surely don't want to do it at the expense of the older men and women who pioneered before them in much the same spirit.

You were right to explode a balloon in Donart's face and rock him back on his heels. He tends to be too big for his britches, and he hasn't yet realized what a lemon that kind of outlook can be in his political future. More important, though, I commend you for advocating a plan whereby our community will play an active role in locating jobs for older residents who want to join, or stay in, the work force. You can count on our firm to participate in this program.

Sincerely,

Commending the Police Department—Crime Prevention Efforts

Dear Chief Parkman:

You have received several complaints from me in the past about crime in our neighborhood.

You have received hundreds—perhaps thousands—of gripes in prior years about what is wrong with your department, your methods, your officers, and who knows what else.

So this letter may come as something of a shock: A real, honest-to-God *commendation* from a private citizen. Personally, I was overwhelmed, as were my tenants, to see how quickly you apprehended the ring of burglars that terrorized our neighbors and looted our abodes. It was a case of very scientific police detection, as well as aggressive action on the part of the members of your force who participated.

Your may not get a thank you note from the four hoods you apprehended, but you certainly have my

Thanks and very best wishes,

To High School Team—League Victory

Dear Coach Sweringen:

Congratulations on your impressive victory!

At the start of the season, there were only a handful of people in Bridger's Falls who had any idea that Lewis & Clarke High would have a winning basketball season, let alone go home with the League Trophy. Remembering my own years on the team more than two decades ago, I could sense a certain vigorous spirit every time I attended the early games and was not as surprised as some of my friends and business associates seemed to be. But I'm sure you were both determined and confident—qualities that really paid off.

We at Acme Sporting Goods and our whole town are proud of you and every member of the time. So this letter is simply an echo of everyone else's feelings. Keep it up!

With best wishes,

Announcing Awards for Long Service

Dear Member:

Please join with us in recognizing the following organizations which this month are celebrating their tenth anniversary of membership in the Small Business Association:

Arrow Construction Company
Bennett Foods, Inc.
Hampshire House Seasonings
Hart & Hart Kennels
March's Air Conditioning & Heating
Ultra Klean Carpet & Upholstery Service

Four of these members have grown more than 50% since joining SBA, one has doubled in size, and one has increased its business by more than 400%. That's pretty impressive, but seems to typify our members as we commemorate their birthdays from month to month.

There are many reasons why our Association has been able to help stimulate economic growth and security. One is that we exchange effective information about ways to develop new business and improve existing functions. Another is that we join forces in promoting community programs that attract customers and clients. And a third is that we establish codes of ethics and principles of performance so that the SBA symbol is meaningful to the public and guarantees satisfaction.

Happy Tenth Birthday, All of You!

Sincerely,

COMMUNICATION WITH MEDIA

See also Chapter 11, Media, Public Relations, and Business and Professional Associations.

Commending Editorial Stand

Dear Ms. Tanager:

Bless you for publishing "Health Is a Many-Splendored Thing." It was a well-rounded article on the firm steps people can take to stay healthy and fit and the wealth of resources at our command for alleviating the problems of body, soul, and mind. This is not the first article on the subject, by any means, but it is the first one I have ever read that placed chiropractors on a par with M.D.s, dentists, psychologists, and others who can help individuals to attain health goals.

We are here to serve. We have our own specialized capabilities. And we appreciate recognition as much as any other professional in the field.

To your good health,

Promoting Help for the Handicapped

Dear Ms. Mattingly:

The article in the *Daily Argus*, "Give a Hand to the Handicapped," was most provocative, and I commend your staff writer for his ability to look at the subject so convincingly through the eyes of handicapped people themselves. We at Western Termite and Pest Control are very familiar with the subject, since more than 20% of the people we hire are handicapped in one way or another, and we have found them to be more dedicated to their jobs, conscientious, and hard-working than the average employees who enjoy all their facilities. Our ranks include people who are deaf, have impaired vision, are crippled, have lost limbs, and—in two cases—are considered to be retarded. Our company president himself was recently elected as honorary chairperson of the Handicapped Research Foundation and is active in its programs.

So, kudos to you and your staff for presenting the picture so graphically and convincingly!

With best wishes,

PS: By the way, I am handicapped myself, having lost a leg in Vietnam. But I manage with the rest of them.

Inviting Public to Ground-breaking Ceremony

Dear Editor:

Having grown up and lived in Davenport most of my life, except when attending college and the veterinary school at Cornell University, I have always wanted to make a meaningful contribution to the community, but never knew quite what. Last year, after having opened the third of my veterinary clinics in the Tri-City area, I decided that the city and citizens alike could benefit from a park devoted specifically to small domesticated animals. The result—"Pet Park"—which has 5 acres of woodland and grassland overlooking the Mississippi River, south of Davenport on the road to Muscatine.

So please come to our dedication and ground-breaking ceremonies at noon on Saturday, June 11. Naturally, bring your dogs, cats, or other pets. We'll have plenty of food for them. And some snacks for you. The high school band has agreed to be there, drums emblazoned with its bulldog emblem. It will play the theme song from the Broadway hit, *Cats*, along with other animal-oriented music.

Oh, yes, there'll be a drawing for prizes: one week in a luxury suite at one of my kennels, a ten-pound sack of cat food, cartons of dog biscuits, and an assortment of flea collars, nail clippers, leashes, and feeding bowls.

Bring a human friend, too, if you like.

Joyfully,

$\mathcal{P}$ERSONAL BUSINESS CORRESPONDENCE

This chapter is anything but a catch-all for letters and other correspondence that do not fit neatly into previous categories. Rather, it covers those subjects of a personal nature that commonly require letters from small-business owners and managers and professional people who deal with the public. These include condolences, congratulations, appreciations, apologies, invitations, presentations, requests for favors, maintaining social relations, and recognitions of achievements, among other topics. As the sample letters demonstrate, very often personal correspondence of this kind, though perhaps triggered by a sense of duty or responsibility, can reflect positively on the writers and the organizations they represent.

Writing a personal letter is frequently a substitute for a face-to-face visit. It helps to continue or cement a better relationship. It can mean that extra little dialog that shows you care or have a special concern for the recipient. Or it can nudge a person to take some form of action that is desired but not yet a reality. Since some of these letters are casual in style and content, why not use the telephone instead? The answer is that you most certainly can, time after time. Yet there is something about a letter, about expressing yourself on paper that is both more substantial and more permanent in its quality than a phone call. The person who takes the time and makes the effort to sit down and write has something of an edge over the phone caller. And, as studies have documented, the visual message is more likely to be remembered than the aural message. Even a brief note is frequently a reminder that can be placed in a conspicuous spot on the desk or tacked to a bulletin board.

Should you use a company letterhead or your personal stationery when writing a letter that is part business? Should it be typed or written by hand? There is no well-defined formula or protocol, and in the end you have to make that judgment yourself, based on your familiarity with the recipient. Generally, the less well you know the recipient, the more formal the format should be.

SOME QUESTIONS TO ASK YOURSELF

1. Who is the proper recipient for the message I am composing?
2. Is this the proper time for the letter to be sent?
3. How important is my own personality in writing and signing this letter?
4. What is the objective of the letter?
5. Am I making it clear what action or opinion is expected of the recipient?
6. If I were the recipient, how would I react to this particular letter and what would I think of the sender?

If the letter is social in its nature and content, but prompted for business reasons, its visual appearance should be more like that of a letter you might write at home, rather than one written in the office. People tend to react negatively to a personal letter they feel has been delegated to a secretary to write and type. "If a correspondent doesn't have time, or the interest, to write in person," is a typical comment, "then the letter shouldn't be sent at all."

HOW TO DO IT

1. Open with a personal comment, to set the tone.
2. Use conversational language instead of formal business terminology.
3. Relate your company to the subject and the recipient in a pleasant, low-key manner.
4. End on an upbeat note.

Even when a personal letter makes critical comments or includes some kind of rebuke, it should get across the fact that you are sympathetic to a problem and are convinced that the writing of the message is for your mutual benefit. In most cases, even a direct reprimand to an acquaintance or associate can conclude with a positive air of assurance and result in action for your common good.

WRITING LETTERS OF CONDOLENCE

The most difficult letter of all to write is one of sympathy on the occasion of a death, life-threatening illness, serious accident, or other tragedy. It is particularly tough to compose when—as is often the case in business situations—neither the victims nor their loved ones are well known to the writer. One way to lessen the burden is to send an appropriate card and include a handwritten note. But the most acceptable, and usually the most comforting, way to communicate is with a personal letter that evidences the time and sympathetic thought you have given to this tragic occasion.

You will find a number of model letters in this chapter, that will help you face this letter-writing challenge.

SOME TIPS FOR WRITING LETTERS OF CONDOLENCE

1. Never start with "I want to express...". Few people ever *want* to write such a letter. In any case, just say what you have in mind.
2. Leave the bereaved with a fond memory of the deceased, especially if you knew him or her well.
3. Don't try to emulate your minister or explain how "time will heal all wounds... " and the like.
4. If you feel you *must* do something "inspirational," enclose a clipping rather than trying to compose immortal words.
5. Offer personal assistance only if you knew the deceased very well and if close relatives are likely to be really in need of help.
6. Be yourself and try to put yourself in the position of the recipient.
7. Don't try to make the deceased out to be something better than he or she really was. The deception always shows through.
8. Remember, the worst consolation letter of all is the one that never gets written!

CONGRATULATIONS

See also Chapter 12, Community Involvement, which has a section entitled Congratulations.

To Daughter of Employee—Fashion League Award

Dear Annette:

We are all so proud of you for winning the Fashion League Design Award and the scholarship that goes with it. Your mother had been so concerned that your shoulder injury and the costs of rehabilitation would prevent you from completing your work and your entry presentation. But you did it and that shows that you have another skill besides your artistic talents: the determination and will to achieve. That will serve you well in your future career.

As your mother has probably told you, we can always provide a part-time job here in our design department when you are looking for work during the summer or whenever else the Fashion School gives you a vacation.

Congratulations and good luck.

With our best wishes,

To Employee—Outstanding Volunteer Award

Dear Ms. Salgado:

Congratulations on winning the "Outstanding Volunteer" award from the May-bank Industrial Association. Our company is proud to have you in its ranks. And our industry has the good sense to recognize real talent and dedication on occasions like this. We wish you great success in your work here and hope that you will continue to look upon community volunteer work as a worthy compliment to a fine career.

Sincerely,

To Business Associate—Outstanding Community Service

Dear Jason:

We were pleased and proud to see your accomplishments mentioned in the enclosed clipping from Today's *Globe*—pleased because we have enjoyed such a fine business relationship with you and your colleagues and proud because your skills and interests have enhanced the image of this neighborly community which we mutually call our hometown.

My first reaction was to wish that there were more people like you in Springfield. And my second reaction was to realize that there actually *are* because of your leadership and guidance. And there will continue to be more because of your influence on the young people who are growing up here.

We thought you'd like an extra clipping for Jason, Jr., to put in his scrapbook. And tell him that the Old Man has a lot of friends who are cheering him on.

Cordially,

ADVICE

To a Young Person Deciding on a Career

Dear Les:

"I wish I'd become a lawyer instead of an engineer—they're the guys making all the dough."

"I've had a good life at the bank, but I would have sure contributed more to mankind if I'd become a conservationist."

"Wouldn't you know, I could have been a successful artist and had a lot more colorful life than if I hadn't been scared about starving and ended up as a teacher."

When you get to be my age, you hear comments like these all the time, usually prefaced by the wish, "If I had it to do all over again, I'd...". But you have to make your mind up and be decisive when you are young and have just gotten your degree and then go striding along the road you picked. It doesn't do any good to limp along and keep looking back and wondering whether you have made the right choice.

Since you asked for my advice it is this: evaluate your career options. Select the one that looks best. Then plunge in and tackle the job with enthusiasm and the conviction that it's the best one in the world for you. Don't look back and don't start comparing, at least not until you reach my age and need something to gab about with your old friends.

I'm sure you'll choose well and I wish you the very, very best.

Sincerely,

To a Widow—Franchise Plans

Dear Sally:

You are right to make plans, now that you are widowed, to occupy yourself with some form of meaningful employment. However, I do not think a franchise like ours is the answer because you expressed the idea that you want to be independent, and that is not always as easy as it sounds in our kind of small business. If you do have a franchise in mind, though, be sure to determine in advance how much control the franchisor can legally exert over the way you run the enterprise. Consider these limitations, for instance:

- You would have to pay the franchisor an upfront fee and then continue to pay royalties, based on gross income.

- You would not really own the business but only the right to handle the products or services being offered.

- A franchisor can legally limit any changes you want to make in business functions or physical designs.
- If the business goes sour through fault of the franchisor, you can sue him, but are likely to get hung up with substantial legal fees and headaches.

Whatever you decide to do, please let me know. I'd be happy to have our attorney look over any contract you are considering and red flag any points that could cause problems.

Affectionately,

THANK YOU

In the hustle and bustle of business and trying to keep abreast of more critical kinds of communications, we tend to ignore courtesy letters or postpone writing them. Yet thank you letters are important and can go a long way toward building a company's image or enhancing personal relationships. Here are a few appropriate examples.

Professional Award

Dear Dr. Schrontz:

On behalf of myself and my partners at Jacobsen, Fox, and Lindner, I am delighted to relay to you our acceptance of the Fairlawn Civic Improvement Award for this year. As you so kindly requested, we will all be present at the Architectural Society Host Breakfast on November 3.

We feel honored that you singled out JF&L for this annual citation. But we are even more gratified that the award is associated with the design of the Lake Wilmington Municipal Boathouse because of the environmental and ecological features incorporated in its construction and maintenance plans. We have focused much of our professional time and energy on preserving and enhancing natural beauty in all our basic renderings and artistic concepts.

Sincerely,

Small-Business Award

Dear Gus:

One of my friends is a noted artist. He has a studio that is lined with award plaques, honor scrolls, medals, and other testimonials to his talents and finesse.

I have only a single award: the one your committee so graciously bestowed on me last week at the media presentation dinner. Yet I am more proud of what it means than my artist friend is of his whole roomful of honors. I say that from the heart. So thank you again for your recognition, and please pass along my appreciation to the others on your committee.

Sincerely,

Professional Favor

Dear Mr. and Mrs. Larue:

You were most thoughtful to recommend our line of fall fashions to your new neighbor, Mrs. Darnley. She seemed to be very pleased, both with our wares and the courtesy of our sales staff. So I just wanted you to know that everything went well, and we appreciate your support of our establishment.

Sincerely,

Gift

Dear Trevor:

You were most thoughtful to send me a battery-operated thesaurus and spelling corrector after you visited our offices last week. It is a most remarkable device and I have placed it in a prominent position on my desk, where I assure you it will get plenty of use. I write at least a dozen letters a day to friends and business associates. Since I am not the world's best speller, I frequently have to look up words in my old, dog-eared dictionary, a time-consuming process. Now, thanks to you, I can eliminate that step with a mere push of the buttons and write more letters in less time.

We enjoyed our discussion, which should prove to be most fruitful for all of us, and we look forward to your next visit.

With best regards,

Professional Club Membership

Dear Dr. Roemer:

Your invitation to join the Executive Affiliate of the Engineering Guild is accepted with appreciation. Until you mentioned it in your letter, I did not realize that I was the first nonengineer in the Guild's history to be admitted to membership. I am deeply honored. I should confess to you, however, that this statistic may soon be a relic of the past. Because of the intensification of my assignments in the field of mechanical engineering, I have been studying at night for a professional degree. If all goes well, I shall hold my B.E. degree within three months.

Sincerely,

Declining an Invitation

Dear Ms. Hugel:

Thank you for inviting me to attend the award luncheon in honor of Denise McConomy. I must regret your kind invitation since it conflicts with a program to which I have long been committed, and which cannot be passed over. Please extend my regrets to the honoree as well.

Cordially

Declining Appeal to Run for State Office

Dear Barry:

It is flattering that you envision me as an aggressive and fiery legislator in Hartford, fighting for the rights of the people and the conservation of our ancestral lands. I have always admired the statesmanship of legislators in our Nutmeg State and considered them many cuts above the norm. However, I have to be realistic and honest and see myself as what I am. Personable? Yes, and good at my job, running a manufacturing business. Bright? To an extent, since I was usually on the dean's list at Trinity. Dedicated? Quite, in my career, but perhaps more so on the home front, where I like to putter around and be with family. A politician? No way. I can't wheel and deal, and I'm a sitting duck for those that can.

Thank you kindly for even thinking of me in the Connecticut Senate. But, for the good of the people, I have to decline to run at this time.

Sincerely,

APOLOGY

Unseemly Conduct

Dear Mr. Messinger:

My emotional outburst during Dr. Praeger's seminar, "The Limits of Liability," was uncalled for and rude. For that I apologize, to you, to our instructor, and to the assembled participants. I have no excuse for such behavior, particularly as an attorney whose professional demeanor calls for retaining control of oneself and remaining calm, even in the most heated clashes of defendants and prosecutors.

Upon reflection, I realize that I should have ignored the naive viewpoint of the participant who made a verbal attack on our firm's integrity. Others in the room did so, while my blowup seemed only to confirm the charge made by the accuser that we were culpable.

Please give my apologies to Dr. Praeger.

Sincerely,

Missed Appointment

Dear Natalie:

It is dismal to think that I could be losing my memory at such a young age. But how else could I forget that we had an appointment for a luncheon that would have been truly delightful, tasty, and bubbling with good cheer? I keep reaching for excuses, but have absolutely none.

Please forgive me and let's reschedule our plans—perhaps for next week. I'll give you a ring.

Sincerely,

ANNOUNCEMENTS

Retirement Plans

Dear Gene:

As it happens to all of us, to use *Time* magazine phraseology, the moment to retire is on my horizon. I see the date as a year from now, give or take a few months, depending largely upon the wishes of a successor. I urge you, therefore, to initiate an early search for likely candidates for the directorship of the school. I have two persons in mind, but would prefer holding their names in abeyance until the Board has submitted its own preliminary list.

If I may make one suggestion, I see the director as one with less of my business background and more with educational qualifications. I have long realized that, while I was adept at stimulating the preparation of sound business courses, I was less successful in instituting the best teaching procedures. A professional educator would, in my opinion, be superior to an executive as the director. But I leave it in your hands.

Sincerely,

Separation from Spouse

Dear Charles:

It may come as a surprise to you, but my wife of 30 years and I have agreed to a separation, effective by the time you receive this letter. One of the problems has been that our two careers have kept us constantly separated during the last five years as our respective businesses have required regular flights to many different parts of the country, and often over long periods of time.

Martha and I are separating in a friendly manner and have both agreed that it is only fair to write all of you who have done business with one, or both, of us over the years. Martha will remain in the condominium at our old address. And I can be reached at the office or, during nonbusiness hours, at the address and phone number on this letterhead.

Thanks in advance for your understanding.

Sincerely,

Postponing a Social Event

Dear Renee:

The anniversary party is off.

I bit off more than I could chew. I wanted it to be the biggest, best, and most congenial event of the season—just for people like you. So I planned it accordingly.

Then the stock market fell. And with it my hopes. Good sense compels me to rethink the immediate future.

But I promise you, as soon as we effect a turnaround, *then* I'll throw a double party: one for this anniversary and one for the next.

In the meantime, my...

Sincere regrets,

SYMPATHY AND CONDOLENCE LETTERS

The following letters are characteristic of those sent by businesspersons to individuals and families, some of whom are known personally to the writer and others known only through their relationship with the deceased.

Death of a Longtime Business Friend

Dear Louise:

It was such a long, long battle, and I don't know anyone who showed more grit and determination than Warren or courage on your part. We all had tremendous admiration and respect for Warren during his illness, right from the time he first wrote us to explain what was happening.

It is comforting to you, I'm sure, to have such great support from family and friends, near and far. And there is little I can say to provide any greater degree of comfort. But it might be of value to you to know that Warren has been a great inspiration. At times—fortunately not too many—when we have had setbacks or I have felt depressed about one thing or another, I have often thought about Warren. How would *he* have handled such problems? Certainly with more fortitude and faith and optimism than I have been displaying. And it will always be thus, as long as I have the mental capacity to think clearly. And for that, I am eternally grateful to Warren—and to all of you who have lived with your problems so graciously and devotedly over the years.

For these things I am thankful, and I feel that Warren's memory keeps him alive in many thoughts besides mine.

Sincerely,

Death of an Immediate Business Associate

Dear Ms. Templeton:

The thoughts of all of us here at your father's office are with you at this time, and particularly so since we knew your late mother as well and remember her when she used to bring you by for a visit with some of us. You can well be proud, as we are, of what your father accomplished during his illustrious career, first at the University and then with our firm. "Doc," as we affectionately called him, was one of those rare people who could lead people into full cooperation on some very difficult and complex projects without ever seeming to pressure them or establish impossible deadlines. He will be missed here more than I can tell you. But our loss can never compare with that of you and your brothers and the grandchildren.

We count our blessings for having known and worked with him as long as we did.

Affectionately,

Death of a Colleague

Dear Mathilda:

The other night, I was working late, actually almost until midnight, when I heard our elevator door click. I jumped because I was alone in the third-floor newsroom and for an instant I thought of but one person. Regularly, for many years when I was meeting our weekly deadline, I would be startled at one or two o'clock in the morning by that familiar click and there would stand Dave. He couldn't sleep, so he would come down to the office to talk.

Often, he would be wearing his overcoat right over his pajamas and I knew it would be a long night because he loved to talk, and I loved to talk to him. We gabbed of many things, fools and kings, sometimes until daylight when the janitor would run us out. He'd tell me how what he really wanted to do was to run a special kind of garage in a little town somewhere in Ohio and talk to people and tinker with cars. What a guy!

I owe so much to him, not alone in warm memories of friendship but in tangible things. I recall, as a newly married, moving into a crackerbox of a house that had no air conditioning. 'What you need is a nice screened porch,' Dave said to me during a visit one sultry afternoon. My wife agreed.

Dave returned the next night to take measurements. He ordered the lumber, the cement blocks, and the following weekend he and I began building a screened porch. He was extremely handy. I was his flunky. But we built that porch together. You truly get to know someone after you've both bashed your thumbs a few times while nailing sheeting for the roof.

In later years, he advised me about a lot of things, particularly about some investments that helped to pay for my son's college education. I was grateful for that, and I'm thankful that my son also showed his gratitude to Dave long before he passed on.

Well, Mathilda, it all came home so forcefully the other night when I heard the elevator click at midnight and thought of Dave. It's funny how the little things like that in life remind you of the truly big things—like Dave.

Affectionately,

Death of a Colleague's Spouse

Dear Sarah:

It does not take a letter from me to tell you how sad we all are at Arthur's passing. Although I never worked with him personally, I knew him as one of the most forthright and reliable people on the business scene, who could always be counted on to live up to his commitments and carry his share of responsibiliies, no matter how heavy. Beyond that, of course, we extend deep sympathy to you for your loss and pray that you are comforted by family and loved ones nearby.

Four of us from the office will be attending the memorial service next week, representing just a few of the many businesspeople in the community who would like to pay our last respects to your husband.

With sympathy,

Death of an Employee's Child

Dear Norma:

My two partners and I join in extending sympathy to you on behalf of the entire firm for the passing of your young son. I only wish I had the gift of expression to be able to comfort you better in this time of great sorrow. But you can be sure that you are in the thoughts and prayers of all of us at this time. May God be with you and grant you a measure of peace in the memory of one who was so loved and loving.

Sincerely,

Death of an Employee's Father

Dear Sheldon:

My wife and I were saddened to read in the *Daily Argus* this morning about the death of your father in Boston. We knew he had been ill for a long time, but that in no way lessens the loss you must be feeling at this time. We hope that you are close to family and friends who will give you fond support and love. Flora joins me in sending our heartfelt condolences to you and your loved ones.

Sincerely,

Belated Condolence

Dear Andrew:

I was grieved to hear that your partner had been killed in an automobile accident two weeks ago. I was in Chicago on business and did not receive the news until yesterday, upon my return. You have my deep sympathy, and even more so since I lost a close associate last year under similar circumstances and still feel a sense of shock when I think back on it. I did not know Alan anywhere nearly as well as I know you, but I'll always recall him as one of the brightest young men in our field and one with a keen sense of humor under fire.

Although I missed the memorial service, I have asked our treasurer to send a company donation to the Heart Association, as mentioned in the newspaper clipping that my wife showed me.

Cordially,

Announcing Death of a Business Partner

Dear Mrs. Proctor:

The death yesterday of our senior partner, Otto Julius Leftwich, was so sudden and unexpected that neither our firm nor our professional association has yet made any plans to commemorate his name and achievements. It would be fitting to answer any inquiries you receive in your capacity as secretary with something like this. "The members of the Association are saddened by the departure of the man who was recognized as a pioneer in accounting procedures and who gave unstintingly of himself in developing programs to attract young people to the profession. Plans are now underway for a memorial scholarship in Dr. Leftwich's name, which will be announced by the Association during its next monthly meeting on October 19."

You might also want to send out a brief profile, which can be copied from the Association's directory. I'll be in touch with further information and suggestions shortly.

Cordially,

Get Well—Serious Illness

Hi, Trevor,

When I was in the hospital two years ago, you paid me almost daily visits and it was great for my morale. Now that I want to return the favor and visit you, I am told that I have to wait a few days. It's just like in the office—one delay after another. In the meantime, I can at least send you this silly card and my hope that you'll be up and about in no time. You'll end up better than ever. Remember, I did. And at one time they didn't think I'd make it through until the next breakfast. See you soon. Mindy sends her love.

Regards,

Get Well—Accident

Dear Stephanie:

Your husband left a message while I was away, telling me about your automobile accident. While I am distressed to hear of your misfortune, I am relieved to know you'll be out of the hospital by the time you get this note. As I think I told you earlier this week, I am going out of town for the financial seminar, so will not have a chance to visit you in person. But I did want you to know that there is no urgency about your returning to the office. The most important matter is to get yourself back in shape. Take all the time you need. And don't worry about the bills—our new accident and health plan will cover you for most of the hospital costs.

I hope to see you back in your usual good health by the time I return.

With best wishes from all of us,

To Father After Accident to His Daughter

Dear Mr. Manninghouse:

As the father of three daughters, I can well understand your apprehension that the accident suffered by your daughter, Melissa, might leave her with a facial disfigurement. Please rest assured that such is not the case. I have conferred with two specialists at the hospital and studied the x-rays. I am told that the healing process itself will eliminate what now looks like a nasty cut. Following that, minor plastic surgery will remove remaining scar tissue and Melissa's skin will show no signs of the injury.

Medical miracles are many, but they cannot erase the memory of the traumatic moments your daughter experienced when her stamping machine malfunctioned or the days of pain that followed. However, you can be certain that the company will accept full responsibility for the accident and do all in its power to ameliorate the distress caused to both patient and family. Everyone here is most sympathetic, and I believe you can judge that yourself, in light of the number of visitors Melissa has had and the way her fellow employees have reacted.

Sincerely,

To Spouse of Accident Victim

Dear Marlene:

My secretary phoned me to report having heard that Chester was seriously injured in a boating accident while deep-sea fishing near your Florida home. While it is a relief for me to know that he is off the critical list and resting more comfortably in the hospital, I wanted you to know that all of us—the ones he calls "the Old Gang"—are rooting for him. We have some cards and little remembrances we'd like to send him as soon as he gets home again. So please keep me apprised of his condition and whereabouts, so I can pass the information around.

In the meantime, my very best to you and your daughters.

Affectionately,

$\mathcal{A}$PPENDIXES

STRUCTURE AND FORMAT
PROPER FORMS OF ADDRESS

A P P E N D I X

$\mathcal{S}$TRUCTURE AND FORMAT

An effective letter is one that not only uses words, expressions, and information to good advantage, but that follows a structure and format that are familiar to the reader. You depart from this format on occasions, but only at risk if you are not sure of yourself. A letter by its very nature is structured. It might contain attachments and inserts that have completely different formats, but its basic layout, arrangement, and design must be uniform. The whole idea is to make the text easier for the reader to follow and understand.

The elements of a business letter are standard:

1. The *letterhead*, with name, address, and usually telephone number
2. The *salutation*, with the name, location, and form of address of the intended recipient
3. The *body* of the letter, containing the message the sender wishes to impart
4. The *closing*, from one to four words
5. The *signature*, and in some cases title, of the writer

The other elements generally standardized are

1. The margins, top and bottom
2. The side margins, which should be similar, and generally about 1 inch
3. The spacing of the lines: most letters are single spaced, occasionally double, rarely triple
4. The typography, standard typewriter design being the most common and least distracting
5. The color, weight, and texture of the paper, which should be of good quality, but not ostentatious

Experienced letter writers plan their communications ahead of time, visualizing in advance such matters as the size and shape of the paper to be used, the area in which the basic message will be contained, and the length, which will also determine whether the letter will be confined to one page or need two or more.

Owners or managers of small businesses who must engage in frequent correspondence agree it is worth the time, thought, and expense to formulate a style that will come to be readily identified with their companies. Since most stationers or printers can show numerous samples of prospective designs, typography, and papers, there is seldom any need for a small business to hire a designer or consultant. At this stage, you should visualize the typeface you will be using on your office typewriters and/or computers, and the average length of the messages you will be transmitting. Computerized typewriters and word processing programs make it possible to "justify" the right hand margin, that is, squared off as is the type in this book. Many writers feel that unjustified right margins are more natural and seem more personal than justified right margins. In either case the length should average out in such a way that the white space on both sides is about the same.

You should use top and bottom margins that give a look of openness to the letter, but they should not be so generous that it looks as though you wanted to display the quality of your paper. If you see you cannot fit the entire message on the first page, but have only two or three lines to move to a second page, you have two options. The first, and more preferable, is to condense your message, which takes a little thought but is often worth the effort to achieve sentences that are tighter. The second option, of course, is to spill over onto the second page, perhaps moving another line or two from the first page. It is not considered good practice to use the *back* of any page, although this is a procedure followed by many companies that send out long sales letters.

HOW TO FOLD LETTERS

Improper folding can be distracting to the reader. So give this matter some thought and, if necessary, try two or three spacing arrangements to arrive at the one that has the neatest look. Letter paper should be slightly narrower than the envelope, simple to fold the long way into three folds that are almost equal. If it is necessary to use a smaller envelope, the acceptable method is to fold the sheet first in half and then in three almost equal folds. The typing should be spaced so the creases in the paper do not cut through any line of type. When possible, have the letterhead and inside address in the top fold, the salutation and body of the letter in the center fold, and the signature and any following notations in the bottom fold. If a letter is particularly important or contains more than two pages, consider mailing it flat in a 9 inch × 12 inch manilla envelope. Such mailings are often light enough to be sent with a single first-class stamp. This kind of mailing is recommended if folding would detract from the appearance of the letter, if you want to make a greater impression on the recipient, or if you hope the letter will remain flat on the addressee's desk for easier reference.

$\mathcal{P}$ROPER FORMS OF ADDRESS

Many letter writers, whether communicating for business or personal reasons, are confused when it comes to writing to people who have titles that should be recognized in the salutation, as well as in the address. It is important to use the proper, conventional form of address if the letter is to be received respectfully and if the writer is to be considered courteous. Common usage dictates the following forms of address when writing to people who hold significant positions and titles.

Position or title	Styling for address	Styling for salutation
Executive branch of the federal government		
The president	The Honorable (full name) President of the United States The White House	Dear Mr. President:
Wife of president	Mrs. (full name) The White House	Dear Mrs. (surname):
Vice president	The Honorable (full name) Vice President of the United States	Dear Mr. Vice President:
Cabinet member	The Honorable (full name) Secretary of _____ The Secretary of _____	Dear Mr. Secretary:
Attorney general	The Honorable (full name)	Dear Mr. Attorney

Position or title	*Styling for address*	*Styling for salutation*
	The General Attorney	General:
Postmaster General	The Honorable (full name)	Dear Mr. Postmaster
	The Postmaster General	General:
Commissioner	The Honorable (full name)	Dear Mr. Commissioner
	Commissioner of _____	
		Dear Madam Commissioner:
		Dear Mr. (full name):
		Dear Ms./Mrs./Miss. (full name):
Chief Justice	The Honorable (full name)	Dear Mr. (Madam)
	The Chief Justice of the United States	Chief Justice:
Federal judge	The Honorable (full name) Judge of _____	Dear Judge of (surname)
Director or head of an agency	The Honorable (full name) (title, name of agency)	Dear Mr./Mrs./Miss./ Ms. (surname):

Congress

Senator	The Honorable (full name) United State Senate	Dear Senator (surname):
Representative	The Honorable (full name) House of representatives	Dear Representative (surname):
Speaker of the House	The Honorable (full name) Speaker of the House of Representatives	Dear Mr. Speaker: Dear Madam Speaker:
Chairman of a Committee	The Honorable (full name) Chairman of _____ Dear Madam Chairman:	Dear Mr. Chairman:
Librarian of Congress	The Honorable (full name) Librarian of Congress	Dear Mr./Mrs./Ms. (surname):

American Diplomatic officials

Ambassador American Ambassador	The Honorable (full name) Ambassador:	Dear Mr./Madam
Minister American Minister	The Honorable (full name) Minister:	Dear Mr./Madam
Charge d'Affaires American Charge d'Affaires	(full name), Esq.	Dear Mr./Madam Charge d'Affaires:

Position or title	Styling for address	Styling for salutation
Consul	(full name), Esq.	Dear Mr./Mrs./Ms.
American Consul	(surname):	
Representative to	The Honorable (full name)	Dear Mr./Ms./Mrs./Miss.
United Nations	United States Representative	(surname):
	to the United Nations	

Foreign Diplomatic Officials

Foreign	His/Her Excellency	Dear Mr./Madam
Ambassador	(full name)	Ambassador:
British	His/Her Excellency The	Dear Mr./Madam
Ambassador	Right Honorable (full name)	Ambassador:
Charge d'Affaires	Mr./Mrs./Ms. (full name)	Dear Mr./Madam
	Charge d'Affaires of ____	Charge d'Affaires:
Consul	The Honorable (full name)	Dear Sir/Madam:
	Consul of ____	
Minister	The Honorable (full name)	Dear Mr./Madam
	Minister of ____	Minister:
Prime Minister	His/Her Excellency (full	Excellency
	name)	Dear Mr./Madam
		Prime Minister:
Premier	His/Her Excellency (full	Excellency
	name)	
	Premier of	Dear Mr./Madam Premier:
President of a	His/Her Excellency (full	Excellency
Republic	name)	Dear Mr./Madame
President:		
Secretary General	His/Her Excellency (full name)	Dear Mr./Madam
of the United	Secretary General of	Secretary General:
Nations	the United Nations	

State and Local Officials

Governor	The Honorable (full name)	Dear Governor
	Governor of ____	(surname):
Lieutenant	The Honorable (full name)	Dear Mr./Ms./Mrs./Miss.
Governor	Lieutenant Governor of ____	(surname):
Secretary of	The Honorable (full name)	Dear Mr./Madam
State	Secretary of State of ____	Secretary:
Chief Justice	The Honorable (full name)	Dear Mr./Madam
of the State	Chief Justice, Supreme	Chief Justice:
Supreme Court	Court of the State of ____	

Position or title	*Styling for address*	*Styling for salutation*
State Senator	The Honorable (full name) The Senate of ____	Dear Senator (surname)
State Representative	The Honorable (full name) House of Representatives	Dear Mr./Ms./Mrs./Miss. (surname):
State Treasurer	The Honorable (full name) Treasurer of (state)	Dear Mr./Ms./Mrs./Miss. (surname):
Local Judge	The Honorable (full name) Judge of the Court of ____	Dear Judge (surname):
Mayor	The Honorable (full name) Mayor of ____ (surname):	Dear Mayor (surname):
City Attorney	The Honorable (full name) (title) for the City of ____	Dear Mr./Ms./Mrs./Miss. (surname):
Commissioner	The Honorable (full name), Commissioner of ____	Dear Commissioner (surname):
Councilperson	The Honorable (full name), Councilman/Councilwoman	Dear Mr./Ms./Mrs./Miss. (surname):

Academic officials and professionals

President of a University or College	President (full name)	Dear Dr. (surname):
President who is a Priest	The Very Reverend (full name)	Dear Father (surname):
Chancellor of a University	Dr./Mr./Mrs./Ms. (full name)	Dear Dr./Mr./Ms./Mrs./Miss. (surname):
Dean of a School, University, or College	Dean (full name)	Dear Dean (surname):
Professor (with Doctorate)	Dr. (full name) Professor of ____	Dear Dr. (surname):
Professor or Instructor (with no Doctorate)	Mr./Mrs./Ms. (full name)	Dear Mr./Ms./Mrs./Miss. (surname):
Attorney	Mr./Mrs./Ms. (full name) Attorney at Law	Dear Mr./Ms./Mrs./Miss. (surname):
Physician or Surgeon	(full name), M.D. or Dr. (full name)	Dear Dr. (surname):
Dentist	(full name), D.D.S. or Dr. (full name)	Dear Dr. (surname):
Veterinarian	(full name), D.V.M. or Dr. (full name)	Dear Dr. (surname):

Position or title	Styling for address	Styling for salutation
Certified Public Accounttant	(full name), C.P.A.	Dear Mr./Ms/.Mrs./Miss. (surname)
Engineer or Scientist (with Doctorate)	Dr. (full name), (title)	Dear Dr. (surname):

Members of the clergy

Position or title	Styling for address	Styling for salutation
Pope	His Holiness the Pope	Your Holiness
Archbishop Archbishop of ____	The Most Reverend (full name) (surname):	Dear Archbishop
Archdeacon	The Venerable (full name) Archdeacon of ___	My Dear Archdeacon:
Cardinal	His Eminence Cardinal (full name)	Your Eminence
Bishop, Roman Catholic	The Most Reverend (full name)	Dear Bishop (surname):
Bishop, Episcopal	The Right Reverend (full name)	Dear Bishop (surname):
Bishop, Other Denominations	The Reverend (full name) Bishop of ____	Dear Bishop (surname):
Dean of a Cathedral	The Very Reverend (full name) Dean of ____	Dear Dean (surname):
Priest	The Reverend (full name)	Dear Father (surname):
Minister or Pastor	The Reverend (full name)	Dear Reverend (surname):
Rabbi	Rabbi (full name)	Dear Rabbi (surname):
Mother Superior	The Reverend Mother Superior Convent of ____	Reverend Mother:
Sister, Roman Catholic	Sister (full name), (order)	Dear Sister (full name):
Military Chaplain	Chaplain (full name), (rank and service)	Dear Chaplain

Military ranks

Position or title	Styling for address	Styling for salutation
General*	General (full name) (branch of service)	Dear General (surname):
Admiral*	Admiral (full name) (branch of service)	Dear Admiral (surname):

Position or title	Styling for address	Styling for salutation
Colonel	Colonel (full name) (branch of service)	Dear Colonel (surname):
Major	Major (full name) (branch of service)	Dear Major (surname):
Captain	Captain (full name) (branch of service)	Dear Captain (surname):
Commander	Commander (full name) (branch of service)	Dear Commander (surname):
Lieutenant*	Lieutenant (full name) (branch of service)	Dear Lieutenant (surname):
Chief Warrant Officer	Chief Warrant Officer (full name) (branch of service)	Dear Mr./Ms./Mrs./Miss (surname):
Petty Officer	Petty Officer (full name) (branch of service)	Dear Mr./Ms./Mrs./Miss (surname):
Ensign	Ensign (full name) (branch of srvice)	Dear Ensign (surname):
Master Sergeant	Master Sergeant (full name), (branch of service)	Dear Sergeant (surname):
Cadet	Cadet (full name) (branch of service)	Dear Cadet (surname):
Midshipman	Midshipman (full name), (branch of service)	Dear Midshipman (surname):

*It is common practice to show the specific rank, such as *Major* General, *Lieutenant* General, *Rear* Admiral, *Vice* Admiral, *First* Lieutenant Lieutenant, Lieutenant, *j.g.*, if that rank is known to the sender. This distinction, however, is not made in the salutation.

$\mathcal{G}$LOSSARY

Terms and phrases relating to letters and other correspondence and the use of the mails.

Acronym. A name formed from the initial letters of a name, such as UPS, United Parcel Service.

Addressee. The person to whom a letter or other message is sent.

Aerogramme. An economical letter for sending abroad, which is a combined letter and envelope, but does not permit inserts.

Attachment. An insert or enclosure attached to the letter.

Audience. The person to whom a letter or other communication is addressed.

Body. The main text of a letter.

Bond paper. A type of quality paper used for stationery.

Certificate of mailing. A certificate used by a sender to document the fact that an item was actually mailed.

Certified mail. Mail that has been documented as having been sent, but which pays no claim for loss.

Closing. The phrase used before the signature to indicate the letter has ended, such as "Sincerely," "Yours truly," or "Respectfully."

Community relations. Positive plans to encourage better relationships between the community and a business.

Composition. The combining of words, phrases, and other elements to formulate a letter or message.

Condolences. Words of sympathy, written or spoken, on the occasion of death or other misfortune.

Copy. In correspondence, the text, or body, of a letter.

Direct mail. Letters or other mailings sent from a business to prospective customers.

Elite. A size of type on a typewriter, with 12 characters to the inch, commonly used in letter writing.

Embossed. Printing and/or design formed on high-quality paper by pressing the paper against an engraved steel roll to create a textured look.

Enclosure. Printed matter or other material enclosed inside a letter.

Exposition. A precise statement, definition, or explanation.

Express mail. Mail that is sent at a faster than normal rate at a premium price, but with guaranteed overnight delivery to most cities in the United States.

First-class mail. Letter, cards, and business reply mail with a weight of 12 ounces or less, which is sealed and cannot be opened by postal employees.

Focus. Directing the attention, in a letter or message, on a precise subject or threme.

Form letter. A printed document that can be mailed as is, or with minimal changes, to large numbers of people.

Format. The overall design of a letter or printed piece, whose elements consist of design, color, type, and margins.

Forms of Address. The proper nomenclature and title to use in the salutation of a letter, such as "Dear Mr. President," "Dear Judge Swift," or "Excellency."

Fourth-class mail. Domestic parcel post, used for sending packages, library books, and catalogs, generally weighing 16 ounces or more.

Gender-neutral terms. In correspondence, refers to methods of referring to people in a sexless manner so as not to offend either male or female readers. (Examples are: "mail carrier" rather than "postman" and "salesperson" instead of "saleslady.")

Graphics. The visual elements of layout and design in a letter or other communication.

Heading. In correspondence, the name and address of the recipient as well as the date.

Imprint. A mark or pattern produced on paper, with ink or other marking materials.

Insert. Something inserted or enclosed, usually printed matter, in a letter.

International mail. Letters, printed matter, and small packages destined for foreign countries.

Junk mail. Printed matter, such as form letters, catalogs, and advertising literature sent in quantity at low postal rates. A popular term for unwanted mail.

Justified. Typewritten or printed text in which the edges of both the right and left margins are perfectly even.

Layout. The designer's sketch for the arrangement of type, art, color, and space for a printed piece.

Letter quality. Term used to signify that the typewriter or printer has produced lines and characters that are of good quality.

Letterhead. The name, address, and usually telephone number of the sender. It may also include a title and/or the nature of the business.

Logo. A sign or symbol used by an organization as a graphic means of quick identity. It is called a *trademark* when used with a product.

Mail-order. A request for goods and services that is received and usually filled through the mail.

Mailgram. The trade name for a telegram delivered jointly by the postal service and Western Union.

Mailing list. A list of prospective customers or clients, usually prepared by a professional service.

Margin. In a letter, the white space above the letterhead, below the signature, and on both sides of the page.

Media. A means of mass communications, such as newspapers, magazines, or broadcasting, which companies reach through advertising and publicity.

Memorandum. Also popularly referred to as a *memo*, a form of letter frequently used for inter- and intraoffice communications to numbers of people at the same time.

Metered mail. Mail that bears an imprinted meter mark rather than gummed postage, used largely by organizations that make regular multiple mailings.

Motif. A recurrent graphic element used in various forms of communication.

Newsletter. A typed, printed, or photocopied document that is halfway between a letter and a newspaper and periodically sent to a specialized group of recipients.

Offset paper. An inexpensive, uncoated paper commonly used in offices in photocopying machines.

Optical character reader (OCR). An electronic device used by post offices to scan addresses and sort mail instantly.

Oversize mail. Mail too large to be sorted by electronic or mechanical means that must be hand-processed.

Paper stock. The term used for paper that is to be printed.

Pica. A unit of measure used in printing, which has six to the inch.

Postscript. A brief message appended in type or by hand at the end of a letter, after the writer's signature.

Press relations. The action of contacting media and members of the press to encourage a more favorable image of an organization, group, or individual.

Press release. A form letter printed in quantity by a company or other organization and sent to members of the press to impart news or other information.

Print order. An order specifying how many copies of a publication are to be printed.

Printout. The printed sheets produced singly or in quantity by the printing function of a word processor, computer, or electronic typewriter.

Priority mail. Mail that exceeds 12 ounces but not more than 70 pounds in weight that receives full first-class handling, including shipment by air.

Public relations. The activities pursued by an organization to promote a favorable relationship with the public.

Rag paper. Paper containing at least 25% rag or cotton fiber, thus making it more elegant and expensive.

Recipient. The addressee, the person who receives a letter or other item of correspondence.

Recycled paper. Paper that has been manufactured from waste paper or other materials that have been sanitized and processed.

Registered mail. Domestic first-class and priority mail that has been registered to protect valuable enclosures, not to exceed $25,000.

Reply card. A postal card that is paid for by the sender and returned eventually to document the delivery of certified, registered, or insured mail.

Return receipt. See *reply card*.

Salutation. Derived from the word *salute*, this is the greeting at the start of the letter (Examples are "Dear Mrs. Johnson:" "Dear Joe:" "Dear Customers:".)

Satin finish. Paper with a smooth, satin-like finish.

Second-class mail. Mail that includes newspapers, magazines, and other periodicals mailed quarterly or more frequently.

Self-cover. A mailing piece whose cover is made out of the same paper as the inside pages.

Self-mailer. A folder that can be mailed without being enclosed in an envelope.

Signature. The name of the person signing the letter, often with that person's title underneath.

Simplified letter. A style of form letter that avoids gender and title problems and lends itself to adaptation for numerous communications purposes.

Spacing. In letter writing, refers to the amount of space between lines—generally single or double spaced.

Special delivery. A classification that can be used for all classes of mail except express mail and that virtually assures delivery on the same day the mail is received at the destination post office.

Special handling. Mail, generally third or fourth-class, whose delivery is speeded up through special handling between post offices.

Style. In correspondence, the tone and manner in which the message is written, as distinguished from the substance and subject itself.

Test mailing. Mailing a letter or printing piece to a selected sample of recipients in order to predetermine the reactions to expect from a full-scale mailing.

Text. The body of a letter or other medium of communication.

Theme. A point of view, idea, or proposition on which the text is centered.

Third-class mail. The classification covering booklets, circulars, catalogs, and similar publications, as well as photographs and sketches.

Tracer. A form that can be filled out to try to trace mail within one year of the mailing date.

Trademark. See *logo*.

Transmittal, letter of. A letter, usually brief, that is sent separately or with a communication to record the sending of information or materials.

Treatise. See *theme*.

Typeface. The size, design, and style of a character of type.

Typo. An error in the typing or type.

Typography. The process of printing material from movable type, as well as the arrangement of printed matter.

Unjustified. The body of a letter or a column of type in which one side (usually the right) is not aligned.

Vellum. A top-quality paper, uncoated, relatively absorbent, and with a slightly rough finish.

Widow. A word left hanging on a line by itself, which often produces an undesirable visual image.

Word processor. A computer/typewriter designed specifically for writing and editing texts.

Zip code. The numerical designations assigned to different postal regions in the United States and abroad, which are increasingly vital to the fast, accurate delivery of all classes of mail.

$\mathcal{S}$UGGESTED READING

The following books are listed as supplements to refer to when using the *Prentice-Hall Small-Business Model Letter Book*. They contain information about various forms of written communications for business, in addition to letters.

BRILL, LAURA. *Business Writing Quick & Easy*, 2nd ed. New York: AMACOM, 1989.

CAHILL, BERNARDINE B. *Executive's Portfolio of Business Letters*. Englewood Cliffs, NJ: Prentice Hall, 1985.

CROSS, MARY. *Persuasive Business Writing: Creating Better Memos, Reports & More*. New York: AMACOM, 1987.

CROSS, WILBUR. *Growing Your Small Business Made Simple*. New York: Doubleday, 1992.

CULLINAN, MARY. *Business Communication: Principles & Processes*. New York: Holt, Rinehart and Winston, 1989.

FRUEHLING, ROSEMARY T. *Business Correspondence Essentials*, 4th ed. New York: McGraw-Hill, 1986.

GILSDORF, JEANETTE. *Business Correspondence for Today: Letters, Memos & Short Reports*. New York: John Wiley, 1989.

LEONARD, DONALD. *Effective Letters in Business*, 3rd ed. New York: McGraw-Hill, 1984.

McNALLY, TERRY. *Contemporary Business Writing: A Problem-Solving Approach*. Belmont, Califor.: Wadsworth, 1986.

MEYER, HAROLD E. *Lifetime Encyclopedia of Letters*, revised and expanded edition. Englewood Cliffs, NJ: Prentice Hall, 1991.

NAUHEIM, FERD. *Letter Perfect: How to Write Business Letters that Work*. New York: Van Nostrand Reinhold, 1982.

PEARLMAN, DANIEL. *Letter Perfect: An ABC for Business Writers*. New York: Macmillan, 1985.

REID, JAMES M. *Better Business Letters: A Programmed Book to Develop Skill in Writing*, 3rd ed. New York: Addison-Wesley, 1985.

SEGLIN, JEFFREY L. *The AMA Handbook of Business Letters*. New York: AMACOM, 1989.

SHARP, DEBORAH. *Writing Business Letters with a Personal Touch*. New York: Van Nostrand Reinhold, 1983.

THOMSETT, MICHAEL. *The Little Black Book of Business Letters*. New York: AMACOM, 1988.

$\mathcal{I}$NDEX